THE HUNGRY TIGRESS

BUDDHIST MYTHS,
LEGENDS, AND JATAKA TALES

ALSO BY RAFE MARTIN

BOOKS

The Rough-Face Girl
The Boy Who Lived with the Seals
Will's Mammoth
Foolish Rabbit's Big Mistake
Mysterious Tales of Japan
The Boy Who Loved Mammoths
One Hand Clapping: Zen Stories
A Storyteller's Story
Dear as Salt
The Eagle's Gift
The Monkey Bridge
The Brave Little Parrot

AUDIO TAPES

Rafe Martin Tells His Children's Books
Ghostly Tales of Japan
Animal Dreaming

THE HUNGRY TIGRESS

BUDDHIST MYTHS, LEGENDS, AND JATAKA TALES

Told and with Commentaries by
Rafe Martin

Foreword by Roshi Philip Kapleau

Completely Revised & Expanded Edition

Cover Art: Anomyous Japanese Painting from
the collection of The Rochester Zen Center
Used by Permission

Yellow Moon Press
P.O. Box 381316
Cambridge, MA 02238
(617) 776 - 2230
(617) 776 - 8246 Fax
(800) 497 - 4385 Toll Free Ordering
story@yellowmoon.com
www.yellowmoon.com

Greater is the amount of tears already shed by you in this long journey, forever running through the round of rebirth, than all the water of the four mighty oceans. Greater is the amount of mother's milk already sucked by you in this long journey, forever running through the round of rebirth, than all the water of the four mighty oceans.

—Shakyamuni Buddha

What are human beings without the animals? If all the animals were gone, humankind too would die from a great loneliness of spirit. For whatever happens to the animals soon happens to human beings. All things are connected.

—ascribed to Chief Seattle

The closest thing we have to a planetary mythology is Buddhism. In it all things are potentially Buddha-things.

—Joseph Campbell, The Power of Myth

The unexpected and the incredible belong in this world. Only then is life whole.

—Carl Jung

AUTHOR'S PREFACE

In the years since the original revised edition of The Hungry Tigress was completed, my understanding of Buddhist tradition and teaching, of myth and story, of words and sentences, has simplified and clarified.

So, thanks to Robert Smyth of Yellow Moon Press for encouraging me to rewrite this book as I really wished it to be—which I have. And thanks to Ginger Lazarus, also of Yellow Moon, for her careful editing of the text. The introduction includes new material, all the stories have been retouched, and the commentaries have been added to, redeveloped, and refined as well. In addition, two new sections have been added: one on the relevance of jatakas today and one on how stories teach.

With this rewriting, this particularly protean book has found its final shape.

Special thanks for the continuing support given to this project by Roshi Philip Kapleau. One of the noted first-generation American Zen teachers, his enthusiasm for The Hungry Tigress has remained undiminished, heartening my own efforts to renew its life again. His many years of dedicated Zen teaching clearly lie behind the introduction and the extended commentaries.

Also special thanks to my family—to Rose, Jacob, and Ariya for their constant patience, interest, and support. And to my father, Arthur Martin. In World War II he served in Army Intelligence and Rescue, stationed in the Himalayas, flying the "Hump." He looked at India with youthful, admiring eyes and brought back photos, objects, and tales that enlivened my childhood and established an imaginative and karmic link with the original land of the Buddha. This book is one direct result of that uncanny web of interacting forces that make up our personal histories and the world's.

Finally, thanks to the community of the Rochester Zen Center for having given me the opportunity to develop and refine many of these stories in the actual telling over many years.

Rafe Martin
April 8, 1998

FOREWORD

Readers of Rafe Martin's original Hungry Tigress will find in this completely revised and newly expanded edition a cornucopia of new delights and edifications. Each of the stories has been rewritten in light of the author's deepening and evolving understanding of narrative and of the Buddhist tradition. A very contemporary and insightful afterword on the jatakas has been added, as well as a fascinating yet brief meditation on how stories actually work, how they teach—something particularly useful for those who come—as many do today—with a bias toward "truth" and a suspicion of "mere" story. Perhaps most significantly, the already excellent introduction and commentaries have been carefully rethought and revised as well, making this a truly new book, one that is powerful, resonant, and uniquely valuable. In the commentaries the author not only reveals his deep understanding of Buddhism (from which the jataka tales emerged), but he makes arrestingly clear the ethical and social values lying at the heart of the stories themselves. The jatakas are not simply cautionary tales for children. In these superb recountings as well as in the excellent commentaries which follow, we clearly see how these stories function within the traditional world of the storyteller as well as within the heart and mind of the Buddhist tradition. We see how these stories uphold, at all levels, the universally respected values of patience, courage, compassion, and self-sacrifice—virtues which seem to be in short supply in our fear-dominated, greed-ridden society. In addition, we come to understand the relevance of these stories for us today. Through their drama, humor, compassion, and insight, as well as through the vast scale of their imagination, they speak with special urgency and clarity to us who live today in demythologized time.

Of course, to the casual reader many of the jatakas may seem mere superstition, because the events in them seem at odds with the laws of nature, or just unbelievable, because contrary to reason. For example, how believable is it that the Buddha-to-be was a grown man before he saw for the first time a sick man, an aged man, and a corpse? Or that when the Buddha was born he took seven steps and, raising his right hand, cried, "Above the heavens and below the heavens I am the most honored One"? But wait, here is Rafe Martin's answer: "Myth and legend, it has been well said, reveal a truth too great to be limited by mere fact." And again: "Like cubism in painting, these stories distort ordinary reality enough to make their meaning, not their surfaces, come through all the clearer."

These stories, like all powerful stories, should be felt and intuitively understood, not simply reasoned out. We can be grateful to the author for making this fine selection of Buddhist tales and legends so wonderfully and authentically accessible to a new generation of readers. This is, in short, not only a beautiful book but an important one. It remains one of the very few even today to approach Buddhism the traditional way—through stories that rise from the depths of its mythic vision.

Roshi Philip Kapleau

CONTENTS

SECTION III: LATER STORIES

SECTION IV: COMMENTARIES

INTRODUCTION

JATAKAS IN TH E WEST

Buddhist jataka tales (tales of the Buddha's earlier births, often in animal fable form), have appeared in Western literature since relatively early times. Indeed, there are enough suggestive and interesting parallels between Euripides' Hippolytus and the Buddhist jataka legend "Kunala" to suggest influences or a common root. Aesop's fables and the Arabian Nights show jataka influences. Chaucer's The Pardoner's Tale and Shakespeare's As You Like It and The Merchant of Venice all show quite plausible and likely jataka influences as well. More recently, "The King's Ankus" in Kipling's Second Jungle Book is a retelling of a Buddhist jataka.

How did jatakas find their way into Western literature? For Kipling it was easy. He grew up in India and had an Indian nursemaid. The route of the tales to Chaucer and Shakespeare was more circuitous. Scholar T.W. Rhys Davids believes it began with Alexander the Great's invasion of India around 300 B.C. Jatakas and other tales were translated into Greek in the process of occupation. (Greek art had its reciprocal influence on Indian Buddhism. The first Buddha images were based on Greek statues of Apollo. Until then, the Buddha had been symbolized in Indian art simply by a Wheel of the Law, an Umbrella or Banner of Victory, or some other such image, but never shown as a person.) Almost fifteen hundred years later, crusaders returning from the Middle East brought with them Arabic retellings from the Greek. Jewish scholars of the Middle

Ages, taken with the idea of the animal fable as a philosophic form and with the compassion so evident in the tales, became skillful translators and adapters of the stories. Through them, the jatakas found their way throughout Europe.

It wasn't until the later part of the nineteenth century, however, that stories clearly identified as jatakas became available in translation for interested Western readers. These translations were mostly from Pali texts by scholars of religion and folklore working outside of the Buddhist tradition. Early in the twentieth century, more popular but simplistic versions were created from these translations specifically for children, giving the jatakas a reputation as quaint, Aesop-like animal fables.

Though I am not a translator, I have tried in this collection of jatakas and other Buddhist legends and tales to allow a different spirit to come into play. I have sought to share something of the inner life of these tales as I have come to know it through years of both Zen Buddhist practice and professional story-telling. And I have tried to restore the tales to the twenty-five-hundred-year-old Buddhist tradition out of which they emerged so they might be known again in their original contexts.

I wanted, too, to let them speak and be as relevant for modern readers as they had been for their traditional listeners. To create versions that would be authentic at the core, yet alive for readers and listeners today, was my prime interest. An interest in living relevance has been part of the Buddhist tradition since earliest times. The Buddha himself is said to have spoken of the importance of adapting what was said to the needs of listeners. My effort, then, was not to supplant existing translations and versions but to pass on functioning re-creations, valid in their own right.

I also tried to restore something of the lively, direct voice through which these tales originally spoke. They were mostly told stories, after all, and told stories must be spare, must demonstrate their meaning in action. Too much description, too much discourse, and the story slows like a stream that wanders among weeds—and the audience is lost. Ornate description and long discourse are the earmarks of the written tale, the tale meant for quiet reflection and concern with inner states.

But the original narrator of the Pali jatakas was, according to tradition, not a writer but the Buddha himself. Buddhist tradition holds that he told each "birth tale" or "birthlet" as a way of setting some current event of interest to his monks and lay-followers in the context of past-life actions and incidents— rebirth through countless lifetimes being accepted by all schools of Buddhism.

THE JATAKA TRADITIONS

Buddhists accept jataka tales as stories of the Buddha's own earlier births as he evolved, over the course of endless world cycles and countless lifetimes, towards full Enlightenment and Buddhahood. As such, they form the backbone of the literary and artistic traditions of Buddhist Asia. " is words," writes ama ovinda, "according to changing times may be interpreted in a variety of ways his living example, however, speaks an eternal language, which will be understood at all times, as long as there are human beings" oundations of Tibetan Mysticism, . As the fundamental expression of that "living example," the jatakas empower and dramati e some of the deepest values and beliefs of the culture. A compassionate reverence for all life as well as faith in the dynamic workings of cause and effect, or karma, are two such implicit values and beliefs that extend throughout the jataka tradition. They have been immensely popular stories, too, with a long history of being told, carved, drawn, sculpted, and performed. Indeed, their artistic lineage goes back almost as far as the time of the Buddha himself. By the time of the ouncil of esali—a gathering of the Buddhist community, or angha, some one hundred years after the Buddha's death—jataka stories had been accepted as an authentic part of the canon. arved and sculpted railings surrounding the relic shrines of anchi, Amaravati, and Bharut in India, dating from the third century B.C., clearly depict scenes from jataka tales. In Tibet, at the Monlam henmo, or reat Prayer estival, begun by the great religious leader Tsong hapa in the year , commentaries on the jataka tales—specifically those in Aryasura's famous collection, The atakamala—were made annually before many tens of thousands of gathered monastics and lay people. The alai amas continued this practice, which still goes on today in the Tibetan exile communities in India.

All parenthetical citations refer to works listed in the bibliography at the back of this book.

Interestingly, the great Thirteenth Dalai Lama (the present is the Fourteenth) commented each year of his adult life on one jataka—"The Hungry Tigress." He saw this tale of compassion as the most central of all.

Two major strands of jataka tales have come down to us today out of what was originally a much vaster oral tradition. The largest and oldest is the Pali Jataka, a collection of 547 jatakas and their verses simply arranged in order of complexity (actually according to the number of verses in each tale). The verses are canonical, the tales being essentially commentaries on, or illustrations of, the verses. Each of the tales is preceded by a brief introductory story and followed by a brief identification of the characters, i.e., who they are now, in their present lives. This written collection was put together in its final form (some say, translated from a lost original) about 500 A.D. in Southeast Asia. However, Ananda Coomaraswamy points out that while the final work is a literary creation, a formal, patterned structure that evolved over time, the stories preserved in this structure are part of a much older tradition extending back to the third century B.C. The Pali Jataka collection as a finished work, then, is not that old. But the verses and stories contained in it have considerable antiquity. One wonders, too, how many of the tales have a purely Buddhistic origin. Though some clearly do, many seem to have roots that extend far down into the truly ancient world of Indian storytelling itself.

The Pali jataka tales are purportedly the record of the historical Buddha's past lives. (Buddha is a title meaning "Awakened" or "Enlightened One.") Ideally, they reveal that whether born as human or animal, spirit or god, he strove for perfection of character and deeper wisdom. They make it clear, too, that while the actual historical figure—the Indian prince of twenty-five hundred years ago, Siddhartha Gautama, known to the world after Enlightenment as Shakyamuni Buddha—was a person of extraordinary character and depth, he was a man, not a god. Long ago, jataka tradition holds, having grown aware of the unsatisfactory nature of unenlightened existence, he became determined to realize enlightenment and to develop his understanding and compassion endlessly. After this, through countless lifetimes of unfolding karma as either a human, nonhuman, or superhuman being, he continued to work towards this Goal. Ideally, the jataka tradition is the record of that astounding effort, and its keynote is that the Buddha's attainment of the ultimate state of omniscience and compassion was the outcome of his own unceasing exertion.

While many of the tales in the Pali Jataka do fit this ideal, archetypal model—i.e., are tales of heroic action, wisdom, and compassion—there are also many stories of seemingly much older story stock. Formed of fragments of epics and hero tales arising from deep in the collective Indian past, this already ancient material was taken over and revised, reworked, and reused by later Buddhist storytellers for their own purposes. Such transformations and reworkings (essentially a kind of thrifty recycling of still potent and viable story stuff) are typical of oral traditions in general and reflect the essential vitality of these traditions around the world.

There is, unfortunately, also a sizeable amount of narrow-minded, ascetic-monastic moralizing in the Pali Jataka, with roots in yogic-ascetic traditions as well as in the lives of the monastic Buddhist writers who put the collection together. While heroines do appear, there is simply too much about the so-called dangerous wiles of women to make the Jataka a really good contemporary read. This is doubly unfortunate, for the very grab-bag-like quality of the Pali Jataka, its lavish mix of sources and themes, prompted one early Western commentator (T.W. Rhys Davids) to call it "the most complete and the most ancient collection of folklore extant" (Buddhist Birth Stories, iii). Whether this is still true today, given the wealth of traditional material now appearing, is open to question. That the jatakas do return us to some of the truly core plots of literature seems irrefutable.

Caroline A.F. Rhys Davids, wife of T.W. Rhys Davids and also a noted Pali scholar, described the Pali Jataka and its traditional introduction (see note for "Sumedha Meets Dipankara Buddha") in this way:

> For all the foolishness we find in [the jatakas], the oddities, the inconsistencies, the many distortions in ideals and in the quest of them, they are collectively the greatest epic in literature of the Ascent of Man, the greatest ballad-book on the theme that man willing the better becomes the better. . . . We are given the life history of the individual; not as a type . . . but as a human unit, with a long life history of his own. (Stories of the Buddha, xviii-xix)

The other main grouping of jatakas are the more thematic and self-consciously literary Mahayana collections, which were written not in Pali but Sanskrit. The most highly influential example of these is the famous fourth-, or possibly even third-century A.D. Jatakamala ("Garland of Jatakas") of Aryasura (or Arya Sura), a collection of thirty-four jatakas which dramatize the Perfections of generosity, morality, and patience.

It was these versions of the jatakas that were used as the basis for the beautiful sixth- and seventh-century paintings on the walls of the Ajanta caves of India, and as the inspiration for the magnificent monumental structures of the ninth century at Borobudur, Java. Interestingly, Aryasura's own elegant re-creations of the jatakas may have themselves been based on texts very much like that of the Pali Jataka. Indeed, there is obvious overlapping of individual stories between the two strands of the jataka tradition, and jatakas appear in sutras—purportedly the direct oral teachings of the Buddha—as well.

Still, in such collections as Aryasura's, tales of compassion and of heroic self-sacrifice come to the fore, and the theme of Buddhism as a path of compassion emerges clearly. Tales that may, in the Pali Jataka, do little more than reveal the workings of karma are now retold so as to bring out the overwhelming goodness—and eloquence—of the Bodhisattva. The theme of deep compassion, thinly spread throughout the Pali Jataka, is much more clearly emphasized in these Mahayana Sanskrit collections. One enters a refined and rarified world whose atmosphere is characterized by elegance and beauty. Polished philosophical passages are part of the steady pleasure of these works: "Earth with its forests, noble mountains and seas may perish a hundred times by fire, water and wind, as each eon comes to an end, but the great compassion of the Bodhisattva, never" ("The Great Ape" jataka in Khoroche, tr., Once the Buddha Was a Monkey, 166). There is a surer literary sense. Dialogue tends to be richer, scenes more intimate and dramatic. Inner motivations, the thoughts and feelings of the characters, are given fuller imaginative expression and life. Descriptions of nature and of settings become lavish. There is a tenderness that suffuses these tales, as well as a lofty religious sensibility.

In the words of Wendy Doniger, mythologist and professor of religious history, the Pali Jataka tends to be "rather rough-hewn," whereas the Jatakamala "combines . . . the simple joys of rough peasant fare and the more epicurean (often even gourmand) pleasures of the cuisine of Sanskrit court poetry" (Forward to Once the Buddha Was a Monkey, vii). In the Jatakamala, language itself is one of the heroes. Action, the lifeblood of the folktale, becomes hidden within discourse. Indeed, rhetorical action, the debate between good and evil, right and wrong, often seems to take center stage. A well-known story like "The Banyan Deer" in the Pali Jataka would seem likely to make a successful transition to, and be upheld by, the Mahayana tradition. After all, it dramatizes selfless compassion, the Great Vow to save all beings, and a complex awareness of the interrelation of all living beings. And it delights in debate. Yet, strangely, it is a tale Aryasura ignores. I say strangely, for the triumph of the mind is one of the key interests of the Jatakamala; discourse, combined with joy in thinking about goodness, is the focus. In keeping with this, each story, rather than opening and closing with a quasi-historical context as in the Pali Jataka, opens and closes with a moral. "The pure in heart cannot succumb to the enticements of evil. Try, therefore, to make your hearts pure"—such is a typical opening and closing of a jataka in the Jatakamala. The emphasis has shifted. No longer is it simply on what happened at one time in the historical Buddha's path towards enlightenment, but on a way of living and being that is to be emulated by believers. The Jatakamala is a devotional work created to inspire. Says Aryasura in his prologue, "These praiseworthy exploits are like conspicuous signs pointing the way to perfection. As such may they soften even the hardest of hearts. And may these edifying tales give greater enjoyment than ever before" (Once the Buddha Was a Monkey, 3).

Still, as beautiful as it is, the later Jatakamala does not supersede the Pali Jataka. Some of the most powerful, beautiful (in meaning, if not in conscious artistry), and compassionate jatakas —tales, for example, like "The Banyan Deer"—are found in the Pali Jataka and not in the Jatakamala. Perhaps they appeared in other, now lost, Mahayana collections. Or perhaps they were so well known at the time there was no need to anthologize them further. So there they remain, told less artfully but more directly and simply, in the old folktale-like way. If they are somewhat rough hewn, they are also sturdy. Filled most often with action rather than with discourse and thought (again, "The Banyan Deer" is a puzzling exception—its missed potential for Aryasura seems almost stunning), they clearly beg to be told, shared and used, rather than quietly reflected upon.

USES AND MEANINGS OF JATAKAS

If we approach the jataka tradition with an open mind and really look at it ideally and as a whole, we see that the jatakas explore the ultimate meanings of life and death. They reveal life's often hidden, deeply spiritual purposes. They present a vision of the unity of all life. They also raise the animal fable to unexpected spiritual heights. And they give expression to a powerful impulse towards compassion. Whether they were first told by the Buddha or whether they came into being later through the efforts of unknown sages, teachers, and wandering storytellers, the best of these tales ring true, opening the imagination to a coherent world teeming with life and energy, meaning and wonder. (Again, there are many shortsighted stumblings from this ideal vision littering the jataka Path—a lack of acknowledgment of, and respect for, the Feminine being, perhaps, primary). Frank Waters, in describing Navajo and Pueblo ceremonialism, makes a statement that could be equally well applied to the world of the jatakas—both Pali and Sanskrit:

> It is an assurance which avoids the terror that a soul exists on earth for the short space of only one lifetime, and that it is irretrievably committed to the horrors of Hell or the celestial raptures of Heaven for all eternity on the basis of this short span. On the contrary it reaffirms the belief in the ultimate evolution of every living thing, subhuman, human and superhuman. (Masked Gods: Navajo and Pueblo Ceremonialism, 302)

As the so-called Mahayana or Great Vehicle (the vehicle capable of carrying all beings towards the goal of Buddhahood) flourished, tales of compassion, especially, came to be seen as the "classic" jatakas, the ones which transmitted the heart of the tradition. It is such tales which most deeply affected the popular imagination. Interestingly, one of the most famous of all jatakas, "The Hungry Tigress," does not appear in the Pali Jataka at all. Either it is a Mahayana original, or it was retained by Mahayana authors from yet earlier sources lost to Southeast Asia. As is often the case, through stories a tradition both creates and re-creates itself. As Lama Govinda says:

> The Bodhisattva ideal, in spite of its relatively late verbal formulation, is not some "invention" of the centuries after the Buddha's Parinirvana, but is one of the basic ideas of earlier Buddhism. (A Living Buddhism for the West, 12)

Jataka stories have traditionally been seen as entertainments of the highest order, bringing delight to listeners and imparting wisdom. They explore a wide range of Buddhist teachings and make them dramatic and particular. They do what all narrative art does—make their subjects live. Themes that might have remained abstract or philosophical become intimate, are clothed in flesh and blood, fur and feather. What might have been distant and conceptual now pulses with life, emotion, and personality. Scholar Giuseppi Tucci, travelling in Tibet prior to the Chinese invasion, relates how the roughest sort of men, the muleteers and horse traders of his caravan, would listen as jatakas were told around the campfires at night and weep unrestrainedly, like babies. Lama Govinda says:

> It was only when Buddhists again began to turn more consciously towards the figure of the Buddha, whose life and deeds were the most vital expression of his teachings, that Buddhism emerged from a number of quarreling sects as a world religion. In the cross-fire of conflicting views and opinions, what greater certainty could there be than to follow the example of the Buddha? . . . The exalted figure of the Buddha and the profound symbolism of his real as well as legendary life, in which his inner development is portrayed—and from which grew the immortal works of Buddhist art and literature—all this is of infinitely greater importance to humanity than all the philosophical systems and all the abstract classifications of the Abhidharma. Can there be a more profound demonstration of selflessness, of the Non-Ego Doctrine (anatma-vada), of the Eightfold Path, of the Four Noble Truths, of the Law of Dependent Origination, enlightenment and liberation, than that of the Buddha's way, which encompassed all the heights and depths of the universe?

> "Whatever be the highest perfection of the human
> mind, may I realize it for the benefit of all that lives!"
> This is the gist of the Bodhisattva vow. (Foundations
> of Tibetan Mysticism, 45)

Our own times seem to grow daily more sympathetic to a
jataka-like vision. The findings of contemporary astrophysics
suggest that we might do well to settle ourselves imaginatively
into an endlessly transforming universe without fixed beginning
or end. Chemistry, microbiology, and the behavioral sciences
confirm a fundamental kinship extending from the earth itself
through all living things, from the tiniest bacteria to the largest
blue whale. The recent discovery of possible bacteria on rocks
from Mars may reveal that such kinship extends throughout the
solar system—and much further. Our deepening awareness of
the impermanence of even the most solid and stable-seeming
structures—mountains, seas, the atmosphere, the countless,
wheeling galaxies—has become poignant. Human life, indeed,
all life, can now be seen as more interconnected, and simultaneously more fragile, than past generations of Western thinkers
could concede. In the ongoing effort to gain moral control over
our own relentless defensive and economic drives—including
learning to control our own masterworks of impermanence: our
nuclear weapons—we must now struggle with spiritual responsibilities to the earth and all its future generations, nonhuman
as well as human.

We are, it seems, reawakening to realms of imagination, which
traditional cultures as far back as the Paleolithic knew well. In
this long-sustained "Old Ways" vision, all life is interconnected;
what happens to one living thing here happens to all. As the
eighteenth-century English visionary, artist, and poet, William
Blake, reminds us, "Everything that lives is holy!" The archetypal
thinking of Carl Jung, the transformative possibilities implicit in
Einstein's general theory of relativity, the thoughts and deeds of
compassionate peacemakers like Gandhi and Dr. Martin Luther
King reinforce for us today, at the end of the twentieth century,
a natural responsiveness to the worldview which the jatakas
fundamentally uphold.

Cosmic dimensions of time and space are natural to the jatakas. The tales speak of kalpas—units of time so unbelievably
vast as to include the widest spans of geologic time, spans in

which mountains rise and fall like waves and continents drift and flow. The jatakas revive in us an evolutionary viewpoint in which we rediscover ourselves in the many varied life forms around us. (At the deepest level, these other life forms are us. At relative levels, we have been them; they are the bodies we have passed through to be who and what we are now; they are our ancestor-parents.) How modern, then, rather than simply quaint, to have stories in which humans learn wisdom from animals. In these stories, too, the Great Teacher, the Buddha, has not just human but many animal births. Rather than claiming the spiritual high ground, the stories present us with a religious figure who literally rises up out of the most common ground of all—the realm of the animals. Simple narratives can point us towards profound truths.

Traditional cultures have taken almost for granted—yet have treated with the utmost sacredness and respect—the truth that animals were here first. To the traditional imagination, this suggests that animals are closer to the Source, that they are wise and embody numinous, oracular power.

That such a tribal, even Paleolithic, awareness should be retained so strongly in the jatakas—the story tradition of a culture of cities, courts, and written tradition—is unusual. Though there are parallels between India and ancient Celtic traditions, classical Western traditions (Greek and Biblical) have tended to emphasize an alternate view. Humans, this view holds, having arrived late on the scene, are the "manifest destiny" of all earlier forms. Humans are the real reason, the true Purpose towards which earlier forms stumbled. We are the masters of a clearly anthropocentric universe.

The jatakas strike a middle ground. The stories are not about the worth or significance of certain animals, i.e., the intent is not shamanistic or totemic. It is not a way of saying that we should honor deer, bear, lion, oxen, or monkey, for example, because once the Buddha himself was such a being. Tribal cultures might do that. The Buddhist tradition does not. But it does not seek to make human beings the masters, either. Rather, the thrust of the jatakas, as in all traditions of Buddhist teaching, is towards a perception of the ultimate worth of all living things, of each individual living thing just as it is. "Wonder of Wonders" said the Awakened One at the moment of Enlightenment. "All living things are Buddha!"

Deep ecology, which, as poet Gary Snyder has neatly put it, gives equal weight to the needs of the nonhuman, was thus already dramatized twenty-five hundred years ago in these tales. Their perennial significance is renewed by contemporary need, and so they become current. In the jatakas, a prince gives his own body to save a tigress and her cubs from starvation; a king gives portions of his own flesh so that a dove will not be taken by a hawk—and so the predatory hawk itself will not starve! These tales can be weird, even unnerving, from our ordinary perspective. Yet they push us into some of the most pressing ethical dilemmas of our time. Where do humans fit in? What are our responsibilities to the nonhuman beings—the four-leggeds, two-leggeds, and no-leggeds—with whom we share this earth?

Such elements allow the tales at their best to speak naturally to our contemporary, ecologically sensitive, galaxy-filled imaginations. They are not stories whose contextual structures have been outdated by advances in scientific, social, environmental, or even psychological thinking. (As a visit to the psychology or spiritual section of most any bookstore will reveal, the subject of rebirth, for example, is of quite contemporary interest.) Indeed, one would have to look to contemporary science fiction to regain the scale of the jataka imagination. Novelist Doris Lessing, in her Canopus in Argos series, has taken this seriously, weaving rebirth, vast time frames, levels of consciousness, and galactic space into the fabric of her fiction. The jataka tales, when taken as a whole, give us a body of folk literature that is similar. In them, the role, the thoughts and deeds of the individual are examined in relation to, not isolated from, the whole living universe. As Huston Smith states in his introduction to Roshi Philip Kapleau's The Three Pillars of Zen:

> Why should the West, dominated to the extent it currently is by scientific modes of thought, go to school to a perspective forged before the rise of modern science? Some think the answer lies in the extent to which Buddhist cosmology anticipated what contemporary science has empirically discovered. The parallels are impressive. Astronomical time and space, which irrevocably smashed the West's previous world view, slipped into the folds of Buddhist cosmology without a ripple. If we turn from macrocosm to mi-

crocosm we find the same uncanny prescience. . . .
    "Very interesting," says the Buddhist, this being what
his cosmology has taught him all along. (xii)

ABOUT THIS BOOK

The stories in this collection have been arranged as follows:

1) Legendary material leading up to and including the Buddha's historical life—enlightenment, teaching stories, and the tale of the Buddha's Parinirvana, or entrance into Nirvana.

2) Folktales said to have been told by the Buddha himself during his teaching career, i.e., a wide-ranging selection of jatakas.

3) Tales set after the Buddha's historical life, including a group of traditional Buddhist tales—"Most Lovely Fugen," "The Dog's Tooth," and "The Legend of Avalokitesvara"—and several modern, original tales of my own which extend jataka-like patterns into our own time. In these stories I tried to both raise and suggest some answers to such questions as: Are the jatakas just old tales or can they give us insight into the perennial nature of things? If so, what happens if we extend the tradition jataka into our own times? What would a jataka look like if it were occurring now?

4) A long section of in-depth commentaries on the stories, containing information—historical, literary, Buddhistic, and mythic—for each story.

The commentaries are integral to this book. Through them the stories can function much closer to the way they actually would have for traditional audiences. Through them readers can become something of a traditional audience themselves. The Hungry Tigress can be read as a set of stories with commentaries that reveal the stories' hidden function and depth, or as a collection of commentaries with stories that demonstrate the meanings revealed in the commentaries. The commentaries give relevant Buddhistic background and explain obscure technical terms and principles so that readers can more easily see the significance of a particular tale. Mythic and symbolic information is presented and discussed. Stories which might have seemed totally implausible to modern readers may assume dignity, relevance, and meaning.

In the jatakas, surfaces may be distorted so that meanings can come to the fore. What the heart knows, not what the eye sees, is often primary. This kind of thinking is part of the worldview out of which these stories arose and which once probably existed worldwide. The commentaries are, in part, a doorway back into this way of seeing.

As I am not a scholar of Buddhism, none of these commentaries are definitive. I have not been exhaustive in my research. Rather, I have tried to identify interesting sources for the versions I have created, as well as to share information which I found to be of particular interest and resonance. My motivation in working on the stories was not so much to produce authoritative texts as to re-create tellings which might live authentically for readers and listeners today. I was interested, as traditional Buddhist storytellers and writers have been through the centuries, in keeping these tales alive. In traditional cultures, storytellers are not mere memorizers but creative participants in the life of the culture. It is traditional, then, for storytellers to comment meaningfully on the stories they tell so that the tales may live more fully for those who have gathered to hear. In a sense that is what The Hungry Tigress is about.

5) Two essays, one exploring how traditional tales teach, the other presenting the contemporary relevance of the jatakas. These two new pieces extend the contexts in which both the tales and commentaries may be read.

By necessity, the stories presented here reflect subjective criteria. The storyteller's job, after all, is to pass on stories that have actually spoken to him or her, to share stories that have been heard not just with the ears but with the heart. As this is a storyteller's book, the principle guiding both the selection of stories as well as the choice of information recorded in the commentaries was informal and natural. As the nineteenth-century Japanese Zen monk, poet, and calligrapher, Ryokan, says:

> The wind brings
> Enough of fallen leaves
> To make a fire.

(Blyth, Haiku, vol. 4, 357)

As a storyteller it is my hope that readers will find stories in this collection suitable for reading and sharing aloud. Something unique happens when the human voice carries and embodies oral tales. A kind of unrecognized life that printed words can only suggest stirs again. I hope that others will be tempted to try such readings and tellings for themselves.

A bibliography has been included, and in the commentaries, where it is appropriate, each jataka is listed with its traditional number as it appears in the Cowell translation from the Pali. If it appears in the Jatakamala, that is noted as well. In this way, those interested may go to the original sources and see more clearly what has been done—for better or worse—to the versions that exist in currently available translations of the original texts.

The more I work with these stories, the more I think about, write, and tell them, the more true they seem to me. Stories, of course, are true—true to the imagination in which they live. For me, these stories are especially so. After having worked on these stories, I find myself observing flocks of pigeons wheeling between the houses on our block, and thinking, as I watch, of the Buddha's lives as various birds. Or I now observe our family dog and cat in a new light. The bodhisattvic presence, the jatakas suggest, is potentially everywhere. The ninth-century Japanese Buddhist pilgrim, Ennin, relates in his journals that when he arrived at Mount Wu-Tai in China, the mountain sacred to the Bodhisattva Monjushri, Bodhisattva of Wisdom, he discovered that when resident monks or pilgrims to the mountain saw a lowly person, or even a donkey, none dared think a contemptuous thought. Rather they would spontaneously think, "Perhaps it is He!"—and act accordingly.

Such transformation of our own thoughts and lives is what traditional stories are all about. While among the oldest, and seemingly frailest, of humanity's creations—they are only sounds in the air, squiggles on a page—they remain, even today, among our most significant tools for bringing about positive inner change.

SECTION I

BUDDHIST LEGENDS

BEGINNINGS

Once, many long ages ago, in a time beyond all reckoning, the Buddha was a king named Suprabhasa.

One day this king, Suprabhasa, told his elephant trainer to ready the great white elephant so that he might ride.

"My Lord," replied the trainer, "I cannot bring him. The great white elephant has broken his golden chains and gone back to the jungle. It is only temporary, being the time of rut. He will return. He is well trained."

The king, disappointed, lost all self-control, and, shouting at the trainer, angrily dismissed him.

The next morning the elephant trainer again came before the king and announced, "My Lord, it is as I predicted—the great white elephant has returned. The training was good. We have conquered over his wild ways."

Those words touched the king's own fault. "Though I am king," he suddenly realized, "holding great power over others, I have as yet failed to conquer what is closest—myself. I was not even able to control my own anger. This will not do."

"Tell me, trainer," he now asked, "are there any who have truly conquered themselves? For harder it must be, it now seems to me, to conquer oneself than it is to control an elephant in the time of its rut."

"My Lord," answered the trainer, "there are the Conquerors, the Buddhas. Having triumphed over all greeds and desires, over all anger, hatred, and fear, they must surely be the noblest of all beings. Free from all self-centered delusions, they live in peace, seeing things as they really are."

At once a great yearning, like a fire, arose in King Suprabhasa's heart, a yearning to conquer himself and also be free.

In this way Shakyamuni, the Buddha of our own age, many many long ages ago first awoke to what was to be an ever-deepening longing for Wisdom and Truth.

Commentary on page 192

SUMEDHA MEETS DIPANKARA BUDDHA

Ages passed. From the seed of that yearning, life after life, now in high station, now in low, now as god, now as human, now as a spirit, bird, or animal, the Future Buddha strove towards the realization of his Goal.

Four asankheya kalpas and a hundred thousand world cycles ago a decisive moment was reached.

At that time the future Buddha was born into a wealthy Brahmin family in the city of Amaravati. He was named Sumedha.

He was blessed with all goodness—physical beauty, intelligence, friendliness, kindness, moral vigor.

His parents died when he was still a young man, and as the steward went through the list of all of Sumedha's inherited properties and wealth, noting so much from his mother, so much from his father, so much from his grandparents, so much from his great-grandparents, and so on, back and back for seven generations, this young man, Sumedha, began to think: "My family has amassed wealth for seven generations. Yet neither my parents nor my grandparents nor any other of my ancestors were able to take any of it with them upon leaving this world. What is the point of amassing more? One day I too will die. As there is a road that leads beyond the sufferings of this world should I just remain idle? No, I will leave this sheltered life and find that Way."

Announcing his intention to the king, he gave away his money to the poor and entered the forests.

The hermit Sumedha ate wild fruit and wore clothing of bark. His hair and beard grew long and matted. Striving energetically, whether standing, sitting, or lying down, looking deeply into his own mind, in a short time he gained profound insight into the True Nature of existence. For many days he sat absorbed in the bliss of his newly won freedom and Knowledge.

At this time the Buddha Dipankara, surrounded by thousands of monks, nuns, and laypeople, was making his way to the city of Amaravati. Workers were busy smoothing and leveling the road before the city in expectation of the great Teacher's arrival.

The hermit Sumedha was roused from his trance. Seated cross-legged he rose up into the air and flew over the forest until he came to the road. Calling down to those working there he enquired, "What is the excitement? Why are you laboring in the midday heat? Why is the road being leveled and strewn with golden sands? Why these flowers and perfumes?"

"Venerable Sumedha!" replied the workers, calling up to where the hermit sat hovering in the clear air, "Do you not know! The Buddha Dipankara is approaching the city. This evening he is to give public talks and reveal his Dharma!"

And Sumedha's heart leapt for joy! "A Buddha!" he thought. "Rare, indeed, is it to even hear that word—'Buddha.' Rare beyond all comprehending to actually meet such a fully Realized One."

Descending from the air, he alighted beside the workers. "Let me help you level this road for the Buddha Dipankara," he said. Seeing that his powers were supernatural, the foreman assigned him a stretch of low, swampy ground to fill.

Then, with his heart pounding in expectation, his mind lit with joy, repeating over and over "a Buddha! a Buddha!" Sumedha began filling in the marshy ground with dry soil.

Up ahead, near the city, drums beat, trumpets sounded, and flutes trilled. Crowds called and murmured like a sea. Looking up, Sumedha saw bright banners swirling, flowers and jewels tossing in the air. At the center of all that noise and commotion walked a calm figure. It was the Buddha Dipankara approaching.

Sumedha saw six-hued rays of light, linked in pairs of colors, extending from the Buddha. He saw a halo of golden light and wreaths of pulsing light like lightning rippling across a star-studded sky, encircling him. Devas, tossing celestial flowers and strumming instruments of pure gold, flew overhead as an exquisite music filled the air.

Then thoughts arose in Sumedha's mind: "Here, at last, is one who has attained all the super-knowledges, all wisdom. Here, at last, is one free from all greed, anger, and ego-delusion. Here, at last, is one in whom all goodness has been realized. I shall make an offering to the Buddha Dipankara for the sake of Buddha-knowledge."

Loosening his long hair, Sumedha spread his bark-cloth cloak before him in the mud. Then he thought, "Like the Buddha Dipankara I, too, want only to help all beings. How can I be content with mere personal liberation while others still suffer? I am determined. Despite difficulties and dangers I will never turn back. I am resolved to attain what the Buddha Dipankara has attained and benefit all beings."

Then Sumedha lay down upon the bark-cloth cape and spread his long hair, making a dry passage for the Buddha Dipankara to walk over the mud.

The Buddha Dipankara arrived at the spot and stood by Sumedha's head. Looking down, he thought, "This hermit has formed the resolution to be a Buddha. Will he be successful?" And casting his mind far into the future, he saw that four asankheya kalpas and one hundred thousand world cycles from that time, Sumedha would indeed become a fully realized, omniscient Buddha, an Awakened One. And that his family name would be Gautama.

And standing there, surrounded by his disciples, the thousands of monks, nuns, men, women, and children of all stations from beggar to king, the Buddha Dipankara made this prophecy: "Four asenkheyas and one hundred thousand cycles from now, far far in the future, the hermit lying here in the mud before us will fulfill his great vow. He will be a Buddha named Gautama. His birth will be in the city of Kapilavasthu. His mother's name will be Maya; his father's, Suddhodhana. His clan will be the Shakyas. When he is grown he will see the four signs—old age, sickness, death, a monk—

and he will leave the world. After great exertions he will receive, when he is near death on the banks of the Naranjana River, a lifesaving meal of milk-rice. Then, strength renewed, he will make his way to the foot of a Bo-tree, seat himself there, and continuing his exertions to the utmost, he will attain Supreme Buddhahood."

Lying in the mire, Sumedha became delirious with joy. "My deepest wish shall be attained! I shall be a Buddha!"

And the crowd murmured, "Here is a Buddha-shoot, a Buddha-seed. We too shall make efforts, and if we should fail to attain the Path of Freedom in this life under the guidance of the Buddha Dipankara, we shall surely succeed in the time of the Buddha Gautama. We too shall triumph."

Then the Buddha Dipankara praised the Bodhisattva and encouraged him. Making an offering of flowers, he saluted him palm to palm and, accompanied by the thousands of monks, nuns, and lay followers, departed.

The Bodhisattva, Sumedha, arose and exclaimed, "The words of a Buddha cannot fail. They are certain. Like an arrow, which once shot from a bow must fall to earth, so, too, these words are destined to be fulfilled. I shall become a Buddha." He rose from the mud up into the clear air and flew back again to his retreat high in the mountains. There he remained, steadfastly striving towards his ultimate Goal.

Commentary on page 195

THE BIRTH OF THE BUDDHA

It was long ago, in India, that Queen Maya, wife of King Suddhodhana, dreamed of a six-tusked white elephant that entered her room and touched her right side with a lotus flower.

The king called for his wisemen to interpret the dream. They all predicted that a child, destined for greatness, would soon be born. "If he follows a worldly path," they announced, "he will become a great ruler, even Emperor of the World. If he recognizes the truth of impermanence, he will seek a higher life. He will leave the palace in quest of Enlightenment. Undergoing much hardship, he will finally attain complete Understanding and become a teacher to gods, beasts, and humankind."

The queen was overjoyed but King Suddhodhana, while rejoicing, was troubled. He could not help but think of how he might protect his son from hardship and danger, and of how he might help him become the great man who would rule the world.

One day, almost ten months later, Queen Maya set out to give birth in the home of her parents. On the way she passed a magnificent park near the town of Lumbini. There, she and her attendants stopped to rest in a grove of ancient Sala trees.

Queen Maya wandered through the gardens until she stood beneath the largest and oldest tree in the grove. She reached up to touch the petals of an opened blossom. White and golden-yellow lotus petals tumbled from the skies in a rain of flowers. The earth breathed forth delicate odors—jasmine, rose, and sandalwood. From the air itself came magically sounding a music of silvery bells and of high, clear voices singing in a language of delight.

Her child was born. Sky-walking devas appeared at the mother's side and washed the child in streams of heavenly dew. The baby Buddha took seven steps, and, at each step, a lotus blossom sprang up to support his feet. Raising one hand up towards the heavens and pointing the other down towards the earth, he fearlessly sounded the Buddhas' lion's roar: "Above the heavens, below the heavens, I am the only One."

Queen Maya gathered her long-awaited child into her arms, and as she did, the infant lapsed from all signs of special consciousness or power. However, the queen had heard and seen. That day there could be no one happier than she.

Unless it was the Buddha himself. Though just a newborn child, he already looked on each deva, man, woman, child, animal, flower, tree, and stone with a parent's tender love. After many ages of sustained effort, he had at last come into life prepared to aid them all.

Commentary on page 197

LEAVING HOME

Two thousand five hundred years ago, he who was to be the Buddha was born as a prince in the foothills of the Himalaya mountains. Sages had prophesied that the child's merit, accumulated over countless lives, was now so great that he was destined to become either a mighty king, a world ruler, or an Awakened Buddha.

But one very old sage, Asita, prophesied that there could be no doubt—the child would be a Buddha. And he wept, for he saw that he himself would die before the child attained the Goal.

King Suddhodhana wanted his son to be a great king. And he wanted to protect his child from pain and suffering. So he named the boy "Siddhartha," meaning "He Whose Wishes Are Fulfilled," and, despite the death of the child's mother, Maya, within days of the birth, strove to keep his life happy and pleasant.

Siddhartha played in beautiful gardens. During the fierce heat of summer he roamed the cool halls of marble palaces. Anything he desired was immediately his. Playmates, friends, and loving attendants constantly surrounded him.

King Suddhodhana was happy and his people were happy too. Their king had provided them with a worthy heir.

But Siddhartha, "He Whose Wishes Are Fulfilled," was not happy. He saw what his father and the others would no longer see: cobras hunting frogs in the garden pools, falcons dropping upon terrified pigeons and doves, dead deer slung on the hunters' poles. He saw, too, the many fleeting sadnesses of his companions and friends. In vain, he tried to recall the face of the mother he had never known.

As he grew, these impressions gathered within him, piling up like dry sticks a spark might ignite.

When he was a young man, strong and in his prime, his father had three palaces built for him—one for the hot, one for the cold, and one for the rainy season. Female musicians, dancers and attendants chosen for their beauty surrounded him. Yasodhara, daughter of a neighboring king, became his wife.

One day, the thought struck him that he had never really seen the world of his subjects, of ordinary women and men. He went to his charioteer, Channa, and said, "Take me, Channa, out from the palace and into the streets of the city. I want to see my people. I want to see how they live."

"Very good, Sire," answered Channa. "Let us go tomorrow. I will make the necessary arrangements."

And the prince was content.

Siddhartha's father, King Suddhodhana, and Prajapatti, his foster mother and maternal aunt, had long been dreading this moment—a sign of the prophecy's unfolding. Soon Siddhartha might see what his father had worked so hard to keep from him—old age and sickness, change and death. And the king knew that should that happen, they would lose him.

Then the king ordered the captain of the guards to go into the villages and see to it that the beggars, the aged, the sick and infirm were all hidden from view. "Strew the roads with flowers and perfumes!" he commanded. "Make sure that only the young and able-bodied, the handsome and healthy are on the streets when Siddhartha arrives."

The preparations were carried out as King Suddhodhana had ordered. Yet his fears remained unrelieved.

The sun rose. The day broke. Siddhartha and Channa set off. The horses raced along the road. Birds sang and soared among the trees. White clouds drifted overhead. A cool breeze blew, and the mountains, rising behind them, glowed in the early light.

They entered the city streets. Wreaths of bright flowers hung everywhere. Crowds of smiling people cheered. Children laughed. Handsome couples strolled arm in arm. "So this is life," thought Siddhartha. "Why, then, have I been sad and troubled? My people are happy."

But what was this! Suddenly a wrinkled and toothless old man, clothed in rags, bent and twisted with the burden of his years, tottered from the crowd. There he stood, leaning on a stick, blinking blindly and pitifully in the sunlight. Then, suddenly, he was gone!

The prince's horses laid back their ears and neighed in terror. Rearing up, they tried to back away. Siddhartha leapt from the chariot and grabbed their reins. "Channa!" he cried. "What was that? Was that a man or some other kind of creature?"

"Noble Prince," replied Channa, for the gods themselves had loosened his tongue, "that was indeed a man, even as you and I. But it was an old, old man, Sire."

"Tell me, Channa," the prince asked, "do all, then, become like this? Do all grow 'old'?"

"Yes," sighed Channa, for despite the king's orders to keep this hidden, the gods were at work, knowing the destined time had come. "Yes, they do. Infants become men and women. Men and women age. All creatures on this earth at last grow old, noble Prince."

Shaken, the prince remounted his golden chariot. "Channa," he said, "let us turn the horses round and return. Though I am still young, black-haired, and in the full flush of my manhood, this is a bitter truth. Here is reason enough to spill an ocean of tears." Channa turned the horses and they rode back, dispirited, to the palace once again.

Then the king, Suddhodhana, had his men redouble their efforts. Once more the guards scoured the villages and cleared the streets of the city in preparation.

That night Siddhartha tossed and turned feverishly. It was as if a blaze had begun burning within him.

But the next morning when the sun rose, the prince woke Channa, saying, "Whatever lies ahead must be faced. Let us face it bravely. Prepare the chariot and horses. We shall return. It is not yet over."

Once again, the horses raced along the road. Once again, fine breezes blew and, as before, they rode down garlanded streets where happy crowds smiled and cheered. Suddenly a sick man tottered forth. He was thin, sweaty, wild-eyed, and disheveled. He coughed horribly and so violently he almost fell. The happy people recoiled in alarm.

"What is that!" cried the prince. "Channa! What has happened to that man—if man it is!"

"It is a man, my Prince, and he is sick," answered Channa, "feverish and tormented."

"Was he born like this?" asked the prince.

"No, Lord," Channa replied slowly, like a man being dragged to his doom, "he was in all likelihood born as sound as you or I."

"Can we all, then, become 'sick'?" asked the prince.

"Yes," admitted Channa, impelled again by the gods to speak the truth. "We can."

"Turn the horses round," exclaimed the prince in dismay. "With old age on one hand and sickness on the other, how can I wander so heedlessly? My faith in health and happy youth are gone. My love of festivity is over."

Once again, they travelled in silence back to the palace through the burning midday heat. As they passed through the crowds it seemed to the prince as if all those smiling people stood unawares at the edge of an abyss. It was to him as if they were pieces of paper about to be blown by unknown winds into a mountain of flames.

Cool night fell at last. But, though the stars shone sparkling overhead, what delight could the prince take in them? All night long he again lay feverishly tossing, consumed by thoughts of sickness and age. His wife, father, foster mother, Channa, friends, even his great horse, Kanthaka, the crowds of people, himself—he now saw that all were bound to the inexorable law of change.

That night King Suddhodhana also tossed and turned. He had sent out companies of soldiers under the strictest orders. No infirm, aged, or sick persons were to be allowed on the streets. Not one. All through the night his soldiers labored, going from house to house, so that the young prince would be sheltered from suffering's truth.

But when the sun rose over the mountains, hope awoke in the prince's heart. "Let what is to come, come," he thought. "Whatever it is, I shall meet it face on and find a way through." Somehow he was certain that this was not yet the end of the road he was destined to travel.

So, once again, Siddhartha and Channa set off from the palace.

And, once again, all seemed exactly as before. Smiling people gathered, tossing flowers. Children played. Doves and pigeons flew wheeling in the sunlight. Yet, as they travelled on through those happy streets, the prince's mind remained roused, alert, unbound by and unattached to all he saw. He was vigilant, resolved to know the truth.

Suddenly Siddhartha heard wailing cries. "Channa," he exclaimed, "what is that?"

"It is a funeral, Sire," said Channa with a shiver. "It marks a death."

Though Channa did not pull on the reins the horses stopped of their own accord. "Channa, that sleeping one there, why does he not move?" asked the prince with a sense of foreboding. "They cry loudly. They lift him up onto a hard bed of wood, yet still he does not open his eyes or rise from sleep. But what are they doing now? There are flames all around him! His hair, his clothes are burning, are on fire!"

"Calm yourself, my Lord," said Channa. "He does not feel the flames. He is dead."

"What?" cried the prince. "What do you mean, 'He is dead'?"

"His life is over, Lord," said Channa. "There will be no more movement or action or decision, no more sight or smell or taste or touch, no more hopes or dreams, no more laughter or tears for him. It is over, finished. His days are done. Friends and relatives may weep all they want. They will never see him again." These words of Channa's were again guided by the ever-watchful gods. They knew the time was ripe for Siddhartha to set out and complete what he himself had begun so long ago.

"Channa," asked Siddhartha, "does this happen to everyone?"

Channa turned away. But the gods would have him speak. "It does, my Lord. It happens to each, to all. After old age and sickness comes death."

"To all?" repeated the prince, staggering like a bull struck by the ax. "To father, mother, wife—to friends, oneself—to all?"

They turned away and rode back through the crowds as flames and smoke rose around the uncaring corpse. Again the smiling, garlanded crowds gathered, but this time the prince hardly saw. In his mind, the crackling flames and billowing smoke persisted still.

"Old age and sickness await," said the prince. "And then comes death. No one knows when either sickness or death itself will strike. Yet, like the sure coming of old age, strike they must. So, is this it, then, the end I have sought? Is there nothing more?"

"No, brave Prince," said a steady voice. "It is not the end. It is not yet the end at all." There stood a homeless, wandering truth seeker grasping a wooden staff and carrying a begging bowl. "This is simply where we begin. Walk on, young Prince, walk on! The further you go into these mountains the higher they get. You are still only in the foothills. Seek the heights, Siddhartha, the heights! There your wishes will indeed be fulfilled." Then suddenly he was gone!

A messenger from the palace stood at the prince's side. "Your wife," he said, "Yasodhara, sends you greetings. She is well and shares with you her joy. This day she has borne you a son."

It was complete. Birth, old age, sickness, death, and the knowledge of a Path that led beyond them all was now clear to him. "Old age approaches. Sickness and death may strike at any moment," thought the prince. "Having been born, all are subject to these despoilers. Yet there is a Path beyond such sorrow. I shall take it and walk it to the end. I shall find a way to help all beings, trapped as they are by age, sickness, and death. I am resolved. I will not turn back."

Mounting his chariot as if in a dream, the prince, Siddhartha, and Channa, his charioteer, rode back in silence to the palace once again. Words arose in the prince's mind, sounding over and over to the rhythm of the horse's hooves: "Now is the time to enter the mountains. Now is the time to seek the great heights!"

Like a flood, a river of hope and courage surged through the prince's heart. Standing firmly in the rocking chariot, he saw the mountains looming closer and closer, rising higher and higher as the horses sped on.

Commentary on page 198

ENLIGHTENMENT

At the age of twenty-nine, in the midst of his life of luxury, the prince of the Shakya Clan, Siddhartha Gautama, saw for the first time an old man, a sick man, a dead man, and last of all, a solitary monk—and was sorely troubled. He saw now that his life of privilege brought neither real happiness nor freedom. His pleasure was an illusion, for it was temporary, without substance. Even as he strolled in his gardens and the palace women danced, they all grew older. Sickness stalked the land. Death came to every house, every palace and hut. Yes, his people suffered.

Late in the night he awoke. The dancing girls lay in sleep as if felled: their limbs tossed about and twisted, their bodies uncovered. In that instant, all delight in desire was gone. It was like awakening in a charnel ground. He went to the bedside of Yasodhara, his wife. His newborn son lay beside her. To hold them now might wake them. If they woke, he knew that he might never leave. "I will return," he vowed, "when sickness, age, and death are conquered." Then he roused Channa, his charioteer, mounted the horse, Kanthaka, left the palace, and rode to the river-boundary of his father's kingdom. Channa begged him to forbear and return. But beneath the dark sky and shining stars, he cut his long hair with a sword's stroke, severing his attachment to palace life. Then, crossing the river, he passed forever from that sheltered life of wealth and ease and disappeared alone into the dark forests and snow-covered mountains.

He made his way to the hermitages of the two greatest religious teachers of his time and mastered their methods, matching their inner attainments. But still he found no free-

dom from birth, old age, sickness, and death. So he again
moved on, alone.

He sought the most isolated of places: the deep forests,
the graveyards and charnel grounds. There, the delicate
and once carefully sheltered ex-prince exerted his will. He
forced himself to face all the terrors of darkness and isolation
in which voices seemed to cry "Flee!" and the rustlings and
snappings of branches made his hair stand on end in pure
fear. He persevered through the most fearsome austerities.
He baked himself between great fires during the stifling heat
of midday, then sat silent and naked through freezing nights
on the mountainsides. He stood erect on one leg, unmoving. He held one arm aloft, unmoving. Weeks passed. The
nails grew and pierced his flesh. The muscles shrivelled and
cramped. But in these things he found no freedom.

Then he gradually reduced his intake of food until he was
eating first a thousand, then a hundred, then ten, then at last
just one single sesame seed a day. His flesh withered. His
eyes sank so deep into their sockets they became like the
faint gleam of light reflecting from the water at the bottom
of a well. His hair rotted and, when he rubbed his limbs,
fell out. Every rib, each bony socket and joint stood clearly
exposed, like the wreck of a ship when the tide withdraws.

After six years of continuous effort, exhausted and near the
point of death, he collapsed, more a skeleton wound with
sinews and veins than a living man.

In all this he had found no liberating truth, no freedom,
and it seemed that he must die without attaining his Goal.
The bitterness of that moment, after those six years of unrelenting but now seemingly wasted effort, was keener than a
knife.

Suddenly, there flashed into his mind the memory of a
festival from his childhood. He had been seated quietly under a rose apple tree watching his father, all the nobles, and
the poor men plowing the earth together. He saw the earth
breaking open in even, wavelike furrows, the heat shimmering up off the freshly opened soil and shining on the sweat-
slick brows and straining bodies of men and oxen alike. He
saw the sun continuously flashing off the gilded traces and

horns of the oxen and he heard that senseless, plodding rhythm of hooves and cowbells rolling in a solemn, sealike way. He heard the shrill shouts of the men and the whirring cries of the birds as they dove to devour the billowing hordes of insects, glistening grubs, cut worms, and broken bodies of mice which men, oxen, and plows left in their wake.

The terribly obvious laboring, devouring, suffering, and dying that went on interminably beneath all the gay, surface tinseling of his festival'd days had broken in upon him then and weighed heavily on his mind.

Seated alone beneath the sweet-smelling rose apple tree, reflecting deeply on the scene before him, he suddenly entered a profound experience of samadhi. Trees and mountains, insects and animals, the earth and people, while remaining each themselves all now formed one vast, living Whole.

Now, at the brink of death and in the depths of despair, this memory returned to him, filling him with energy and sureness. "If I already glimpsed the ancient Way," he thought, "while still just a child, well fed and clothed, then Truth-seeking cannot consist of mere punishment of the body. I shall take proper nourishment once again."

As if in response to this unvoiced decision, Sujata, a maiden from a neighboring village, came before him and humbly offered a bowl of milk-rice.

He accepted her offering. His five fellow ascetics, disciples who had followed him throughout his six years of heroic effort, were outraged. Convinced that the ex-prince had abandoned the quest for Truth, they summarily left him.

Alone, he ate in silence. When he had finished, somehow he felt strong enough to stand, and leaning on his staff, he rose and made his way to the shore of the Naranjana River which flowed nearby. He bathed in the water, letting six years of matted filth and dirt wash away.

Climbing up onto the shore again he announced, "If this is the day of my Supreme Enlightenment, may the bowl float upstream!" And he cast his empty offering bowl onto the waters.

As soon as the bowl touched the surface of the river it forged upstream against the current until it came to the whirlpool of Kala Naga Raja, the Black Snake King who dwells on the river bottom. There it whirled down down into the jewelled chambers of the Naga King's palace. It stopped against an endless row of identically formed bowls. And hearing that little noise—"clink!"—the Black Naga King opened his eyes. Slowly he raised his great, hooded head and announced, "Only yesterday a Buddha arose. Today, there shall be another Buddha! Awake! Rejoice!" Then, swaying in that shimmering light, he began to chant his ancient songs in praise of the Bodhisattva's assured triumph and victory.

And the Bodhisattva, Siddhartha Gautama, strode like a roused lion towards the Bo-tree.

There, in the cool, soft light of the late afternoon, he met a poor grass cutter named Sothiya, who offered him eight bundles of freshly cut grass as a sitting cushion and mat.

Then the Future Buddha, spreading the grass on the earth at the base of the Tree, seated himself in the lotus posture and made this determination: "Though only my skin, sinews and bones remain and my blood and flesh dry up and wither away, yet never from this seat will I stir until I have attained Full Enlightenment."

And he pressed forward once again in deep meditation.

Then, many fearsome and foul, as well as many seductive and pleasant, visions arose before and all around him. All the forces of life's desire for joy, comfort, and ease came swaying to him in the form of three women: the three beautiful daughters of Mara, the Tempter. They danced before him offering exquisite pleasure, unceasing comfort, endless rest, while all of life's terrors—fears of death and suffering, fears of hells, horrors, pain, ugliness, the unknown—mobbed him shrieking of torment and deformity, of all manner of terrible and disgusting experience should he persist. Mara's army descended upon him: horse-headed, ten-eyed, tiger-faced, many-armed, with faces in their chests, with sharp yellow teeth and blood-dripping mouths, with spiders for hands and hissing with adders' tongues. On they came, heaving stones, knives, spears; hurling flaming discs, mud, filth. Screaming madly, they whirled down upon him like a flock of hunger-maddened crows wildly striving to peck and tear some slight scraps of nourishment from a huge smooth stone. But they could not.

The Future Buddha sat on, viewing all these wild displays evenly, surely, calmly, completely unmoved. It was as if he were watching the antics of children at play. The knives and spears turned into flowers and garlands, the mud and filth became incense and perfume. The beautiful women grew old and the howling armies stood silent.

Then Mara, the Tempter, himself approached the Future Buddha. Assuming the voice of Gautama's own innerness, the habitual voice of his own thoughts, he began to question the Future Buddha with these words: "Are you sure you are the one? Sure you have this Buddha-Nature? Sure you are worthy of coming to Supreme Enlightenment today? Right now? Think of it. Supreme Enlightenment! Supreme! Enlightenment!"

But the Future Buddha only touched the earth lightly with his right hand and asked the earth to witness for him.

And the earth replied with a hundred, a thousand, a hundred thousand voices—the voices of furrows and graves, voices of youth and age, of man, woman and child, the unheeded cries of beasts, the quick, unknown silvery language of fish, the sweet twinings of plants and the warm, grey crumblings of stone. For all were one voice now, thundering, "He is worthy! There is not one spot on this globe where he has not offered himself selflessly, through countless lifetimes, for the attainment of Enlightenment and the welfare of all living beings!"

Mara's hosts dropped their weapons and fled. His daughters prostrated themselves and asked forgiveness. His great war elephant, "Mountain-Girded," crashed to the ground like a heap of stones. The flowers faded, and the incense and perfume drifted away. All, all was gone.

Alone beneath the tree, the Future Buddha only pressed on, deeper and deeper, without stopping anywhere, transcending all limitations, swallowing up the darkness with his own light, until with the dawn, his Mind rose clear and radiant and obvious as the daybreak. And when he glanced at the Morning Star he found Enlightenment itself, crying out, "Wonder of wonders! Intrinsically, all living beings are Buddhas, fully endowed with wisdom and virtue!"

It was December eighth. He was thirty-five years of age and had broken through to what others as yet only half-dreamed. The Path had been reopened. The Dharma was once again accessible to the efforts of humans and devas. In the steadily rising morning light, a Fully Realized Buddha now sat beneath the suddenly blossoming tree.

Commentary on page 200

THE STORY OF
ANGULIMALA, THE ROBBER

Long ago a child was born to a noble family that dwelt in the city of Savaat, in the kingdom of Kosala. At the moment of his birth, every weapon in the city, from the most elegant ivory-inlaid hunting spear to the crudest cold-hammered iron sword, glittered with a piercing light.

No one had ever seen such a thing. Disturbed, the king called for his wise men to explain this strange event. Studying the heavens, they announced that the newborn child, having been born under the constellation of the Robber, was destined to become a robber when he matured.

"Will he be a lone robber?" asked the king, "or the leader of a gang?"

"A lone robber, Sire."

The king announced, "Let the child live. His father has been a faithful minister. What harm, after all, can one lone robber do?"

So it was decreed. And because of the king's words, the child was named Ahimsaka, meaning, "the Harmless One."

As the years passed, Ahimsaka grew to be a sensitive and intelligent child. When he was sixteen his father sent him to a noted Brahmin teacher to complete his education.

The teacher, impressed with the boy's kindness, intelligence, and willingness to learn, devoted special efforts to Ahimsaka's education. The other students, growing jealous, began to plot against him.

Sometimes alone, sometimes in groups of two or three, they came before the teacher claiming to have seen Ahimsaka embracing the teacher's young wife.

The teacher laughed them out. But in time, a seed of doubt was planted. The teacher's love for the boy turned to hatred. Then, the teacher devised a plan to send Ahimsaka to his death.

He called the boy to him and said, "My son, your spiritual training is almost completed. Only one task remains. When it is finished, your life of suffering will be over. Listen carefully: You must slay one thousand men."

"What?" cried the boy. "Kill a thousand men! I couldn't even kill one. No, not even a dog! Please, Master, do not say such a thing, not even as a joke. You know that killing is the worst of sins."

"This is no joke," replied the teacher severely. "I have pondered long, and it is clear to me. Slay a thousand men and your freedom is assured. Fail, and you are lost. Come, Ahimsaka, my instruction has always brought you happiness, has it not? Don't be confused, child. Have courage! The race is almost won. Don't stumble or falter now! All shall be well. You shall see."

That night, Ahimsaka paced his little room. "To kill is a grievous sin. That I know. My teacher has always praised kindness. Yet he has always taught me well. Always his words have brought me benefit. Perhaps, then," he thought on, "there is some teaching here which I do not, cannot, as yet understand. Can I refuse his command? Yet how can I carry out such a horrible task? I cannot do this. Yet I must."

At last, against the deepest promptings of his own intuition and the warnings of his judgment and reason, Ahimsaka took up a sword, a spear, a bow, and a quiver of barbed arrows, and set out alone into the dark forest.

A curved, yellowed tooth of a moon slid above the clouds. Ghostly mists coiled from beneath the shadows of the trees. In the distance a jackal mournfully howled. An owl hooted, and Ahimsaka started with dread. For one last time he cast a lingering glance back towards the safety of the little compound of shrines and huts he had come to call home. Then, steeling himself, he moved on, letting the darkness swallow him.

Soon, in horrible, silent, guilty despair, he began to slay travellers on the road. Dropping them in the dust singly and in pairs, he counted, "one, two. . ." as they fell. His bright, quick mind grew grim and dark. His graceful, slender form turned lumpish and thick. His fists dangled awkwardly at his sides like stones. He neither laughed nor spoke. He took no delight in the singing of the birds or the rustling of the green leaves. Prowling the forests like a beast with tangled locks, starting eyes, and bloodstained hands, he simply drew his weapons, and without a thought, slew all he met.

In time, Ahimsaka could not maintain his count. Numbers slithered madly through his mind without sequence or meaning, giving him no peace.

Then, he devised a simple way to maintain his count. Each time he killed, he cut a finger from his dead victim's hand and strung it on a cord, the remnant of an earlier Brahmanic initiation.

In time, a necklace of severed fingers dangled at his throat.

Then, throughout the land, the people whispered a new name, a name like the rattling of dry leaves in a hot wind. The name was Angulimala, "Grisly-Garland." This name the people themselves gave to the one who killed caravans of men, waylaid companies of soldiers, struck down the armed and unarmed alike however they might plead and weep. It was the name of the murderous robber who took a finger from every corpse.

Then the people hid themselves in their homes and stayed far from the forest roads. Such a great silence fell on the land it was as if a famine or blight stalked the kingdom, not just a lone man.

And Angulimala, once Ahimsaka, counting his garland of fingers in dark simplicity—"one, two, three. . ."—found that he neared his goal. Only one finger more was needed and the horrid task would be done.

A tremor of joy tore through his mind like a hound bounding through a thicket. For a moment his eyes grew clear. Gripping his heavy spear and polished bow, he slung a quiver of rattling arrows over his shoulder and set off to find his last victim and release.

Now, at this time, the Buddha was residing with his monks in a grove of trees not far from the city of Savaat. As he sat beneath the trees, he heard a woman sobbing and wailing. He rose and came to the road.

"What grieves you, mother?" asked the Buddha.

"Blessed One!" she sobbed, "It is my son, Ahimsaka, my gentle son. He is the robber, the one they call Angulimala. It is he and no other. I know it. I awoke in the night, and my heart cried out beneath my breast, and suddenly," she moaned, "I knew. The king's army is searching. They will find him and slay him. But I shall find him first. I will bring him home. He shall return with me and beg for his pardon."

"I will bring him home for you," said the Buddha. "Be patient. Dry your eyes. The boy shall not die by the king's hand. I promise you he shall come safely home. Return and do not grieve."

And the Buddha set off on the dusty road that led through the forest.

Soon the robber, Angulimala, lying in the shadows beneath the trees, saw a lone traveller approaching. Rising to his feet, he raised his spear and called, "Stop, traveller. Your destiny awaits!"

But the Buddha, without turning his head, only walked on. The robber Angulimala laughed bitterly. "Walk or run. Do your utmost, friend. These are your final moments. Do with them as you will. They are your last." Then, slinging on his sword and a quiver of arrows, taking up his bow and spear, he began to run after the Buddha.

But, strangely, no matter how fast he ran or how far he ran he could not get within spear range or bow shot. The Buddha just walked calmly while Angulimala, dripping sweat, his sides heaving, gasping for his breath, ran and ran. Yet it was to no avail. He could not approach.

At last Angulimala stopped and stood bent over, leaning on his spear, gasping for breath. His lungs ached. His eyes burned with sweat. His glistening sides heaved like those of a dog winded from a long chase. He raised his eyes, and the road, trees, and hills seemed to ripple. Spots of light danced before him. Leaning on his spear, he strove to catch his breath.

Then the Buddha, walking still, turned back and calmly spoke. "I have stopped," he said, "yet you have not."

"Oh, monk," panted Angulimala, near tears from both his great exertion and confusion, "some great trickster you must be. For while you only walked, I ran, and running, could not catch you. Now you walk on saying you have stopped, and I, you say, while I stand here, still go on. Come, I beg you, what can you mean?"

"It means, 'Harmless One,'" answered the Buddha, "that I have stopped harming others while you most certainly have not."

And for Angulimala a veil was lifted. Recovering himself, he was Ahimsaka once more. Covering his face with his hands he dropped into the dust, his weapons clattering around him, and cried out, bellowing in horror at the depth of his error and shame.

Then the Buddha asked if he would be willing to give up this life. And he who had been the boy, Ahimsaka, said, "Yes, I am most certainly willing to leave this life behind."

"Then rise," said the Buddha, "and follow."

But Angulimala said, "No, I cannot. Send for the king and his men. Tell them I shall not lift a finger against them. They must bind me and slay me for I cannot live with this knowledge of my deeds."

"Patience," said the Buddha. "Tie up your despair and your grief. There will always be time to surrender and die. But the time is short in which to struggle and live. Rise, I say, and follow."

So Angulimala rose. He followed. And he became a monk.

As a monk, Angulimala discovered that he had the power to help women in childbirth. Those exhausted by the difficulties of labor had only to be brought before him and instantly their sufferings would cease. Then, with the ease of water flowing from a pitcher, their children would be born. Even animals could be brought before him and they too would quickly and painlessly deliver healthy young.

It was a great mystery. How could a man who had slain so many without a single thought of compassion now have such compassion on those struggling to bring forth new life? Still, for the soothing and healing presence that he brought, the women praised and blessed him.

But Angulimala himself was not soothed or healed. Day and night images of his own past cruelties arose in his mind. He saw tear-stained, bloodied, terrified faces. He saw hands raised protectively as if to ward off heavy blows. He felt dying fingers gripping his ankles in final, loosening supplication. He heard sighs, screams, and groans. In the muscles of his arm, he knew again the heft of a sword, felt the shock of blade hitting bone. Voices screamed, "I have a wife. I have children. I have an aged mother! Spare me." Over and over he heard the cries of those who had wept for mercy and had yet been slain.

And as the hot tears gushed down his own cheeks, he cried out many times, "What have I done! How could I have been so blind! I have opened the gates of hell."

But always the Buddha counseled him, saying, "Patience, monk, patience."

One hot, dusty morning the monk, Angulimala, walked slowly through the city of Savaat, the place of his birth, collecting alms for his meal. Though he had become a familiar figure, many still became silent or hurried away at his approach. Others turned their backs or shut their doors. Now and then, a woman with a nursing child stepped quietly from the shelter of her doorway to place an offering of fruit or rice in his bowl. In silence, head down, Angulimala, with a bow to his donor, received his alms and walked on.

Then suddenly Angulimala staggered and fell. His begging bowl was knocked from his hands and shattered. His robes were torn from his shoulders as every stone flung at any mangy dog or crow, every whip or goad raised against horse or ox, every club, stick, dagger, knife, or sword lifted by any man against another throughout that land struck, not their intended victims, but the monk, Angulimala, alone.

Bleeding, in great pain, with even the bones of his fingers broken, Angulimala gathered his robes to him and groped his way to the Buddha like a blind man.

Then the Buddha sat in the dust with the monk Angulimala and said, "This is the time for patience, monk. The time for great patience has come. This moment brings the payment for all your debts. Your chance for freedom has come."

Then Angulimala roused himself and raised a great determination. Pushing his mind on and on, he allowed it to settle nowhere. He refused to give in to agony or to seek refuge in hope, fear, or grief. The awful memories came again. He let them go. Visions of his childhood, of rippling laughter, running water, sunlight on flowers—a stream of sweet images— flowed through his mind. He clung to nothing. Moment by moment he continued patiently on, enduring all. Suddenly, his pain vanished and his doubting, seeking mind lay shattered. For a timeless instant he knew the taste of Nirvana, the fruit of the Buddha's Path.

Flooded with joy, like one cured of a long illness at last, he cried out:

> "Lesser men subdue with swords, hooks, and
>   sticks.
> But, to my eternal relief, I have been subdued
>   by the Buddha
> Who needs neither weapon nor whip."

And Ahimsaka, free at last, sighed once, twice, and peacefully died.

In the city of Savaat, the treetops tossed in a sudden, cooling wind, and, once again, the weapons glittered, but now as if with a cleansing flame. The long wandering was over. The Harmless One had come safely home.

Commentary on page 201

NALAGIRI, THE ELEPHANT

Nalagiri was an elephant, a great bull tusker. And he was a brute. Huge, violent, ugly-tempered, as much like other elephants as an untamed stallion is like a child's pony.

The king had been warned. Nonetheless, he liked the sense of power that came from owning and riding such a beast. It was said, too, that rival kings hesitated to attack for fear of facing Nalagiri in battle.

Devadatta, the Buddha's cousin, while a monk, remained proud, cruel, and selfish. Like Nalagiri he was undisciplined. In his unbridled quest for power, Devadatta knew no restraints, and had even made attempts—through courtesans, poison, thugs—on the Buddha's life.

Somehow, the efforts had all failed. Devadatta himself had even once pushed a boulder down towards the Buddha as he walked along a deserted forest path. The boulder, hurtling down, bounced and miraculously split. Only a tiny splinter of stone pierced the Buddha's foot.

Still, Devadatta persisted, his mind twisting and turning, to find some final, foolproof plan. One day, he hit upon a stratagem so simple, yet so perfect, that he wept for joy. "Nalagiri shall be my emissary!" Devadatta cried. "I shall get the monster drunk, madden him with noise, prod him with spears, and release him on the Buddha's path. The perfect, unpunishable murder will commit itself."

And off he hurried to the royal elephant stables. There Devadatta found a man raking the yard clean of soiled straw and elephant dung. Devadatta saw the anger burning there.

"Friend," said Devadatta, "I seek a man who desires to rise in this world, a man willing to take hold of the golden chances that fortune offers."

"Speak on," said the man.

Devadatta smiled. "I have a problem. A cousin, mad with power, will not share the reins of his office. If you would help, your task will be simple. Fill Nalagiri's trough with wine and let Nalagiri drink. Let the fire in the beast be soothed so that he may know peace. Let him be released from his bondage. Yes, at the right time, let him know freedom. Release him from his chains, and you shall let him release me from my problem. Do you understand?"

"Are you not Devadatta, cousin to the Buddha?"

Devadatta bowed. "At your service."

"It might prove expensive."

Devadatta smiled again. " Friend," he said, "kings wait upon me. Women, gold, jewels—just name what you desire, and you shall have it. Do not fear. Your fortune is made. You shall soon see the last of the land of elephant dung. Bring friends. I shall liberate them from their difficulties too."

And so the plan was made.

The next night, in the early hours before dawn, six men carried three large clay jugs into Nalagiri's stall. Nalagiri's ears fanned forward as he heard liquid splashing into his trough. He lifted up his trunk, and smelling sweetness, walked forward, his chain clanking. He drank. And it was sweet, as sweet as flowers, sweet as sugar cane.

Nalagiri's eyes grew soft, half-lidded, and flecked with gold. His trunk twirled this way and that. His ears slowly flapped. Slowly, the great beast swayed, first to one side, then the other. He lifted a hind foot, then a front. He gurgled as if singing to himself some long-forgotten, peaceful, elephant lullaby.

The stall cleaner watched from the shadows of the doorway. Slowly, the darkness around him lightened. A warmth touched his neck, and a shadow stretched before him as the sun crept over the palace wall. It was time. The stall keeper picked up a spear, and signalling the others to follow, crept forward towards where Nalagiri swayed and gurgled in the darkness. All had drunk of the palm wine, and the air was sickly sweet with the smell of it. Now they were set, crouched in place, directly behind Nalagiri. Their eyes shone with greed and wine, excitement and fear.

"Now!" shouted their leader, and they yelled, screaming loudly. Cymbals crashed. Drums thundered. Spears jabbed. Nalagiri screamed a wild, mad cacophonous scream, trumpeting so loudly and so shrilly that the walls of the stable shook and the straw dust billowed up in swirling, choking clouds.

Then, Nalagiri whirled on his tormentors, straining with his trunk and tusks to reach and destroy them. The men, terrified, ran. But the chains held. Then the men, released from their fear, laughed and grew angry. One picked up a jagged stone and hurled it so that it struck with a great "thump!" on the bulging dome of Nalagiri's forehead. They laughed again. Nalagiri's eyes blazed with red fire. He trumpeted madly and dug at the earth with his tusks in his rage. But the men, made bold by the wine and trusting in the strength of the chains, raced behind and jabbed with their spears. Again, Nalagiri screamed and whirled. But the men raced behind him. Again, the cymbals crashed. Again, the spear points pierced the tender folds of Nalagiri's skin.

"Enough!" shouted the stall cleaner. "Unbar the gates! Let Nalagiri charge out onto the streets. Prepare to release the chains!" But it was too late. Nalagiri, in his frenzy, had a strength they had not bargained for.

With a scream Nalagiri hurled himself forward. The chains snapped. On he came, the broken chains whipping his ankles like goads, straight on at his tormentors he charged in his fury, and he caught them still inside the stable. He pounded them with his head and gored them with his tusks. He kneeled upon them, crushing them into the mud and dung and straw. He beat them into the earth with his tusks until only a bloody froth remained. He put his trunk into his mouth, and in his madness, trumpeted loudly. Then, Nalagiri, like some demon of unspeakable power, smashed down the still-unbarred gates and stormed out into the early morning streets.

As the Buddha quietly walked through the streets of the city gathering offerings for his morning meal, he heard cries and screams. Crowds streamed past, racing through the streets. "Run, Master!" they yelled. "Run! Nalagiri is loose, and he is furious!"

In a great splintering of beams and planks, nearby walls collapsed. There was a great roaring as masonry, stone and brick came tumbling and crashing down. A black cloud of churning dust and smoke rose up. With a loud flapping of wings, flocks of screaming, terrified birds wheeled through the sky. Cattle bellowed. And above it all rose the wild trumpeting of Nalagiri raging in his madness.

The Buddha walked towards the sounds of destruction. At a safe distance behind him a crowd of men, women, and children gathered. Many gathered, too, on the rooftops and balconies to see what might happen when Nalagiri and the Buddha met.

Ananda, the Buddha's attendant and cousin, walked by his side. He had already decided that when the dreaded moment came he would throw himself before Nalagiri so that the Buddha himself might yet be saved.

As they approached the place of Nalagiri's rampage, a hush fell on the crowd. Those on the rooftops also grew silent. Now the only sound was that of Nalagiri in his rage.

The Buddha stopped. At the end of the street Nalagiri kicked at an already crumbling mud-brick wall. He lifted up a shattered bed and flung it into the air. Broken carts, pots, tables, chairs littered the ground. The body of a bull, its neck broken, lay crumpled against a half-demolished house.

"Come, Nalagiri. Come, friend," called the Buddha.

Nalagiri spun to face this new threat. He lifted his trunk, sniffing the dust-laden air. Then, trumpeting wildly, he charged.

The crowds, screaming, scattered wildly. Even the monks broke ranks and fled, their orange robes fluttering like great, panicked butterflies around them. But the Buddha, with Ananda struggling mightily with his rising fear still by his side, stood firm.

Nalagiri, like a great black cloud, his tusks gleaming like lightning, hurtled towards them. The Buddha smiled, and advising Ananda to remain where he was, stepped forward saying, "Come then, Nalagiri. Since you seek, you shall find." And he extended an infinite tenderness towards Nalagiri, lost and alone in his madness.

Like a shadow of the wind racing along the bending grass blades, like a white, glimmering wave spreading along the shore, like a faint whirring and whirling in the sunlight, like the curling of heated air over the paved roads, something raced towards Nalagiri and broke against the rock of his brow.

Nalagiri staggered, slowed. His ears fanned back and forth. His trunk lifted this way and that, sniffing, searching the wind. Uncertainly, he stepped now this way, now that, like one lost, confused. The fire in his eyes softened. Tears hung from the long lashes and rolled down the thick, gray-black, wrinkled hide.

"Come, Nalagiri, come, friend," repeated the Buddha in a voice sweet as honey.

And Nalagiri, trunk extended, eyes half-closed, stumbled blindly forward, like a lost child that hears its mother calling, like a calf seeking the teat.

The Buddha reached forward his hand and gently touched the curled, thick-skinned, bristly trunk tip.

Every hair on Nalagiri's body stood erect. His eyes opened wide, rolled upward. His knees buckled, and slowly, like a mountain sinking into the sea, like a mound of sand washing away in the tide, Nalagiri sank down before the Buddha, sighed once, and rested his great tusked head upon the earth.

"Suffering, friend Nalagiri," said the Buddha, stroking lightly the great dome of Nalagiri's forehead, "is the condition of all life. But there is a Path that leads beyond it. No more killing, Nalagiri. Walk on, friend, with no thoughts of harm towards any living thing. Then shall the darkness lift. Rise now, Nalagiri, and be at peace."

Then Nalagiri arose, and flinging his trunk back up upon his head, trumpeted the royal salute. After that he stood calmly, quietly swinging his trunk and tail, until his frightened trainer came hesistantly forward and led him back to the palace stables.

Then the people cheered, tossing scarves, coins and flowers into the air. Musicians beat drums and played flutes and pipes. The king himself exclaimed, "Today we have seen such a miracle as never before. The Buddha, without weapons or force, has stopped Nalagiri in his rampage. He has pacified the heart of that great beast. So let us celebrate! Whoever has suffered losses, even so little as the smallest grain of rice, let them come forward. They shall have compensation from my own hands. Tonight, World-Honored One, dine with me. Speak, and I shall listen! This day a flower of faith has opened in my heart!"

In a nearby alley one lone angry face brooded from the shadows. It was Devadatta. For an instant the walls of his pride had fallen, and he, too, had gazed with wonder upon the unlikely scene. In that instant a sudden, wild impulse had arisen in his heart, an impulse to rush forward and, like Nalagiri, throw himself down and find peace. But he would not give in to it. Wrapping his robes even more tightly around him, he withdrew further yet into the shadows.

The Buddha saw that slight movement and sorrowed. Yet, at the same time he saw, too, that distant day, ages hence, when Devadatta himself would step from the darkness. After endless kalpas in the deepest hells, he would rise, restored to himself at last, and be a Buddha.

So, with the faithful Ananda by his side, and amidst the great joyful noise of the people, the Buddha set off through the city towards the palace of his host, the king.

Commentary on page 203

KISA GOTAMI

O nce a young woman named Kisa Gotami married into a
wealthy family. She was not well regarded in her new
home, but when a child was born—a son—she was, at last,
fully accepted. Kisa Gotami doted on her child. She loved
its every perfect, tiny bone, its dark eyes, curling toes, smiles
and sighs.

Kisa Gotami's child became sick. Despite all efforts, to save
its life, it died. She became crazed. She would let no one
take the child from her. In her unbalanced mind, she clung
to one thought: the Buddha, the Teacher, the Great Physician,
would save her from this nightmare and restore her child.

With the child on her hip, she left her husband's home and
set off to find the Buddha. She arrived at the assembly, and
approaching the Buddha, made her request. "World-Honored
One," she begged, "please restore my child."

The Buddha said to this heartbroken woman, Kisa Gotami,
"I will do so under one condition. You must bring to me one
tiny little mustard seed from a house in which no one has
died. Then I shall bring your child to life again."

Kisa Gotami ran off in joy. She knocked on the first door.
"Have you," she breathlessly asked, "any mustard seed? It is
for my child."

The woman of the house said, "Yes, my dear, I can give you
some mustard seed."

"I need only one," said Kisa Gotami.

"One seed?" asked the woman, surprised.

"Yes, one."

"I can give you one mustard seed."

Kisa Gotami's heart leapt. Soon her child would live, would smile and sigh and laugh and cling to her with tiny perfect hands. "Excuse me, but no one has died in this house, have they?" asked Kisa Gotami.

"My dear," answered the woman at the door, "my father died only last week."

"Oh," said Kisa Gotami, "I must find my seed elsewhere."

Again she knocked, and again she requested a mustard seed, and again a mustard seed was offered. Who did not have one tiny mustard seed to spare for a distraught woman and her child?

"Excuse me," said Kisa Gotami. "You have not had a death here recently?"

"My dear, my husband passed away a month ago."

"I must search elsewhere," said Kisa Gotami.

To house after house she went. Household after household freely offered her the mustard seed she required. But from house after house Kisa Gotami turned away with a sinking heart. In each house the story was the same: "My mother has died, my aunt, my mother-in-law, my wife, my daughter; my brother, my uncle, my father, my nephew, my cousin, my father-in-law, my son." On and on went the endless lament rising from every household. Indeed, there was not a single household in the city, from the palace of the king to the poorest beggars' hovel, in which such a magical mustard seed could be found, a mustard seed from a household in which no one had died.

Kisa Gotami found herself walking the streets of the city with her dead baby on her hip. She had come back to herself. Her eyes were clear, her mind alert. The sorrow she bore was no longer her sorrow alone. It was the sorrow of all. All that is born, she now knew, dies. All that comes into being must, sooner or later, exit again from being. There is no household that death spares. This was the hard, simple truth. She knew it now. It was her own. It was the truth.

She took up her dead child in her arms and kissed it gently. She kissed the perfect forehead, the curling fingers, the tiny toes. She brought her baby home, wrapped a tiny mustard seed in its funeral garments, and at last, said her farewell.

When the funeral was completed, she left that house and returned to the Buddha.

"Well, Kisa Gotami," asked the Buddha, "was your quest successful? Did you, my sister, find the mustard seed that brings life from death?"

"World-Honored One," she answered, "the mustard seed that I could find I have already left with my own beloved child. All that is born dies. Every child, mother, king, man, woman. Every cow, dog, tree, star. All go the same route. I have found the mustard seed. Now I make of you one request. Accept me into the Order. I was dead. I have come to learn to live."

So Kisa Gotami was received by the Buddha into the Order, and working hard, gained Liberation.

Commentary on page 205

PARINIRVANA

In his eightieth year the Buddha became ill. He admitted to Ananda that the time of his departure was near, for, he said, his body was like a worn-out cart that could only be kept going with difficulty. Only in meditation, he added, when all sense of the body had been transcended, was he at ease.

The Buddha then addressed his monks, saying, "All component things grow old. Work out your liberation with diligence. Time waits for no one. In three months the Tathagata, 'He Who Is Thus Come,' will enter Nirvana!"

Then the Buddha, accompanied by many monks and with Ananda by his side, walked to Pava, stopping at the Mango Grove of the smith, Cunda. The smith received instruction from the Teacher, then, with his heart gladdened, fed the assembly a lavish meal.

During that meal the Buddha ate some mushrooms. Immediately he told Ananda to set the dish aside and let no one else eat of it for the mushrooms were spoiled. Shortly after this, he was struck with such pain that he could hardly stand. When the pain abated, he and Ananda set off for Kusinara.

The Buddha was weak, and they walked slowly, taking their time to complete the journey, resting by the river banks and beneath the trees as they went. During that journey, the Buddha counseled Ananda that no one was to blame Cunda the Smith, nor was the smith himself to feel any blame. "Two meals are supremely precious to all Buddhas," he said. "One is received just before the One-Who-Has-Thus-Come attains Perfect Enlightenment, and the second is the one received just prior to a Buddha's entrance into Nirvana. Therefore," he added, "everyone should know that, with this final meal, Cunda the Smith has established a very good karma, beneficial to himself and to others. There is no reason at all for him to grieve."

At last they arrived at the Sala tree grove of the Mallas at Kusinara, on the far shore of the Hiranyavati River. It was almost three months to the day from the time of the Buddha's initial pronouncement of his going forth into Nirvana. Then, the Buddha turned to Ananda and said, "Ananda, please set up a couch for me between the twin Sala trees, with my head lying to the North. I must lie down now. I can go no further."

Weeping, Ananda did as the Buddha requested, spreading and folding a cloth over the great stone couch that lay between the trees. The Buddha then reclined on his right side upon this couch, and ever mindful, alert, and self-possessed, rested beneath the trees.

Though it was out of season, the twin Sala trees flowered, and blossoms rained down from the branches and from the sky. Unearthly music sounded. Ananda was astonished by these miracles, but the Buddha said, "It is not thus that the World-Honored One is truly reverenced. Those who do good, who uphold the practices and precepts of good character, who fulfill their duties in life both great and small, those who gain an entry into the Dharma and discover that they and all beings are intrinsically Buddhas—it is such as these who, whether monks or nuns, laymen or women, of this faith or any other, truly reverence the Tathagata. Now know, Ananda, this very night the Tathagata will enter Nirvana. There will be no more limited return in store for me, no further error or suffering."

The birds grew very quiet and uttered no sound, sitting along the branches as if in trance, their bodies relaxed. Ordained practitioners, advanced disciples and beginners, their faces covered with tears, gathered in the grove as the light of the afternoon deepened and gathered.

"Go, Ananda," said the Buddha, "and tell the Mallas that it is time. They will be stricken with grief if they are not permitted to attend me now, before my Nirvana." Ananda obeyed the order.

The Mallas, their eyes streaming tears, came at once, and Ananda presented them to the reclining Buddha, family by family. Then, anguish in their minds, they stood weeping among the trees of their Sala grove.

A lone truth seeker named Subhadda, troubled with doubts, arrived hoping to see the Buddha while time remained. But Ananda refused him an interview, saying, "The Exalted One is growing weaker, friend. The hour is late. Do not trouble him now." But the Buddha, overhearing, asked that the wanderer, Subhadda, be admitted to him. Subhadda questioned the Buddha, and with the Buddha's replies, his doubts were resolved. He was admitted into the Order, the last disciple to be personally accepted by the Buddha.

Then the World-Honored One, seeing the Mallas still caught in the nets of distress, spoke as follows: "In this hour of joy it is not proper for you to grieve. Your despair is quite inappropriate and you should regain your composure! The goal, so hard to win, which for so many eons I have worked hard for, is now at hand. When that is won, there is no earth, water, fire, wind, or air present, but unchanging bliss, beyond all objects of the senses, and a peace which nothing can ever take away. When you hear of that, and know that no becoming mars it, and that nothing there can ever pass away—how then can there still be any room in your minds for grief? At Bodhi Gaya, when I won Enlightenment, I got rid of the causes of becoming which are really nothing but a gang of harmful vipers. Now the hour nears when I also will get rid of this body, the crystallization of my own thoughts and deeds arising from an endless past. Now that at last the frightful dangers of becoming are about to become extinct, now that they are to be blown out, like a candle's flame is blown out by the wind, now that at last I emerge from the vast and endless suffering—is this really a time that you should grieve?"

So spoke the sage of the Shakyas, the Buddha Shakyamuni.

The oldest of the Mallas alone found strength to reply. "We all weep, but why? We should look upon the Awakened One

as a man who has escaped from the dangers of a house on
fire! The gods see it like that. So should we, too. Yet the
cause of our grief remains. This mighty man, the Tathagata,
once he has won Nirvana, will pass beyond our knowledge
and sight. When those who travel in the wilderness lose
their guide they fall into distress. That is how we feel. People who walk away from a gold mine with no riches are to
be pitied. Likewise, those who have seen the great Teacher
ought to have gained some spiritual achievement of their
own! World-Honored One, this is why we weep!" The old
man spoke to the point.

Then the Buddha, the Best of Men, aiming at their welfare,
addressed them a final time. "Liberation cannot come from
the mere sight of me. It demands serious efforts in actual
spiritual practice. But if someone has truly seen my Dharma,
then that person is released from the net of suffering, even
though they have never seen me at all. Similarly, the mere
sight of a physician cures no illness. One must actually take
the medicine to be well. The mere sight of me enables no
one to conquer suffering; each person has to meditate and
discover the truth themselves. If disciplined, a man or woman may live as far away from me as can be. If he or she only
sees my Dharma, then that person truly sees me as well. But
if a person should neglect to strive in concentrated calm for
higher things, then, though they may live quite near to me, it
will be as if they are far away. So, work hard for Truth's sake.
Do good deeds and strive resolutely for Mindfulness. Be vigilant! Remember life is continually shaken by many kinds of
suffering even as the flame of a lamp is shaken by the wind."

In this way the Sage, the Best of All Who Live, encouraged
and fortified the Mallas. But as they went back to Kusinara,
each one felt helpless and alone as if crossing a swollen river
on a dark and stormy night.

Then the Buddha turned to his close disciples and said,
"Everything comes to an end though it may last an eon. I
have done all I could do, both for myself and for others. I
have disciplined, in heaven and earth, all those I could discipline. I have trained them and motivated them and set them
in the stream that leads to Liberation. Hereafter, my Dharma

shall abide for generations among living beings. Recognize the true nature of the living world and do not be anxious. Separation cannot be avoided. All that lives is subject to this law—yet strive from this day onwards that it shall be no more! When the light of wisdom has dispelled the darkness of ignorance, when all existence has been seen as without abiding substance, peace ensues when life draws to an end, a peace which seems to cure a long sickness at last. Everything, whether stationary or moveable, is bound to perish in the end. Be mindful and vigilant! The time for my entry into Nirvana has arrived! These are my last words!"

As the Buddha entered Nirvana, the earth quivered and firebrands fell from the sky. Rivers boiled. The heavens were lit with fire. Thunderbolts crashed, winds raged. The moon's light waned, and in spite of a cloudless sky, darkness spread everywhere. Beautiful flowers opened out of season on the Sala trees above the Buddha's couch, and the trees bent down over him and showered his golden body with flowers.

The mighty five-headed nagas, the great serpents, stood motionless in the sky, their eyes red with grief, their hoods closed as, with deep devotion, they gazed on the body of the Sage. The gods of the Pure Abode remained composed, deep in their non-attachment to the things of this world. The kings of the gandharavas and nagas, as well as the yakshas and devas, who rejoice in the Dharma, all appeared in the sky, mourning and absorbed in the utmost grief.

The world, when the great Sage had passed beyond, became like a mountain whose peak had been shattered by a thunderbolt; it became like the sky without the moon, like a pond whose lotuses the frost has withered.

Only those who truly understood the deep import of the Buddha's teachings were not shaken to their depths. For, like the Buddha himself, they knew well that it is the nature of all things to pass away.

On the seventh day after the passing into Nirvana, the body of the Buddha was borne to the shrine of the Mallas where it was set upon a perfumed pyre and consigned to the flames. The bones that remained were honored for another seven days. Then, at last, these final relics were divided into eight portions and distributed equally to those clans and territories among whom the Buddha had, while alive, most often travelled and taught.

Commentary on page 205

SECTION II
JATAKA TALES

GIVE IT ALL YOU'VE GOT

In a certain lifetime, long ago, the Buddha was a merchant and traveller. He gathered his goods in one part of the vast land of India, traded what he had brought with him, then sold his new merchandise in yet another part of the land. In this way he gained much experience of life, survived many hardships, and learned about the ways of differing peoples. He became wise and gathered some wealth.

At one time, when he was already a grey-bearded and dignified man, he was bringing a caravan of goods across a sandy desert. He had almost one hundred ox-drawn carts filled with cloth, spices, and grain. Many men were in his employ at that time, and he hired, in addition, a desert pilot to guide them safely through the vast wasteland.

Now, a desert pilot is a man who knows the land and knows the stars. Like a pilot at sea he navigates by starlight, and so, can lead a caravan safely across the most featureless desert terrain.

Because of the terrible heat, the caravan rested during the day under awnings, men and oxen both. Then at night, in the coolness after the sun had gone down, the men would hitch up the oxen and set off again under the stars. In this way, they travelled safely some six days across the sands. They had water and wood, and food enough for yet another day or so, but men and oxen were tired.

That night the pilot, seated in the lead wagon, announced that by morning they would be beyond the desert. Wood, water, food all again would be plentiful. So they unloaded the remaining water jars, the sacks of rice, and the wood they carried for building cooking fires, and, with their loads lightened, set off on the final trek.

The pilot had been up on constant watch for six nights. The excessive heat and glaring light of the day had made sleep difficult. Now, as they neared their destination, he dozed off. The wagons rolled on. The oxen marched steadily through the darkness. The stars glittered overhead in the clear desert air. Men laughed and joked.

Just before dawn the pilot awoke with a start. He glanced at the stars and cried out in alarm. Rather than going straight and true on their course, they had been veering in a great half-circle through the night. They were no nearer the desert's ending than they had been at the sun's going down! Men and oxen were already terribly thirsty. In an hour the sun would rise like a great ball of fire. The desert would become hot as a blast furnace. Soon, they would be consumed by thirst. Their water had been left behind. "Halt!" cried the pilot. "Stop the wagons! Stop!"

The open cloth shelter was erected, and all huddled beneath the protection it offered from the searing rays of the desert sun.

The merchant leader of the caravan was no newcomer to danger. He stepped out from the shade of the shelter and began to walk along the dunes.

Soon he spied what he had been searching for: a few pale tufts of grass rising from the sand.

"Bring shovels!" he called, "and quickly!" His men hurried forward, shovels and picks in hand. "Dig," he said, "where this grass grows. Dig, for our lives depend upon it."

Down they dug into the sands, deeper and deeper. The exertion in that heat was terrible. Men gasped and fainted. Many times they thought to just give up and wait for death. But the merchant stood firmly by them. "Dig," he said. "I know it is hard, but where grass grows there is water. Just trust me and do your best." So on they dug.

At last they had a narrow well pit extending some twelve or fifteen feet straight down. At the very bottom of that shaft the sand was cool and carried some moisture in it. So, parched and exhausted as they were, they had hope and took

turns going down to the well bottom and digging on with a
will. Soon, it seemed, they would have cool water. But, alas,
their efforts were doomed to fail. After another foot or two
of digging they hit a great stone blocking their way. There
was no way to dig around it. The narrow shaft, already sliding with sand, would collapse if the base were widened any
further. In despair, they all lay exposed on the hot sands and
wept.

"Don't give up yet," said the grizzled merchant. "Tie a rope
around me and lower me down into the well."

As they lowered him down, loose, shifting sand slid and
hissed ominously down around him. He knelt upon the
stone and put his ear to it. He could hear, like a distant hum,
the movement of water beneath the stone. "Up!" he called.
"Draw me up."

The tunnel was treacherous. With every pull he had to
keep from brushing the well's sides and causing the whole
shaft to collapse. He came out covered with sand. He was
grim, but smiling.

"The water is just below the stone," said the wise merchant.
"Get a sledge hammer and bring to me the strongest and
most well-rested man among you."

A sledge hammer was brought and a large-framed, big-
boned youth was led before the merchant.

"Son," said the merchant, "it's up to you. The stone at the
well bottom must be broken. The water is flowing just below
that stone. Rouse your every confidence. You are the strongest among us. Our lives depend on your determination.
Take this hammer and break that stone."

The youth was lowered carefully down into the hole and
landed safely upon the stone. There was hardly room for
him to swing the hammer, but he lifted it up and struck the
stone a great blow. The stone didn't budge. He tried again.
And again. It was nerve-wracking work. The water was defi-
nitely just below. He could feel the whole stone humming
with the force of its flow. But if one careless swing were to
hit the tunnel wall, the whole shaft might cave in upon him.
He wiped his brow, again carefully lifted up the hammer, and
again brought it down with a great jarring blow. Again, he
swung, and again. Still the stone would not break.

The youth could not go on. The constant threat of the tunnel's collapse, his own thirst and weakness, the solidity of that unyielding stone, the hissing of the sands sliding down the shaft, all conspired to sap his deepest reserves of strength.

"Pull me up!" he cried. "Get me out! It's hopeless."

The merchant stuck his head down into the dry well shaft. "Son, it's difficult, but not hopeless. You can do it. The stone will break. Don't give up. If there was ever a time to exert your strength to the limit, this is it. Give it one more shot and give it all you've got!"

Heartened, the youth lifted up the hammer one more time and swung it with his whole heart and strength. The rock cracked, split, and a geyser of cool water shot up.

Quickly, they hoisted him out of the well as the water shot up bubbling and dancing out of the hole.

The merchant's fortitude and the youth's strength had saved them.

After filling their vessels and drinking their fill, they tended to the oxen, then made their way safely out of the desert.

In that desert the well bubbles still. Even today, travellers in the wasteland praise the men who left this bounty for them.

Commentary on page 207

THE BRAVE LION AND THE FOOLISH RABBIT

Once, a little rabbit was resting peacefully in the shade beneath a mango tree. He wasn't wide awake, and he wasn't completely asleep. He just lay there drifting between waking and sleeping. As he lay there, a foolish thought crossed his mind. "What if the earth broke up?" He sat up, now wide awake. "What if the earth broke up today?!" Suddenly, he heard a loud CRASH! right behind him. And, without turning to see what it was, he jumped up and ran off crying, "The earth is breaking up! The earth is breaking up! Run! Run!"

As he ran, he passed a second little rabbit. "Say, friend," called out this second rabbit, "what's the hurry? Why are you running?"

But the first rabbit was too scared. He wouldn't stop. He wouldn't tell his friend what it was that was bothering him. He just turned, looked over his shoulder, and shouted out, "The earth is breaking up! The earth is breaking up! Run! Run!"

"The earth's breaking up?! The earth's breaking up!" cried the second rabbit. "Why, then, wait for me!" And off he ran, too.

Pretty soon, they passed a third rabbit. "What's happening?" called the third rabbit. "Why are you both running?"

But those two rabbits were too scared. They wouldn't stop. They just looked over their shoulders as they ran past, and shouted out loudly, "Run! Run! The earth's breaking up!"

And that third rabbit said, "The earth's breaking up!! Well, wait for me!"

So now there were three rabbits running along. Pretty soon there were four rabbits, then five rabbits, then ten rabbits, twenty rabbits, thirty rabbits, forty rabbits, fifty rabbits, one hundred rabbits all running along.

And they all ran past a big, sleepy bear. The bear rubbed his sleepy eyes and said, "Wha-at's hap-pen-ing? Why are you all run-ning?"

But the rabbits were too scared to stop. They just shouted over their shoulders, "The earth's breaking up! Run! Run!"

"The earth's break-ing up?" repeated the bear in shock. "The earth's break-ing up? Why, why, why, if the earth's break-ing up, I'd better get go-ing too!"

And off he ran, crying out in his slow, sturdy bear's voice, "The earth's break-ing up! The earth's break-ing up! Run! Run!"

Soon, he passed another bear. And that bear called, "What's going on? Why are you running?" But that first bear was too scared. He just looked over his shoulder as he ran past and shouted, "Run! Run! The earth's break-ing up!"

And that second bear said, "The earth's break-ing up? The earth's break-ing up?! Why, why, if the earth's breaking up, wait for me!" So now there were two bears running along.

Pretty soon they passed a third bear. He was sitting on the ground chewing on a piece of dripping honeycomb and batting at the bees buzzing all around him. "Hey," he called out. "Where are you going? Why are you running? Stop and tell me!"

But those two bears were too scared to stop. They wouldn't even stop for some of that sweet honeycomb. They just turned, looked over their shoulders, and shouted out, "The earth's breaking up! Run! Run!" And they kept on running.

"What! What's that you say?" exclaimed the third bear, rising to his feet. "The earth's breaking up? The earth's breaking up! Well, wait for me!" And pushing all of the remaining honeycomb into his mouth, he scrambled off leaving the bees buzzing angrily in the empty air.

Now there were three bears running along. Pretty soon there were four bears, then five bears, then ten bears, twenty bears, thirty bears, forty bears, fifty bears, one hundred frightened bears all running along. Oh, what a howling and growling din they made!

And they all ran past an elephant. The elephant stood dozing under a great shade tree. His huge ears fanned slowly back and forth. His tail swished behind him, this way and that, sweeping off the droning flies. Suddenly, his ears swung forward and stopped. His eyes opened wide. One hundred screaming rabbits and one hundred moaning bears burst through the bushes and rushed right past him. "What's going on?" trumpeted the elephant. "Why are you all running?" he demanded. "Stop and tell me!"

But those animals were too scared. They wouldn't stop. They just turned, looked over their shoulders, and shouted out, "The earth's breaking up! The earth's breaking up! Run! Run!" And they were gone!

The elephant was wide awake now! "The earth's breaking up?" he exclaimed. "The earth's breaking up?! Why, I'm the biggest and heaviest of all creatures. If the earth's breaking up, I'd be the first one to fall in!" And trumpeting in terror, he too charged off, his tail pointed straight out behind him, running madly after the others.

Soon they ran past a second elephant. Then another, and another. Soon there were five trumpeting elephants stampeding along behind the rabbits and the bears. Then ten elephants, twenty elephants, thirty elephants, forty elephants, fifty elephants, one hundred elephants all trumpeting loudly in their fear and charging along as fast as they could. On they went, tearing up trees and bushes, tossing boulders, pounding the earth with their great feet, raising up a great cloud of dust and a great, wild, trumpeting cry.

They passed a snake sunning itself on a warm rock ledge. "Sssssssay," hissed the snake, anxiously lifting his smooth, scaled head. "What'ssss happening? Why are you all running? The earth isss ssshaking sssso. Isssss it an earthquake?"

"The earth's breaking up!" trumpeted the elephants with their snakelike trunks, "run, run!"

"The earth'sssss breaking up?" hissed the snake. "The earth'sssss breaking up? Why, if the earth'ssss breaking up, it'sss the end. I'd better get sssssliding." And off he went, sliding over boulders, under bushes, around trees. Soon they passed another snake.

"Sssssssay," hissed that snake. "What'sssss the hurry? What'sssss happening?"

"The earth'sssss breaking up!" called the first snake. "Sssssssssslither! Ssssssslide!" And without pausing an instant or diverting his ruby eyes, he flowed quickly on over stones and stumps, following the great crowd of animals running ahead, and was gone!

"The earth'ssssss breaking up!" repeated that second snake in shock! And then off he slid too.

Soon they passed another snake. And another. Then there were four, five, ten, twenty, thirty, forty, fifty, one hundred snakes all sliding along. One hundred elephants charging straight ahead, one hundred bears barreling through the bushes, one hundred rabbits leaping leaping leaping. And all of them were so scared they were shouting loudly, at the tops of their lungs, "Help! help! The earth's breaking up! Run! Run!" Soon the buffalos had joined in this great flight of the beasts, as did the rhinoceros, the boar, and the deer. Now a great host of beasts was charging through the jungle.

Up on top of a mountain overlooking this jungle was a brave lion, asleep. The lion—the Buddha in an earlier birth—heard all those screams and cries. Opening his golden eyes, he looked out over the jungle and saw all those animals running madly in great terror. But he couldn't see why they were running. As he watched, he saw that, unless someone stopped them quickly, they would run over the edge of a cliff and die.

"Someone should help those frightened animals," said the lion to himself. "Why," he said, "I'll help."

Rising to his feet, he shook his heavy mane. Rousing all his great lion's strength, he LEAPED out over the jungle, his golden mane streaming behind him, and landed in front of all those terrified animals.

"ARRRRAAAUGHHHHRROARRRRR!" roared the lion loudly, stopping the flight of the maddened beasts. "Why are you all running?"

"Because the earth's breaking up! The earth's breaking up!" cried the frightened animals. "Let us go, mighty lion, before we are all killed!"

"The earth's not breaking up. Look," said the lion. "Here's the earth, right under your feet, solid as it's ever been. Who told you that the earth was breaking up?"

The deer said, "Boars," the boars, "Rhinoceros," the rhinoceros, "Buffalo," the buffalo, "Snakes." "It wassss the elephantsssss," hissed the snakes. "Bears!" trumpeted the elephants. "Uh, rab-bits," said the bears. "Him, him, him, him, him, him, him, him, him!" said the rabbits, pointing down the whole long line of rabbits until they came to the foolish little rabbit. "He told us," they all said.

"Well, little rabbit," asked the lion gently, "where did you see the earth breaking up?"

"I heard it," said the little rabbit. "Back there." And he pointed back into the forest. "Under a great mango tree."

"You heard it?" repeated the lion to himself, "and under a mango tree. Why," he thought to himself, "this little rabbit must have heard a ripe fruit falling from the tree and hitting the earth. I must show these animals they have nothing to fear."

"Come, little rabbit," said the lion, "get up on my back. Let's go back to the tree together and see what it was that really scared you."

"Oh no," said the little rabbit, shaking still with fear. "I couldn't do that. It's much too dangerous."

"Do not worry," said the lion gently. "There is nothing to fear. But as you alone can guide me to your tree you must come with me." Then, placing the frightened rabbit on his back, he set off in great lion leaps back along the trail the animals had travelled.

Soon they reached the tree. The lion stalked around the tree. He sniffed the earth. Then he picked up something with his paw, and he laughed.

There, indeed, was the mango, a ripe mango that had fallen from the tree.

"Here's your earth breaking up, little rabbit," said the lion. "You heard this ripened fruit fall from the tree and you thought it was the earth breaking up!" And he handed the mango to the rabbit. "Now let us return and tell the others."

Then, once again, with the great speed of a lion, he raced back along the trail to where the others waited.

"Friends," said the lion when they had returned, "I have been to the rabbit's tree myself and can tell you that it was only a ripe fruit falling from the tree that led to your mad flight. Here is that fruit. The thud of this falling mango, this was your 'earth breaking up.' Remember this next time something frightens you. Take a good look at it for yourselves and do not be afraid. Maybe you'll discover that, like this falling mango, it is nothing that can really hurt you."

Then the animals returned in gladness to their homes.

The lion leaped back up onto his mountaintop, lay down, and calmly surveyed the now peaceful jungle below.

The little rabbit, still holding his mango, hopped back to his tree, lay down under it, and took a big bite of the mango. Ummm, but it was sweet!

Commentary on page 208

THE QUAIL AND THE FALCON

Once, the Buddha was a little quail who one day decided he had enough of pecking out his living on the hard, sunbaked earth.

"I'll make my way to greener fields," he said. "I need a change."

Flapping his wings, he rose up, and without a single regret, sailed out over the dry plains. Soon he was flying over entirely new terrain. Green grass waved in the sunlight. Streams rippled and ran. The little quail was beside himself with delight. "This is it," he said to himself. "Paradise!" And down he spiralled towards his new home.

But he was not alone. A great falcon flying high above saw the little quail, and folding his wings, dove down upon him. In less than a minute the little quail had been plucked from the sky and, in shock, found himself in the falcon's grasp.

"I'm lost! What chance do I have!" thought the little quail in despair. But before sinking into a final fluttering panic, he said to himself, "He is a fierce falcon, and I'm just a little quail. Still, if I keep my wits about me, I may even the odds yet." And, instead of weeping and crying, he now shouted loudly, "Unfair! Unfair!"

"What?" said the falcon, surprised. "Why, little bird, whatever can you mean?"

"Just that you caught me at a disadvantage, that's all!" exclaimed the little quail. "You caught me far from home. But on my own home ground you never could have caught me. There you'd find it impossible to turn me into a meal!"

The falcon was intrigued. No quail had ever said such things to him before. The others had wept or screamed, had fainted away or pleaded for their lives. Yet, in the end, he had eaten them all. This was a new twist. "Little bird," he said, bending his sharp beak and fierce yellow eyes down towards the little quail, "whatever do you mean?"

"I mean that on my home ground I'm free. Just try and get me there. Big as you are, you'd be no match for me there!"

"Surely you jest," said the falcon, bringing the razor edge of his beak even closer.

The little quail closed his eyes, took a deep breath, and said, "Why should I jest? If I'm wrong, you'll eat me. I'll be your supper anyway. But what's the matter?" he added bravely, opening his eyes once more, "don't you think you can bring it off?"

"Come," said the falcon, irritated despite himself, "show me your home ground, little braggart, and that," he added with a meaningful squeeze of his claws, "will be that!"

When the little quail felt the falcon's claws closing tighter around him, he almost gave up all hope. But then, catching his breath, he yelled, "Just fly on, fly on. We're almost there." And sure enough, in another minute his own old, dry, dusty patch was directly below. A wave of relief and joy flooded the little quail's heart, and yelling even louder now, he called out, "There it is! Down below!"

"What," said the falcon, peering down, "that sunbaked field? Surely you can't have grown into such a great, big, powerful bird like yourself down there?" And he laughed.

"Well," said the quail, "just set me down in the middle of my field and we'll soon see who's strongest!"

"All right," said the falcon, "I will."

And swooping down, he set the little quail free in the center of the field. The earth was dry and sunbaked. The grasses yellow and stiff. But the little quail hopped up and down with excitement. "This is it. Home sweet home! Watch out now! Just try and get me!"

"Be right back," smiled the falcon, and with a great flapping of his wings, he soared up and up and up, higher and higher and higher. At last he was so high he looked like a tiny dot, almost lost against the bright sky and sun. At the top of his climb, the falcon suddenly turned, folded his wings against his body, and dropped, sharp beak first, straight down like a living stone toward the little quail, who sat exposed and alone in the center of the field. Down down down he fell, faster and faster and faster.

The defenseless quail crouched down low against the hard, sunbaked earth and watched the falcon growing larger and larger above him. First the falcon seemed to be only a speck, then a dot, then a pebble, then at last a great, fierce, yellow-eyed bird, talons outstretched, dropping like a lightning bolt directly upon him. The time had come.

With a sudden motion the little quail hopped up and leapt aside. And the falcon, wide-eyed, tearing down at his top-most speed, had no chance to swerve aside. CRASH! He hurtled into the rock-hard earth and instantly died.

Then the little quail flapped his wings, whistled, and danced for joy. His home ground had, indeed, saved him.

Commentary on page 209

The Steadfast Parrot

Once there was a parrot. His feathers were beautiful— green, red, and yellow. His eyes were shiny and black, his beak pale yellow. Altogether he was a most handsome bird.

This parrot lived in a fig tree. How he loved that tree! He loved if for the way its leaves shaded him from the harsh, glaring midday sun and for the cool shade it cast over him. He loved it for its endless whisperings, its creakings and rus- tlings. He loved it for the way its branches quietly rose and fell, swaying with every breeze. He loved it for the feel of the cool, smooth bark beneath his toes. He loved it, too, for the sweet fruit it so freely gave him.

Every evening, as he settled on the branches of his tree- home, he would say, "How happy I am. How content. How peaceful and free. I owe this tree so very much. I'll never abandon it for another refuge." And closing his eyes, he would listen with delight to the music of the tree's fluttering leaves.

Shakra, King of the Gods, heard the parrot's words and de- cided to test him. He withered the tree and dried it until the leaves blackened and died. Dust now lay on the branches where sweet dews once gathered.

But the parrot would not leave. He sat on the dead branches. Slowly lifting his claws he climbed from branch to branch, circling the tree to keep from the glaring sunlight which beat down upon him. In his mind's eye he could see it, covered not with dust but with bright leaves, still swaying and rustling in the breeze. "Should friends part just because bitter fortune has struck?" said the parrot to himself. "Days pass and fortunes change.

> My words were sincere and true
> And my tree, I'll not leave you."

And he would not leave. Though days passed, the parrot remained steadfast and content. Perched on the dead branches among the dry, rattling leaves, he watched the sun rise and he watched it set. But he did not abandon his tree-home.

Then Shakra, watching, smiled, and a golden breeze blew. Buds formed, green leaves unfolded, fruits swelled, and the dust, whirling, blew away. Amazed, the parrot sat sheltered once again among the green, leafy branches of his beloved tree.

"Little bird," said the King of the Gods, "the whole universe is brought to life by a steadfast and faithful heart. Even the lofty gods smile when meeting one who has attained unwavering contentment. While outwardly you may only be a little bird, inwardly you bear the gift of life.

> Live contented with your tree
> And may all beings so contented be."

And laughing, the great god Shakra rose up into the bluest of blue skies.

The steadfast little parrot, once again sipping the sweet dews, rubbed his beak against the cool, smooth bark. Oh, how contented he was!

Commentary on page 210

PRINCE FIVE-WEAPONS

Long ago there was a prince. When he was sixteen, his father, the king, said to him, "My son, soon you shall be old enough to help me rule. Therefore the time has come for you to journey to the city of Takkasila, where the greatest weapons masters live. Learn from them how to master the five weapons, then return. Are you ready for this journey?"

"Of course, Father!" said the boy. And the next morning, just as the sun was rising and the birds were beginning to sing, he set off on the roads. He walked and walked. He climbed high mountains, crossed swift rivers, and went through dark forests. At last he arrived at the city of Takkasila, that city famed for its wise weapons masters. And there, under the direction of a skillful teacher, he began to train in the use of the five weapons.

Each day, just as the sun was rising, out he would go into the practice yard to shoot arrow after arrow from his sturdy bow. When his arrows were gone, he'd lift his spear and hurl it. Then, drawing his sword, he'd slash and lunge and parry. Finally, he'd raise a great club to smash and pound. Over and over he did these things. When the sun set, the boy, exhausted, collapsed onto his little bed and slept until the sun rose again.

And when the sun rose, once more out the young prince would go, and all would begin as before—shooting and throwing and slashing and smashing. Gradually the prince became stronger and faster. His eyes grew keener, his aim surer. Days turned into weeks. Weeks became months. Months were soon a year. Still the young prince practiced on.

One day, the old weapons master called the boy to him and said, "Young Prince, you are disciplined and accomplished. The time has come for you to return and help your father rule his kingdom. I give you a new name. You shall be called Prince Five-Weapons. Use your powers for good and luck will go with you."

The prince thanked his old teacher, lifted up his weapons, and set off on the roads. He walked and walked.

Now, at one point on his journey, just where the road narrowed to enter a dark forest, the prince came upon a barricade of hewn logs blocking his path. Armed soldiers standing there called out, "Stop, young Prince! Don't go down this path!"

"And why not?" asked Prince Five-Weapons.

"Because," said the soldiers, "a monster named Sticky-Hair lives down this road, and he is heartless. He grabs people and gobbles them up. If you value your life, take some other road."

"What?" exclaimed the prince, "turn and run when danger threatens? Absolutely not! I've made up my mind to be of some good in this world. I've spent a year learning to use the five weapons. I'll go down this path and make it safe for all to travel on."

So the prince went around the logs and set off down the forest path. As he walked on, the trees grew taller on either side of the road. Their arching branches blocked the sun. The bushes, too, grew more wild and tangled. With every step his path became darker and darker. Yet, was the prince afraid? No, he was not. He just walked straight forward along the forest path.

Soon the prince heard rustlings and creakings from the bushes ahead. Then, flap, flap, flap! a glossy black crow flew across the path before him. "Hooo! Hooo! Hooo!" an owl hooted from the tangled gloom above. Suddenly, with a great crash, the tops of the tallest trees came splintering to the ground.

There, peering down, one hundred feet tall, was the monster Sticky-Hair!

The monster's eyes were as big as doors, and his nostrils like great round boulders. His hands were as wide as carts and his fingernails as long as broom sticks. His crooked yellow teeth had holes in them so big that birds were nesting there, flying in and out. He was immense. He was horrible. And he was covered with sticky sticky hair.

But was the prince afraid? No, he was not afraid! He was not afraid at all! He put an arrow to his bow, drew the bowstring back, and said, "One more step, you monster Sticky-Hair, and I'll send this arrow through your heart. For I'm Prince Five-Weapons and I've come into this dark forest to make you change your evil ways or to strike you dead."

But the monster Sticky-Hair just laughed loudly, in a booming voice, "Ha ha ha ha ha ha!" and strode forward, trees crashing down around him as on he came.

So the prince let his arrow fly. Woooooooosh! Straight as a falcon it flew, straight to the monster's heart and thuuuuuup! it struck! But what was this! The arrow hadn't hurt him at all. It just stuck to the monster's sticky sticky hair!

Then the prince put another arrow to his bow, and another, and another. Fifty arrows in all he shot, straight and true at the monster's heart. Thuuuup, thuuup, thuuup, thuuup, thuuup! They all struck! But what was this? Not one had hurt the monster at all! They all just hung there, stuck to the sticky hair. The monster laughed and shook himself like a wet dog. The arrows rattled together and flew off in every direction. And on the monster came.

Was the prince afraid? No, he was not afraid! He was not afraid at all! He lifted up his spear and hurled it straight at the monster's heart. Thuuuuuump. It struck! But what was this? It too just stuck, dangling from the sticky sticky hair. And on the monster came, closer and closer.

Then the prince drew his shining sword, swung it once, twice, three times and slaaaassssh, struck the monster's gigantic leg. But what was this? Why, the sword, too, just stuck to the sticky sticky hair. The monster loomed over the prince ready to grab him and gobble him up. Did the prince turn away? Did he run? No! He just lifted up his club, made of ironwood and knotted like a great fist, and brought it down, crash! on the monster's foot. But what was this? The club, too, just stuck to the sticky sticky hair. It hadn't hurt the monster at all.

Now the monster was bending down to grab the prince and gobble him up. But was the prince afraid? No, he was not afraid! He was not afraid at all! He said to himself, "When I came into this forest, I didn't just trust in my weapons. I trusted in myself. If I have to, I'll beat this monster to dust with my fists."

And drawing back with his right fist, he swung at the monster with all his strength. Bop! But what was this? His right fist was stuck to the sticky hair! "Oho," said the prince. "My left fist is by far the stronger. This is the end for you, Sticky-Hair!" Then the prince drew back with his left fist and bop! once again struck the monster with all his might. But what was this? His left fist, too, was stuck to the sticky hair!

Then the prince said, "My right leg is stronger than my fists. Prepare to meet your doom, you monster Sticky-Hair!" And drawing back with his right leg, whaap! He kicked that monster as hard as he could. But what was this? Why, the prince's right leg was stuck to the sticky hair!

"Well," said the prince, "my left leg is even stronger than my right. One kick and I shatter boulders, knock them to dust. It's the end for you, monster Sticky-Hair!" And drawing back with his left leg, whaack! he kicked that monster a terrible and a mighty kick. But what was this? The prince's left leg just stuck to the monster's sticky hair.

Then the prince said to himself, "The time has come for me to use my head." And drawing back with his head, crash! He hit that monster a terrible blow—with his head! But what was this? Why, the prince's head, too, just stuck to the monster's sticky sticky hair. The prince was stuck head, hands, and feet. He couldn't move this way. He couldn't move that way. He couldn't move at all.

But was he afraid? NO! He was not afraid. He was not afraid at all!

And the monster could tell. He could sense no quiver of fear in the prince at all. And now he began to get nervous. He hesitated. "I don't like this," said the monster to himself. "Everyone else, as soon as they see me, they turn and run. But this prince came straight on like a lion, like a hero. He didn't turn. He didn't run. And now that I've got him completely stuck, he's still fearless. Something's not right. He must have a secret weapon protecting him. Yes, that must be it. Even though he's completely stuck—head, hands and feet—he has no fear. I'd better look into this before I do something rash. I could get hurt."

And bending down towards the prince, the monster said, "Ahem, Prince?"

"Yes!" said the prince.

"Do you have some kind of secret, er, weapon about you?"

"Yes!" said the prince.

"I thought so," lamented the monster. "What is it?"

"I have a sword of Truth within me," said the prince. "And if you try to eat me, it will cut you open so that I may leap out, completely free. Why should I fear? You can never hold me."

"I believe you!" exclaimed the monster. "Don't hurt me. I knew I could never eat you up. No, I could never have digested the tiniest piece of a hero like you. Not even a piece as big as a bean. I'll let you go!" And bending down, the monster pulled Prince Five-Weapons from the sticky hair and set him free, saying, "I set you free like the moon when it comes out at last from behind the clouds."

But the prince, collecting his weapons, said, "I don't set you free. Don't you know that you've become a miserable monster because you treat others so unkindly? Stop that, and you'll become happier. Someday you'll be a real human being, and a whole new world will open to you."

"It's true," said the monster, "I have been pretty miserable. So I'll . . . I'll do it! I will treat others with kindness. I'll protect travellers from lions and tigers, from robbers and other dangers. I won't gobble them up ever again. From now on, I'll help."

"That's good!" said the prince. "Now see that you do as you say—or I'll be back to check up on you." And shouldering his weapons, he once again set off down the path. When he reached the forest's other side, he announced to the astonished soldiers, "The way is clear. The path is open. All may walk safely through this forest now." Then the prince returned home and helped his father rule. Years later he himself became king and was known as "King Five-Weapons, the Opener of the Ways."

As for the monster, he did just as the prince had told him to do. He was kinder. He helped travellers who took that forest path, and he protected them from dangers. With his long-clawed hands, he pushed apart the tangled branches. Sunlight streamed down into the dark forest. Flowers began to grow. In time it became bright and beautiful there.

The monster became happier. Happier and happier. Years went by. Life after life. The monster became smaller. His sticky fur disappeared. He was born as tiger, lion, bear, wolf, horse, elephant, monkey, and human being. Recently, he was born as a boy or girl, I can't remember which, and lives happily right here in our own city.

Commentary on page 210

THE WISE QUAIL

Once the Buddha was a quail, and he was leader of the flock. One day, a hunter came into the forest where the quail and his flock lived. Imitating the quails' own calls, he began to trap unwary birds.

The quail noticed that something was amiss. Calling his flock together, he announced, "My fellow quail, I fear that a hunter has found us. Many of our brothers and sisters are missing. Danger is all around us. Still, if we work together we can keep our freedom. Please listen to my plan. If you hear a whistling call—'twe whee! twe whee! twe whee!'—as if a brother or sister were calling, and you go running off to help them, be very watchful! Suddenly, darkness may descend upon you, and your wings may be pinned so that you cannot fly. The fear of death will then grip your heart. But do not panic. Just understand that you have been trapped by the hunter's net and do not give up! If you work together you can yet be free. Stick your heads out through webs of the net, then flap your wings together. As a group, though still bound in the net, you will rise up into the air. Fly to a bush. Let the net drape on its branches so you can each drop to the ground, and fly away, this way and that, to freedom. Do you understand? Can you do this?"

"We do understand," answered all the quail as one. "And we will do it! We will work together and be free."

The wise quail was well satisfied.

The very next day a group of quail were pecking on the ground when they heard a long, whistling call: "Twe whee! twe whee! twe whee!" It was the cry of a quail in distress!

Off they rushed. Suddenly darkness descended upon them, and their wings were pinned. They had indeed been trapped by the hunter's net. But, remembering the wise quail's words, they didn't panic. Sticking their heads through the net they flapped their wings together, harder and harder, and slowly, slowly, with the net still draped upon them, they rose as a group and flew through the air to a bush. They dropped down through the branches and leaves of the bush, leaving the net hanging empty on it, and then flew away, each in his or her own direction, this way and that, to freedom. The plan had worked! They were safe! They had escaped from the jaws of death. And oh, they were happy!

But the hunter was not happy. He could not understand how the quail had escaped him. And this happened not just once, but many times. At last he realized the truth. "Why," he said, amazed, "those quail are cooperating! They are actually working together! Bah! It can't last. They are only birds, mere featherbrains, after all. Sooner or later they will argue. And when they do, I shall have them." And so he was patient.

Now, the wise quail had had the same thought. Sooner or later the birds of his flock would argue. And when that happened they would be lost. And so he decided to take them deeper into the forest, far from the present danger.

That very day something happened to confirm the wise quail's thought.

A quail was pecking on the ground for seeds when another bird, descending rapidly, accidentally struck it with a wing tip. "Hey! Watch it, stupid!" called the first quail in anger.

"Stupid, is it!" responded the newly landed quail, flustered because he had been careless. "Why are you so high and mighty? You were too dumb to move out of my way! Yes, you were too dumb—you dumb cluck!"

"Dumb cluck, is it!" cried the first quail, enraged. "Dumb cluck! Why, talking of dumb, it's clear that you can't even land without slapping someone. If that isn't 'dumb' I don't know what is! Who taught you to fly, anyway—the naked wings? The bats?"

"Bats, is it?" yelled the second quail, enraged. "Bats! Why, I'll give you a bat, you feathered ninny!" And with a loud chirruping whistle, he hurled himself straight at the other quail.

Chasing furiously after one another, loudly hurling insults and threats back and forth, they flew twisting and turning between the great, silent trees of the grove. An argument had started, and as is the way of arguments, no end was in sight.

The wise quail was nearby and heard it all. At once he knew that danger was again upon them. If they couldn't work harmoniously together, the hunter was sure to have them.

So, again he called his flock together and said, "My brother and sister quail. The hunter is here. Let us go deeper into the forest and, in seclusion, discipline ourselves, practicing our skills so that we can work harmoniously together. In this way we shall become free from danger."

Then many of the birds said, "Though we love our present home, we shall go with you, Wise Quail. The danger is indeed great."

But others said, "Why go from this pleasant spot? You yourself, Wise Quail, have taught us all we need to know in order to be free. We know what to do. We just have to stick our heads out, flap our wings together, and fly away. No. We're going to stay."

So some of the birds flew off with the wise quail while others stayed.

A few days later, while some of those who had remained were scratching around for their dinner, they heard a whistling call: "twe whee! twe whee! twe whee!" They ran to answer the call, when suddenly darkness descended upon them. Fear gripped their hearts. They were trapped in the hunter's net! Remembering the wise quail's teaching, they stuck their heads through the net and one bird said, "On the count of three we all flap. Ready? One two, thr—. . ."

"Hey!" called another bird. "Who made you boss? Who said you could give the orders?"

"I'm the hardest worker and the strongest," said the first

bird. "When I flap my wings, I flap so hard that the dust rises from the earth and whirls up among the clouds. Without me, you'd never get this net off the ground. So I give the orders, see?"

"No! I don't see!" shouted another bird. "What you've just described is nothing. Why, when I flap my wings, I flap so hard that the leaves shake on the trees, the branches bend, and even the tree trunks sway. That's how strong I am. So if anyone should be giving orders around here, it's me!"

"No, me!" shouted a third bird.

"Me!" yelled a fourth.

"No! No! Listen to me!" screamed the first bird again, above the rising din. "Flap! Flap! Flap! I tell you. Flap your wings all together when I say 'three!'"

But no one flapped; they just argued and argued. And as they argued, the hunter came along and found them, and alas, their fate was not a happy one.

But the other quail, those who had gone off deeper into the safety of the great forest, learned, under the wise quail's guidance, how to really cooperate. They practiced constantly until they were able to work together without anger or argument.

Though the hunter tried many times to catch them, he never could.

And if he never caught them, why, they're still free today.

Commentary on page 211

THE MONKEY AND THE CROCODILE

Once there was a crocodile who liked nothing better than to lie in the sun on the warm, muddy banks of his lazy, green river. He would stretch out at the water's edge and, shutting his eyes tight, open his mouth wide in a great, toothy grin. Then the little birds would fly in and out of his jaws, pecking at the scraps of food stuck between his yellowed teeth.

"Ah," he thought contentedly, digging his claws into the soft, gray mud, "but this is the life!"

One day his wife crawled over to him and said, "Have you noticed that monkey swinging around on the island lately?"

"Uh-huh," grunted the crocodile, keeping his eyes shut and his mouth open wide.

"Well," she went on, "he looks large and juicy. I bet his heart is very tender. Oh," she exclaimed at last, "how I wish I had that monkey's tender heart! Won't you get it for me?"

"Uh-huh," sighed the crocodile. Closing his jaws with a snap, he quietly opened his cold, yellow eyes and slowly crawled down the bank into the river. He moved his broad tail from side to side and slid through the cool, green water with hardly a ripple. But when he was only halfway across, he slowly swung around in the water and swam back to the shore. His wife lay on the bank sunning herself. Her eyes were shut tight and her mouth was open wide.

"Dear," he said.

"Uh-huh?" she said.

"How am I going to catch that monkey?" he asked. "He's up in the trees and I'm down here in the water!"

"Well," she answered, "you're big and strong, aren't you?"

"Uh-huh!" he exclaimed.

"Then it's simple," she said. "Just offer to carry him across on your back to where all the sweet coconuts are ripening. Be a friend. You can do that, can't you?"

"Uh-huh!" he agreed. So once again, the crocodile turned around and slowly swam off, moving his broad tail steadily from side to side.

At this time, the monkey was swinging around on the trees of his island. He was eating sweet fruits and enjoying himself in the warmth of the sun. "Ah," he reflected as he sat among the bright green leaves and fluttering orange butterflies, "but life is good!"

At that moment, the crocodile reached the shore of the monkey's island. Crawling along the sandy beach, he raised his knobbed and scaly head up toward the trees and called out in a very gentle-seeming voice, "Brother monkey. Oh, brother monkey."

"Yes," answered the monkey, "what is it? Who is calling me?"

"It's me," answered the crocodile, "your friend from across the deep river, the crocodile. And I was just thinking, as the day is so warm and bright, and the sun is shining so gloriously, that I'd like to do something special for a friend today. My wife has told me that the mangos and coconuts on our side of the river are tender and juicy and ripe. And, as it's a perfect day for a swim, I decided that I'd be glad to take you for a ride over the water to where the sweetest ones are growing. Once there you can eat to your heart's content. In fact," added the crocodile, with a great, toothy grin, "I'd be really glad to do it. Won't you come along?"

"Hmm," said the monkey, scratching his head. "I don't know. It is a nice day, and ripe coconuts and mangos would be nice." Then, calling down, he asked, "Will you promise to go slow?"

"Slow," grinned the crocodile, "slow? Why, slow is my middle name! Just come along. You'll see."

"All right," said the monkey, "I'll go with you." Then he hopped down out of the tree and onto the crocodile's back. Off they went across the river.

As they swam along, the little waves washed and rippled over the crocodile's leathery hide, splashing the rough scales and wetting the monkey's hands and feet. "Ooh, it's cold!" he cried.

"Cold?" leered the crocodile with a cruel and toothy grin. "Cold? You call that cold? Why, that's not cold, that's not cold yet at all!" And with that, he dove down through the green water to the gray, muddy bottom of the river. The terrified monkey held on tight—TIGHT!—and when they broke the surface again in a burst of mud and foam, the poor monkey gasped out from between his chattering teeth, "Friend crocodile, what are you doing? You nearly drowned me with your joke! Please be more careful. Have you forgotten your promise? Remember my home is in the trees!"

"What joke?" said the crocodile with another nasty grin. "I'm taking you back to my wife. She wants your tender heart. And what she wants, she gets!"

"Oh," said the monkey slowly, "I see. Yes, now I SEE. Well, friend," he added after a moment, "it's a good thing you've told me. You almost made a terrible mistake."

"I did?" asked the crocodile, concerned. The smile left his jaws. "Please tell me, friend monkey, how?"

"Why," said the monkey, "everyone knows I don't take anything as important as my tender heart with me on ordinary little everyday kinds of trips. Oh, no. Except for the most special occasions, I always leave my tender heart hanging safely at the top of the tallest tree on my island. A tender heart is a precious thing. Look back, friend crocodile. Don't you see it hanging there on that tall tree by the shore?"

The crocodile looked, and after a moment, thought that maybe he could see it. Yes, he was sure of it! He did see it! He had almost made an awful mistake.

"Listen, friend crocodile," said the monkey, "now that I know the whole story, why don't we just turn around. I'll go back and get my tender heart. It will be no trouble at all. In fact, I'd love to do it. Really. It will take just a minute. I bet your wife would have been upset," he added, as the crocodile turned slowly in the water and began to swim back toward the island once again, "if you had brought me all the way over the water without my tender heart. We would have had to come all the way back then, but now, you see, there's no real harm done."

"You're right," agreed the crocodile, "she never would have understood. You know," he added, "for a monkey you are a very good fellow."

"Thank you," said the monkey. "Glad I could help. Now, just wait here. I'll be back in a moment!"

And with that the monkey took a tremendous leap straight up off the crocodile's back and bounded up into the branches of the tallest tree. Up up up he scampered, straight to the very top, higher and higher. Then, dancing on the highest branch, he called out, "Foolish, foolish crocodile! Tender hearts don't grow on trees! A tender heart is the heart of compassion that feels kindly towards all things—even for silly crocodiles. One day you and your wife will have your own tender hearts. But until then you won't find me riding on your back. Better head home now, my toothy friend. This joke's on you!"

And with that, the crocodile swam off, embarrassed and confused.

The wise monkey sat in the warmth of the golden sunshine drying his wet fur. The sweet fruits hung from the sturdy branches. The clear waves lapped against the shore below. "Ah," he exclaimed, "how could that foolish crocodile have failed to find my tender heart!"

Commentary on page 211

GREAT JOY, THE OX

O nce, long ago, in India, a poor farmer was given an ox calf in repayment of a debt. The farmer delighted in the tiny calf and cared for it well.

And the ox grew and grew until it was a great, big, powerful ox. Yet, strong as it was, it was gentle too. Whatever the farmer asked it to do, it did—and with good spirit. Deeply rooted stumps, big boulders, whatever they might be—if the farmer wanted them pulled from his fields, he had only to tie one end of a rope to his ox's yoke, tie the other end to the boulder or stump, and say, "Pull!" And the ox would pull it up out of the earth and drag it from the fields. Yet the ox was so tame that children could ride on his back. So pleased was the farmer with his great, powerful, and gentle ox that he named it "Great Joy."

One day Great Joy was thinking to himself, "My master, the farmer, is so poor. Yet he has always been so kind to me. I want to use my great strength to repay him."

So Great Joy walked over to the farmer's low, sunbaked mud house, put his great, horned head through the open window, and said, "My master and my friend, you have always been so kind to me, yet you are so poor. I want to use my great strength to help you. Listen, for I have a plan."

And the astonished farmer, his jaw dropping, exclaimed, "I have an ox who can talk?!"

"Certainly, master," replied Great Joy calmly. "Indeed, there are many more wonderful things than that in this world for those whose eyes and ears are open. But listen."

The farmer listened.

"Tomorrow," said Great Joy, "go into the town. Find a wealthy merchant and bet him one thousand pieces of silver that you have an ox who can pull a hundred carts fully loaded with boulders, gravel, and stone."

"It's impossible!" exclaimed the farmer. "No ox has ever pulled so many loaded carts. It can't be done!"

"Trust me," said Great Joy. "Have I ever let you down?"

"Never!" answered the farmer. "You have always been a great joy to me."

"Then trust me," said the ox. So it was agreed.

The next day, when the sun rose, the farmer tied on his worn sandals and headed for the town. Entering a tea shop where the wealthier merchants and farmers gathered during the heat of the day, he sat down alone at a little table. Then, as a wealthy merchant entered, he called out, "My friend, will you join me?"

"Why not?" answered the wealthy merchant.

After pleasantries, a few sweets, and tea, the farmer took a deep breath and said, "I have an ox."

"So?" replied the wealthy merchant. "I have many oxen, and let me tell you, they cost me plenty."

"Yes," said the farmer, "but . . . but my ox is strong."

"Bah!" said the merchant. "It is an ox's nature to be strong. Every ox is strong."

"Not as strong as my ox," continued the farmer, growing bolder. "Why, my ox, Great Joy, is so strong he can pull one hundred carts loaded to the top with boulders, gravel, and stone!"

"Impossible!" laughed the merchant. "Listen, neighbor, no ox, no matter how strong, can pull one hundred loaded carts. This world is one of weights and measures. Everything has its necessary limits. An ox is, after all, just an ox. This can't be done."

"But it can," persisted the poor farmer.

"It can't!" insisted the wealthy merchant.

"Would you like to wager?" asked the poor farmer.

"With pleasure," responded the wealthy merchant.

"One thousand pieces of silver?" asked the poor farmer somewhat hesitantly.

"You're on!" cried the wealthy merchant. "One thousand pieces of silver it shall be! Tomorrow, when the sun rises to the top of the tallest mango tree in the town square, you bring your ox, and I'll have one hundred loaded carts waiting. Until then, my friend, let us call it a day."

And with that, the wealthy merchant rose, and with a flourish of his sleeves, walked smiling from the shop.

Soon the whole town was alight with the news. "One thousand pieces!" exclaimed some. "One hundred carts!" others marvelled. "One ox!" laughed the rest.

Soon money was changing hands, and bets were placed. All waited expectantly for the morning.

That night the poor farmer tossed and turned. Would he win? Would he lose? Could Great Joy really pull all those carts? The odds, after all, were entirely against it.

The farmer awoke early and went at once to Great Joy's stall.

There stood Great Joy, calming chewing the golden straw, quietly flicking his tail from side to side. His great dark eyes looked at the farmer with much good humor as if to say, "So, today's the day, eh? Well, don't worry. All shall be well. We'll win the bet."

But the farmer was preoccupied. Today he couldn't seem to see or hear what Great Joy was so clearly saying.

The farmer began to curry Great Joy, slapping and brushing his sides and broad back so that the dust rose up and danced in the sunbeams like bits of silver and gold. Then he threw a rope around Great Joy's neck and led him through the fields and down the dirt road to the town.

They arrived just as the sun touched the top of the tallest mango tree in the town square. A noisy crowd filled the square. And there were the one hundred loaded carts, waiting.

The poor farmer looked at those carts—and his stomach sank down to his shoes. He had never seen so many carts! And never so many loaded ones! "What a fool I have been to have listened to a mere beast," he thought. "I followed the advice of an animal, and look at the result! I am lost!" Feeling hopeless—but putting on a bold front so that no one would see—he led Great Joy through the crowd.

And there stood the wealthy merchant, waiting. "Are you ready?" he asked,

"Of course we're ready," replied the poor farmer.

The wealthy merchant clapped his hands, and two strong men stepped from the crowd. They lifted up a heavy wooden yoke and set it on Great Joy's shoulders. Then they tied the ropes from the carts firmly to the yoke, knotting them tight.

The crowd grew quiet. It was so quiet, you could hear the birds singing in the trees. It was so quiet, you could hear the sweep of Great Joy's tail. It was so quiet, you could hear the buzz of the glittering flies.

Unconcerned, Great Joy mildly eyed the staring crowd and watched the white clouds drifting slowly overhead. He shook his huge head and snorted loudly as if to say, "What's the fuss?"

Then the poor farmer, finding all eyes focused on him, walked up to Great Joy's side, lifted up a whip, struck Great Joy on a giant shoulder and cried, "On, you beast! On, you wretch! Pull those carts! Show your strength!"

But when Great Joy felt the bite of the whip and heard those harsh words, his eyes opened wide. "Blows and curses, is it," he said to himself. "Well, not for this ox!" And planting his hooves firmly in the earth, he would not move.

The crowd went wild! They yelled, "Pull, you stupid ox!" They laughed and jeered, crying, "Fake! Fraud!" They threw clods of earth. They hurled sticks and stones. But Great Joy would not budge. He wouldn't even try to pull the carts. Not even an inch. He just stood resolute beneath all the shouts and blows.

"My friend," spluttered the merchant, tears of laughter streaming down his cheeks, "that is one ha! ha! ha! powerful ox, indeed!"

At last the proddings, the shouts, and threats ceased, and the crowd drifted away. The wealthy merchant was paid. "Better luck next time!" he joked as he took the poor farmer's last coins. "Truly, that's some great ox you've got, indeed!" Then the poor farmer unhitched Great Joy and led him silently home.

Once there, the poor farmer put his head down on his arms and wept and wept for grief and loss and shame.

Then Great Joy, hearing his sobs, walked again to the farmer's little house, put his big, horned head through the opened window, and said, "My master and my friend, why do you weep?"

And the poor farmer, in great bitterness, exclaimed, "You beast! You wretch! You animal! What you told me to do, I did. Yet I have lost everything. What's more, the whole town has laughed at me. And it's all your fault!"

But Great Joy said sadly, "My master and my friend, let me ask you a question—did I let you down or did you let me down? Have I ever failed you before? Indeed, have I ever cracked a plow, or broken a fence, or smashed a pot? Have I ever injured a child or failed to pull the heaviest load?"

"No," said the farmer, raising his head and looking at Great Joy, "you have always been a great joy to me."

"Then why," asked the Great Joy, the Ox, "did you beat me, and hit me, and call me such names—'wretch' you said, and 'beast.' Was this truly the reward I deserved at your hands—I who only wanted to work hard for you and to serve you?"

Then the farmer sat up and dried his eyes. He looked at his ox in silence—and he grew ashamed.

"You are right," he admitted at last. "You didn't let me down. It was I who let you down, and, Great Joy, I'm . . . I'm sorry."

"Well," said the ox, "since you now feel this way about it, go back to that town, find that merchant, and bet again. Only this time bet two thousand pieces, and if you do not let me down, I will certainly not let you down."

The next day the farmer went quickly to the town and entered the tea shop again. There was the merchant calmly sipping his tea and eating a plate of sweets.

"My friend, may I join you?" asked the farmer.

"By all means," answered the merchant merrily, jingling his bag of coins, "for have you not brought me 'great joy'?"

"My friend," said the farmer, "let us bet again."

"What!" exclaimed the merchant, "don't you know when you are beaten?"

"Come," said the farmer calmly, "one more bet on the ox and the carts, just as before. Only this time let us bet two thousand pieces. What do you say?"

The merchant stroked his beard. "Fools like this," he thought, "don't grow on every tree. He is begging me to take his money. So, why not?"

"All right," he shrugged at last. "Who am I to say no?"

"Then tomorrow," said the poor farmer, "when the sun rises to the top of the tallest mango tree, have your carts ready, for I will bring Great Joy. Until then, my friend," he said. And he left at once for home.

The next morning, as soon as the sun rose, the farmer hurried to the stable where he brushed and curried and combed Great Joy. Then they set off together down the dirt road to the town. They arrived as the sun touched the top of the tallest mango tree.

A noisy crowd was there. Many people were already holding sticks and stones and clods of earth ready to throw. But as Great Joy was led to the carts, spiritedly tossing his great, horned head, the sun suddenly shone down directly upon him. For an instant it seemed that his horns might tear the clouds and that his lashing tail was like the tail of some mighty dragon. Each hair on his glossy hide stood bristling and crackling electrically.

As one, the crowd gasped, crying out, "What an ox! Maybe he will be able to do it!"

Then, as before, the merchant motioned. Then, as before, those strong men set the heavy yoke upon Great Joy's shoulders. Again the ropes were knotted and tied. Then it grew quiet, so quiet you could hear the clouds drifting calmly overhead, so quiet you could hear the buzzing of the glittering flies. The poor farmer, feeling all eyes focused upon him, stepped up to his ox's side, lifted up a wreath of flowers, hung it around Great Joy's neck, patted Great Joy on a giant shoulder, and said, "This is the time, my mighty brother. This is the time, my great friend. So pull, pull with your whole heart, and let the world now see your noble strength!"

And with these kind, encouraging words, Great Joy happily planted his hooves into the sun-warmed earth, stiffened his legs till they stood like ancient trees, and pulled and puuulled and Puuuulllled. And slowly, steadily, the wheels began to turn, faster and faster and faster. Faster and faster and faster rolled the carts as Great Joy pulled those one hundred carts all around the square.

The crowd ran after, laughing and calling for joy! "The ox has won! Great Joy has done it. He's won the bet!" Never would they have believed such a wild and wonderful thing! But they had seen it with their own eyes.

Only one ox, it may have been, and a hundred dusty carts. Still, Great Joy, the Ox, with his dignity, strength, and self-respect had achieved the impossible.

That day, the wealthy merchant lost his money, and the poor farmer was paid. And though this may have all happened long ago and far away, it's still talked about here, today.

Commentary on page 212

THE GOLDEN GOOSE

O nce a poor man lived with his wife and children, a boy
and a girl, at the forest's edge. The man fell ill. Despite all efforts to restore him to health, he grew weaker and
weaker. Finally, as he lay dying, one thought alone filled his
mind: "I want to help my family." Then, he died.

That night both his children had the same dream. Their
father appeared and said, "Dear ones, do not grieve. I will
return and help you. I will not look as I did to you in our
life together. Nonetheless, you will know that it is me."

When they told their mother, she only laughed bitterly.
"Forget this dream, little ones," she said. "Our lives will be
hard enough without such dreams."

So the children didn't mention it to her again. But, when
alone together, they spoke happily about it.

One evening, some months later, as the sun began to sink
below the trees, a large white goose, with golden eyes and
yellow beak and legs, waddled up the path to the little mud-
walled house where this family lived. It approached the
children, stretched out its neck, honked loudly, then spoke in
a human voice, a voice they knew well! "Children," said the
goose, "it is I. Your father."

"It is you!" they shouted. "You told us it would be like this.
You told us in our dream!"

The goose wrapped its wings around them and held them.
Then it said, "I have come to help you. Each day, you must
pluck a feather from my wings and hold it to the sun. It will
turn to gold. With my golden feathers, you and your mother

will be able to buy all you need. But you must tell no one, not even your mother, who I am. And you must pluck only one feather each day, pluck it while the sun still shines.

"Quickly, children," said the goose, "before the sun sets, pluck a feather."

They plucked a feather from the goose's wing and—just like that—it turned to gold!

They ran to their mother, crying "Look, Mother, look! A feather of gold! And Fath— . . . er, . . . the goose said we shall have all we need!" And joining hands, the two children began to dance around and around the astonished woman.

"What are you saying?" she cried. "Where did you get this bright feather? Then, as she touched it, she exclaimed, "Why, it's gold!"

"Of course it's gold," said the children. "Just as the goose said it would be!"

"What goose?"

"Why, the goose in our yard," said the children. "Come, Mother. Look." And taking her hands, they led their mother out into the yard. There, indeed, stood the goose, large and white.

"It's a plump and handsome goose," said the mother. "But its feathers are soft and white. They aren't made of gold."

"No," said the boy, "they only turn to gold when you pluck them and hold them to the sun."

"And," said the girl, "you must pluck only one feather each day. For so the goose told us."

Naturally, their mother found this hard to believe. Still, there was the feather of gold. "We will wait until tomorrow," she said. "We shall pluck another feather tomorrow, and we shall see."

The sun set. The stars came out twinkling overhead. The children petted the goose and spoke softly to it. The goose wrapped them in its wings and lay its head and neck against them. But it spoke no human words, only honked and gabbled like any ordinary goose.

The next morning, as the sun rose bright as gold above the trees, the mother plucked a feather from the goose's wing. Instantly, once again, the plucked feather turned to gold! She gasped and nearly dropped it, so great was her surprise. "It's gold!" she cried. "Gold!"

"Yes, Mother!" cried the children happily. "We told you. We told you. The goose is here to help us."

"Well," she said, recovering from her shock, "we must feed this goose well. This goose is our benefactor. We shall take good care of it."

And so it was. They fed the goose and cared for it well. And every day, as the sun rose over the trees, a feather was plucked from the goose. And the feather turned to gold.

With this gold the mother bought good food and new clothes for them all. She bought shiny copper pots and ladles of polished wood. She bought little mirrors and tinkling bells to hang from the roof poles. She bought carved wooden animals for the children. She applied fresh plaster to the walls of their little house and added a new room, and then another. She put a strong fence around the yard. She bought a buffalo to help them plow the fields and to give them its rich, sweet milk. She bought sweet corn and grain to feed the goose.

They were content. And the goose seemed content as well. Every morning, after a feather had been plucked, it stretched out its neck, flapped its wings, and honked as if for joy. Then, after it had eaten and drunk and preened its feathers, it followed the children protectively out into the fields, guarded them through their day, and returned with them to the house when darkness again fell.

Often, at night, the mother lay awake in the darkness reflecting on their extraordinary luck. She heard her children breathing peacefully in their sleep. She heard the buffalo as it snorted in its stall, and she heard the night birds call. Who, she would marvel, could have ever imagined that a goose with feathers that turned to gold would suddenly appear to save them from hardship. It was a miracle!

But as their life become less burdensome, the mother found it harder to be content. One feather at a time, she realized, had built their security. Yet if she might only pluck the bird bare, they would have a fortune.

Her two children begged her to resist temptation. "The goose told us," they said, "to pluck only one feather each day. We promised not to take more. Please, Mother, please. Let well enough be."

And for a while, she would agree. But after a time, the thought of all that gold would arise once again within her. "It's only a goose, after all," she would reason. "Why should I be so concerned? Though children have tender hearts, they soon forget. And what if the goose should be carried off—by a jackal, perhaps, or by a thief. All would be lost. Besides, I will only use the gold for my children's welfare. What harm can be in that? And as to plucking one feather at a time, why, I never heard the goose say that—or anything else for that matter. It's foolish to wait any longer."

So again, she would decide to pluck the whole goose. But again, the children pleaded and begged and cried. And again, she held off, discomfited and confused.

"It's just a goose," she would tell herself. "A goose. What do children know of life? How can I weigh a single goose against the welfare of my children? It's absurd."

At last, she made up her mind, and this time she was determined. "I shall pluck the goose," she said, "and protect my family with gold."

The next morning, before the sun rose, the mother crept into the yard and caught the goose. While the children slept, she quickly pulled fistfuls of feathers from the uncomplaining bird who shivered uncontrollably, watching her all the while with sad, golden eyes. Feathers flew like whirling snow, but still the woman plucked and plucked, stuffing the soft, white feathers into a sack.

At last she released the bare bird, which ran and hid under the bushes in the corner of the yard. From beneath the broad, green leaves came sounds that were almost human, as if someone were softly sobbing.

With a shiver, the woman set her jaw and lifted up the sack of feathers, opening it to the sun which was now rising above the trees.

The golden light fell upon the sack of feathers. But the sack stayed light as down. She lowered the sack and peered inside. The feathers were all soft and white. Not one had turned to gold. She emptied the feathers out onto the ground and let the sun's light play upon them. But not one showed the slightest sign of change.

The poor woman cried aloud. The children, hearing, ran out to the yard where fistfuls of white feathers now blew like snow from the mountains.

"Oh, Mother!" cried the children. "The goose, the poor poor goose! Oh, Father, Father! We promised we wouldn't tell, but Mother, it is our own father you have plucked so bare. He is the goose! He returned as he said he would in our dream."

The mother sobbed and sobbed. "Your father is gone, children," she said at last. "But feathers grow again. We'll take good care of the goose. Next time, I promise I'll pluck only one feather at a time."

But when the goose's feathers grew in again, they were speckled and grey. And not one ever turned to gold.

One day, the goose spread its wings and flew away. The gold they had already gained would be enough to see them through. They could now make their way unaided.

As the woman grew older, she became known as a hard worker, as well as for the simplicity of her life. "Don't be greedy," she would say to those she met, "everything comes in its own time."

Those who heard her took her words to heart. Somehow, they all felt that here, at last, was someone who really knew what she was talking about.

Commentary on page 213

THE BRAVE LITTLE PARROT

O nce, long ago, the Buddha was born as a little parrot. One day, a storm broke upon his forest home. Lightning flashed, thunder crashed, and a dead tree, struck by lightning, burst into flames. Sparks leapt on the wind and soon the forest was ablaze. Terrified animals ran wildly in every direction, seeking safety from the flames and smoke.

"Fire! Fire!" cried the little parrot. "Run! Run to the river!" Flapping his wings, he flung himself out into the fury of the storm, and, rising higher, flew towards the safety of the river. But as he flew he could see that many animals were trapped, surrounded by the flames below, with no chance of escape.

Suddenly, a desperate idea, a way to save them, came to him.

He darted to the river, dipped himself in the water, and flew back over the now raging fire.

The heat rising up from the burning forest was like the heat of an oven. The thick smoke made breathing almost unbearable. A wall of flames shot up now on one side, now on the other. Crackling flames leapt and danced before him. Twisting and turning through the mad maze of fire, the little parrot flew bravely on. At last, over the center of the forest, he shook his wings and released the few drops of water which still clung to his feathers. The tiny drops tumbled like jewels down into the heart of the blaze and vanished with a hssssssssss.

Then the little parrot once more flew back through the flames and smoke to the river, dipped himself in the cool water, and flew back again over the burning forest. Back and forth he flew, time and time again, from the river to the forest, from the burning forest to the river. His feathers were charred. His feet were scorched. His lungs ached. His eyes, stung by smoke, burned red as coals. His mind spun as dizzily as the spinning sparks. But still the little parrot flew on.

At this time, some of the devas, gods of a happy realm, were floating high overhead in their cloud palaces of ivory and gold. They happened to look down and they saw the little parrot flying through the flames. They pointed at him with perfect hands. Between mouthfuls of honeyed foods they exclaimed, "Look at that foolish bird! He's trying to put out a raging forest fire with a few sprinkles of water! How ridiculous! How absurd!" And they laughed.

But one of those gods did not laugh. Strangely moved, he changed himself into a golden eagle and flew down down towards the little parrot's fiery path.

The little parrot was just nearing the flames again when the great eagle, with eyes like molten gold, appeared at his side. "Go back, little bird!" said the eagle in a solemn and majestic voice. "Your task is hopeless! A few drops of water can't put out a forest fire! Cease now and save yourself—before it is too late."

But the little parrot only continued to fly on through the smoke and flames. He could hear the great eagle flying above him as the heat grew fiercer, calling out, "Stop, foolish little parrot! Save yourself! Save yourself!"

"I don't need a great, shining eagle" coughed the little parrot, "to give me advice like that. My own mother, the dear bird, might have told me such things long ago. Advice! (cough, cough) I don't need advice. I just (cough) need someone to help."

And the god who was that great eagle, seeing the little parrot flying through the flames, thought suddenly of his own privileged kind. He could see them floating high up above. Yes, there they were, the carefree gods, still laughing and talking while many animals cried out in pain and fear from among the flames below. Seeing that, he grew ashamed, and a single desire was kindled in his heart. God though he was, he just wanted to be like that brave little parrot and to help.

"I will help!" he exclaimed, and flushed with these new feelings, he began to weep. Stream after stream of sparkling tears poured from his eyes. Wave upon wave they washed down like cooling rain upon the fire, upon the forest, upon the animals, and upon the little parrot himself.

Where those tears fell, the flames died down, and the smoke began to clear. The little parrot, washed and bright, rocketed about the sky laughing for joy. "Now that's more like it!" he exclaimed.

The eagle's tears dripped from burned branches and soaked into the scorched earth. Where those tears glistened, new life pushed quickly forth—shoots, stems, and leaves. Buds unfurled and blossoms opened. Green grass pushed up from among still-glowing cinders.

Where the teardrops sparkled on the parrot's wings, new feathers now grew. Red feathers, green feathers, yellow feathers too. Such bright colors! Such a handsome bird!

All the animals looked at one another in amazement. Washed by those tears, they were whole and well. Not one had been harmed. Up above, in the clear blue sky, they could see their friend, the little parrot, looping and soaring in delight. When hope was gone, somehow he had saved them. "Hurray!" they cried. "Hurray for the brave little parrot and for this sudden, miraculous rain!"

Commentary on page 213

THE BANYAN DEER

Once, long long ago, the Buddha was born as a Banyan Deer. When he was grown he became leader of the herd.

Now at that time, a new king—one who loved hunting—came to power. As soon as the sun rose, this king would mount his horse and lead his men on a furious chase through fields and forests. Shooting his arrows madly, he would not leave off until the sun set. Then the wagons rolled back to the palace behind him filled with deer, boar, rabbit, pheasant, and monkey, with leopard, bear, tiger, and lion. And the king was happy.

His people, however, were not pleased. Fields were ruined by the royal hunt. Farmers and merchants, forced to leave off their work to beat the jungles and drive the hidden beasts towards the waiting king, saw crops wither and businesses fail. The king's own affairs of state lay unattended.

Determined to bring this to an end, the people devised a simple plan. They built a stockade deep in the forest. "We'll trap a herd or two of deer in the stockade," they said. "Then the king can hunt all he likes, to his heart's content. But we won't have to leave our fields and shops. Let him be happy."

The stockade was built and two herds of deer were driven within its walls. The gates were closed, and the delicate animals, charging and wheeling in frantic circles, sought some way out. But there was none. Exhausted, they stood trembling, awaiting their fate.

The men left happily to tell the king of their success. One of the herds that had been trapped was the herd of the Banyan Deer.

The Banyan Deer walked among his herd. Sunlight played on his many-branched antlers. His black eyes shone and his muzzle was wet. "The blue sky is overhead. Green grass grows at our feet," he told the others. "Do not give up. Where there is life, there is hope. I will find a way." And so he strove to ease their fears.

Soon the king arrived to view the newly captured herds. He strung his bow in preparation for the hunt. Noticing the two deer kings below, he said, "The leaders of both herds are magnificent. No one is to shoot them. They shall be spared." Then, standing on the wall, looking down over the stockade, he sent his arrows flying into the milling herds. The deer became frantic. Racing wildly, they injured one another with horns and hooves as they sought to escape the deadly rain of arrows.

And so it went. Every few days the king and his courtiers returned to the stockade. And every few days more deer were killed and wounded by arrows. Others were injured in the desperate effort to escape.

The king of the Banyan deer met with the leader of the other herd. "Brother," he said with a shake of his antlered head, "we are trapped. I've tried every possible way, but all exits are barred against us. Our subjects suffer unbearably. When the arrows fly, many are hurt just trying to stay alive. Let us hold a lottery. Each day all the deer, one day from your herd, one day from mine, will pick a straw. Then, the one deer on whom the lottery falls can stand before the king to be shot. In this way many can be saved from needless injury and pain."

And the leader of the other herd agreed.

The next day, when the king and his courtiers looked down over the stockade wall, they found one trembling deer standing directly below them. "What is this?" said the king. "Ah, I see. These are noble deer indeed! They have chosen that one deer alone shall die rather than that they all suffer from our hunt. Those deer kings have wisdom." A heaviness descended on the king's heart. "We shall accept their terms," he announced. "We shall shoot only the one deer that stands below." Unstringing his bow he descended from the stockade wall and rode back in silence to the palace.

That night, the king tossed and turned, a radiant deer pacing through his dreams.

One day, the lot fell on a pregnant doe. She went to her king, the leader of the other herd, and said, "I promise to fulfill the lottery once my fawn is born. But if I go now, both I and my unborn child will die. Spare me till then, Sire. I do not ask for myself, but for the sake of the one that is soon to be born."

But her king said, "The law is the law. The lottery has fallen on you, and you must die. There are no exceptions. Justice demands that you go."

In desperation, she ran to the Banyan Deer and begged for aid. He listened quietly, observing her with wide and gentle eyes. "You are right," said the Banyan Deer. "The terms of the lottery require that only one need die. Therefore it is right that you be spared until your fawn is born. I will see that it is done."

Overjoyed, the grateful doe bowed and bounded away.

The Banyan Deer King walked calmly, in great dignity, through his browsing herd. There was no other he would send to take her place. He had spared her, he himself would replace her. How could it be otherwise?

The others watched as he moved among them. His great, curving antlers and strong shoulders, his shining eyes and sharp, black hooves, all reassured and comforted them. Never had their Banyan King let them down. Never had he abandoned them. If there was a way, he would find it. If there was a chance to save another, he would take it. Not once had he lorded it over them. He was a king indeed, and his whole herd took comfort in his presence.

The courtiers were waiting with drawn bows atop the stockade. When they saw that the Deer King himself had come, and that he would not leave, they sent for the king.

"Banyan King," said the human king when he arrived, "Have I not freed you from my hunt?"

"Great King," replied the Banyan Deer, "what ruler can be free if the people suffer? Today a doe with fawn begged for my aid. The lottery, having fallen on her, condemned both her and her unborn fawn to death. Yet, the terms of the lottery require that only one shall die. So I shall take her place.

The lottery shall be fulfilled. This is my right and my duty as king."

A stone rolled from the king's heart. "Noble Banyan Deer," he said, "you are right. A king must care for the least of his subjects. It is a lesson I have been long in learning, but to-day, through your intended sacrifice, you have made it clear. So I shall give you a gift, the payment of a teacher's fee. As you freed the doe and her fawn, so you and your herd shall be freed. That is my promise. You shall not be hunted again. Go now and live in peace."

But the Banyan Deer said, "Great King, this is a noble gift, indeed. Yet how can I leave? If I depart with my herd, the remaining deer will suffer all the more. Your hunters shall shoot only at them. A rain of arrows will fall upon them. While I desire safety for my people above all things, I cannot buy it at the cost of increasing the sufferings of others. So, no. I cannot go and live in peace."

The human king was stunned. "Banyan Deer," he asked, "would you really risk your herd's freedom to benefit others?"

"I would," answered the Banyan Deer. "I will. Think of the anguish of those others, great King. Imagine their sufferings. Then let them, too, go free."

The king paused. He pondered. At last, he lifted his head and smiled. "How can I refuse you? You shall have your wish. The other herd, too, shall go free. Now you may de-part in peace."

But the Banyan Deer answered, "Alas, great King, I cannot. What of all the other wild, four-footed creatures? Like them I have lived a life surrounded by many dangers. How could I live in peace knowing the terrors they must yet endure? Your hunt shall fall entirely on them. Their sufferings shall increase. I beg you, mighty King, have pity. Can there be peace for me unless they, too, are free?"

Again, the human king was astonished. Yet, slowly, the truth of the Banyan Deer's words grew clear to him. "It is true," he said at last. "There is no real peace unless its ben-efits extend to all. Let it be known, then, throughout my realm: never again shall any four-footed creature be slain. All are freed from my hunt—rabbit, boar, bear, lion, leopard, tiger, deer—all. Never again shall any fall to my huntsmen's arrows. Now, my Teacher. Have you at last found peace?"

But the Banyan Deer said, "Great King, I have not. For now I think of the sweet singers, those defenseless ones of the air. The birds, great King, the birds! They shall be surrounded by a net of danger and death. Stones and arrows shall greet them wherever they fly. They shall fall like rain from the skies. They shall know such suffering as can hardly be imagined. Great King, let them, too, go free!"

"Great One," said the human king, "You drive a hard bargain and are determined, it seems, to make farmers of us all. But, yes, I shall free the birds. On this you have my word. They shall fly freely throughout my realm. No one shall hunt them. They shall build their nests and sing their songs in peace. Now, Noble Being, are you satisfied? Are you, at last, at peace?"

"Great King," answered the Banyan Deer, "in whom generosity overflows, think now of those silent ones of your realm—the fish, my Lord. If I do not now speak for them, who will? Hooks, nets, and spears shall soon be poised above them. Can I abide in peace while they alone face that torment? It is impossible! Great King, I beg you, spare them as well. Until then, I cannot be at peace."

"Noble Being," said the human king, tears trickling down his cheeks, "Compassionate One, never—no, never before— have I been moved to think in such a way. But, yes, I do now agree. The fish, too, are of my kingdom, and so they, too, must be free. They shall swim freely throughout my realm. No one shall kill them again."

"Now, all of you assembled courtiers and attendants," announced the king, "hear my words and see that they are posted throughout the land. From this day forth, all beings shall be recognized as my own dear subjects. None shall be trapped, hunted, or killed. This is my lasting decree. See that it is fulfilled."

"Now, tell me, Noble One," he said, turning to the Banyan Deer once more, "are you at peace?"

Birds flew across the blue sky and perched, singing, in the trees. Deer grazed calmly on the green grass.

"Yes," said the Banyan Deer, "Now I am at peace!" A tear trickled from his eye—a tear of pure joy. In that tear was reflected all the world. And he leapt like a fawn, leapt up for joy—sheer joy! He had saved them all!

Gathering his herd, he thanked the king and departed back into the green forest.

Later the king had a pillar of stone set on the spot. Carved upon it was the figure of a deer encircled with these words: Homage to the Noble Banyan Deer, Compassionate Teacher of Kings.

Then he, too, lived on, caring wisely for all things.

Commentary on page 214

THE BLUE BEAR OF THE MOUNTAINS

O nce, long ago, many ages past, a bear with blue fur, silver claws, and ruby red eyes dwelt among the snow-covered Himalayan peaks. Kings and princes offered great rewards to anyone who could capture this bear. They wanted its blue fur and silver claws. And they wanted to eat its flesh, said to be as sweet as honey and give long life. But no one ever caught the bear or brought accurate news of its where-abouts.

One day, a hunter who had come in search of this miracu-lous bear became lost in a snowstorm. He staggered through the drifts and whirling snow, calling desperately for help.

The blue bear, curled up safely asleep in its den, heard those cries and awoke. It was a beast, but somehow those pitiful cries pierced its heart. Rousing itself, the bear raised its paw and, with one blow, broke down the snow wall which blocked its den. Sniffing the air, it shuffled off through the howling storm to find the creature whose cries had awoken it from its long winter's sleep.

The bear found the hunter, near death, half-buried in the snow. Scooping the man up in its paws, the bear carried the hunter to its cave, wrapped its furry arms around him and breathed warmth back into the hunter's near-frozen body.

The hunter's eyes flickered open. He looked up into the face of a bear—the very blue-furred bear he had been seek-ing. Trembling with fear, he gazed up at the furry face, wet muzzle, and ruby eyes. He saw sharp teeth hovering over his own throat. But the bear's eyes were soft, and the breath flowing from its mouth was sweet as lotus honey.

Then the bear spoke in human words. "Hunter," it said, "when I heard your anguished cries, I thought my own heart would break. When you are well you shall go freely, friend. Only promise that you will never reveal where my den is hidden."

And the hunter promised.

However, once the hunter had descended safely from the mountain, he thought of the reward and the desire for riches grew strong within him. "After all, a man is greater than a bear," he growled. "A promise to a beast cannot compare with a man's welfare and comfort. I alone know where this bear's den lies. The gold is mine." And off he marched to tell the king.

The king was overjoyed. "However, if you are lying," said the king, "I'll have your head. Others have tried to trick me before this. Wait here while my hunters seek the bear." And he sent off three of his hunters to the den on the mountain that the faithless hunter had described.

The three hunters crept stealthily up to the bear's den, draped a net over the opening, and sounded their horns. The bear awoke and rushed out from the darkness of its cave into the bright sunlight. Blinded by the light, it stumbled into the net and was caught. The hunters tied the bear's silver-clawed paws together and lifted it up, still alive, onto a pole. But before they tied its jaws, the bear spoke. "I have been betrayed," it said. "Take me to the king and I will reveal the treachery."

The hunters were startled, but they agreed. Then they set off through the snow and down the mountainside. Arriving at the palace, they set the bear before the king, cut its cords, and let it speak.

"Your Majesty," the bear began, "I saved a hunter from death, and in return asked only that he keep the secret of my hidden den. But, for the sake of gold, he has broken his word and has thrown away his honor and my life. Even a beast knows better. I pity him."

The king was astonished to hear the bear speak. And he was angered by its tale. "Bring me the hunter," he ordered.

Surrounded by guards, the hunter was brought to the throne room. Seeing the bear alive, he sought to escape. "Hold him!" ordered the king, "and bring him near."

"Man," said the bear, "do you not see that you have done an evil thing? Did I not give you your life, and did you not promise, in return, to protect me?"

But the hunter turned angrily away. "Your Majesty," he said, "you have the bear. Though it may talk, remember, Sire, you are a king and it is just a beast. You may kill it, cut off its fur, and eat its flesh just as you please. What is that to me? Give me the reward I deserve."

Then the king said, "Release the bear, and with all honors escort it back to its home in the mountains. And as for this hunter he shall, indeed, receive the reward he deserves. Cast him out from our city immediately, but do not harm him. The treasure I give him is his own life, a gift greater than all gold. From this bear I have learned a little of honor and kindness."

The hunter's lips snarled, and his beard bristled in anger. "I'll be revenged," he roared, "revenged on you all!" But before he could lay hold of his weapons, the king's men drove him from the palace and beyond the city walls.

The king bowed to the bear, and with his own hands placed a garland of flowers around the wise beast's neck.

Escorted safely by the king's soldiers, the bear returned to the mountains where it chose another den and lived on, in peace, for many years.

Commentary on page 215

THE GOLDEN DEER

O nce, long ages ago, when Brahmadatta reigned in
Benares, a rich merchant passed on his inheritance to
his son, and then died.

The young man was a wastrel. Quickly going through his
father's fortune, he soon began borrowing and living on the
credit of others. One day he awoke to find himself deep in
debt, the creditors knocking loudly on his door. In desperation, he led them all to the Ganges river, claiming that he had
treasure buried in the sandy bank.

As they neared the riverbank, he seemed to slip, and suddenly, losing his balance, he tumbled in. The current bore
him swiftly away. He called for help, but not one of the
creditors could brave that current. Standing helplessly on
the shore, they watched the youth as he was washed downstream, supposing he would be carried to his death.

All this had been part of the youth's hastily thought-out
plan. His creditors, seeing him washed downstream, would
think him dead, he thought, and so he would be released,
through this trick, from his liabilities.

The plan had a flaw. Swept away by the current, the youth
could not, in reality, regain the shore. His cries grew more
and more desperate. He seemed lost, beyond all hope.

A magnificent deer lay resting in a thicket. Its fur was the
color of gold. Its antlers gleamed like silver. Its hooves glistened as if lacquered. Its eyes shone like jewels. The deer
was indeed the Buddha in a former birth.

Hearing the cries of that drowning man, the great deer said
to himself, "I hear the voice of a man in distress and danger.

While I live, I will not let him die!" Rising to his feet, the Golden Deer plunged through the thicket and leapt into the river. Forging through the swirling water, he came to the drowning man, swam beneath him, lifted him on his back, and carried him safely to the shore. From there he brought him to his own shelter in the thicket among the reeds.

For several days the Golden Deer nurtured the young man, bringing him wild fruits and nuts. When the youth had recovered, the great deer said, "When you return to the world of people and cities and tilled fields, I ask only one thing. Tell no one of my hiding place. It will mean my life. I have risked all to save you. Now do this one thing to save me."

The young man promised he would tell no one. Then, once again, the great deer carried the young man on his back, bringing him to the road. They parted friends, the great deer returning to his hiding place in the forest and the young man setting off back again to the great and ancient city of Benares. He thought he could remain hidden from his creditors now that they thought him dead.

In the city of Benares, Queen Khema, wife to the great king, Brahmadatta, had a dream. She dreamed that a deer whose fur shone like gold, whose antlers were like silver, whose hooves were bright as lacquer, and whose eyes sparkled like jewels appeared to her and taught her the ways of wisdom. She awoke filled with a longing to hear, in actuality, the wise teaching of this Golden Deer. She went to her husband, and relating the dream, begged that he offer a reward to anyone who might find this Golden Deer for her.

Brahmadatta had tablets of gold put up on the walls of the city, offering a great chest of gold and jewels, as well as an elephant from his own stable to carry the treasure, to any one who could lead his men to the Golden Deer.

The young man, reentering the city, read the tablets and was filled with an immediate longing for the treasure. Such wealth would solve all his problems. Despite his promise to the deer, he went to the king and revealed what he knew.

Then the king, Brahmadatta, accompanied by a great company of men bearing spears and nets, had the young wastrel guide them to the Golden Deer's hiding place.

Surrounding the thicket, the men cried out loudly. The great deer, hearing that cry, knew he was trapped. "I shall run to the king," he thought. "There alone I might be safe." Dashing from the thicket, he ran straight towards the king.

The king put an arrow to his bow and watched, thinking, "If this arrow frightens him into stopping, well enough. But if he is for running, I will wound him that we may take him."

The Golden Deer ran like fire in the sunlight, ran straight towards the king, and just before him, stopped. "Great King," he said in a voice like golden honey, "I bear you no ill will. Nor will I run from you. But, tell me, who was it that led you to me?"

The king, enchanted by that wonderful voice, lowered his bow. Pointing to the young man, he said, "It was this one. He guided us here."

Then the great deer recited this verse:

> "Upon the earth are many men of whom the
>   proverb's true
> Better save a sinking log than one like you."

At this the king grew frightened and asked the meaning of the verse. "Of whom do you speak, great Deer?" he asked. "Are you talking of some bird or beast?"

"No, great King," replied the Golden Deer, "I am speaking of a man. This man here. He was drowning in the Ganges. I leapt in and saved him. I nursed him to health and, on my own back, carried him to the road when he was ready to travel. I asked only that he keep my whereabouts hidden. Yet he has betrayed me."

When King Brahmadatta heard of this he drew his bow in wrath, ready to send an arrow through the traitor's heart. "Here is fit repayment for falsehood. Here is the treasure you deserve for such kindness to your benefactor," he proclaimed.

"No, great King," said the Golden Deer. "Shame on this fool, indeed, but no good can come of killing. Let him go and give him the treasure you promised. He has done what you have asked. Keep your word, and I will serve you willingly."

"This deer is goodness itself," the king thought to himself.
"It is worth much treasure, indeed, simply to have met him.
That he will come willingly and share his wisdom is our
good fortune."

"Go," said the king to the wastrel. "Take the reward I have
promised and good riddance to all such faithlessness."

Then the Golden Deer spoke again. "Great King, humans
say one thing with their lips, yet often do another. Truly, it is
hard to trust their words."

"Great Deer," replied the king, "that may be so, but do not
think that all humans are alike. This day I offer you the fulfillment of any wish you choose. And I will keep my word to
you even though it should mean I lose my kingdom or even
my life!"

"Then, great King," replied the Golden Deer, "I choose this.
I choose that all creatures, from this day on, shall be free
from danger. I ask that you give up hunting."

The king granted this request, then led the great deer back
to the city of Benares. Having adorned the city with garlands and having garlanded the great deer as well, he and
the queen and all the people listened as the Great Being
discoursed on truthfulness, charity, resoluteness, vigor, and
the other items of good character. Having strengthened the
entire populace, from king to beggar, in the determination
to attain clear mindfulness and wisdom, he left the city and
returned to his forest where he resided as leader of the herd.

King Brahmadatta sent a drum beater marching through the
land proclaiming, "Great Brahmadatta extends protection to
all creatures!" From that time on all hunting ceased.

Now, after this, herds of deer came fearlessly into the fields
and ate the crops unhindered. All the people suffered. Yet
no one dared kill the deer or drive them away. An angry
crowd gathered before the palace. "Brahmadatta in his
greatness has ruined us!" they complained. "Take back your
proclamation, that we may drive the deer from the fields. Do
it, or your kingdom is lost!"

But Brahmadatta replied, "I have given my word and will
not go back. Though I lose my kingdom or my life, to the
Golden Deer I will be true."

The people left in distress. Word of this spread every-where. The Golden Deer heard of it, and gathering all the deer, gave them this order: "Do not eat the crops in the fields. Brahmadatta has, with his word, given us freedom. Let us, in return, repay him with restraint."

And so it was. Even to this day the deer of that land do not feed in the cultivated fields. Humans and animals share the land equally, and the crops grow straight and tall in the golden sun.

Commentary on page 216

THE LION, THE ELEPHANT, AND THE MERCHANTS' CRIES

Once, the Buddha was born as a fearless lion. Together with his friend, a great bull elephant, he often adventured, exploring the caves, forests, mountains, and seacoasts of his island home.

One day the lion and the elephant were walking at the jungle's edge, not far from the sea. The lion lifted his heavy, golden-maned head and sniffed the salty air. Gulls cried. Waves broke and foamed against the shore just beyond the screen of trees. Suddenly, above the crashing of the waves and the shrieking of the gulls, they heard the sounds of many voices screaming in terror.

The lion gave a great roar and leapt out of the jungle onto the sandy beach. The elephant, too, maddened by those cries, burst through the bushes and trees to follow his friend.

There on the shore, they found a group of shipwrecked merchants running for their lives. A huge and monstrous serpent, its long body still sliding from the sea, swayed above them. Its fangs dripped venom. Its shining scales and cold green eyes glittered like ice.

The lion leaped up on the elephant's domed head. Lashing his tail in fury, he roared a challenge. The elephant, trumpeting shrilly, pointed his tusks towards the great snake and charged, carrying them into battle.

The serpent's head rose up into the air, higher and higher. With a long, murderous hisssssssss it released the merchants, who ran at once for the shelter of the trees. Drawing itself, coil upon armored coil, up out of the foaming sea, the great serpent slid angrily along the beach towards its oncoming foes.

The battle was terrible. The lion's roaring, the elephant's trumpeting, and the serpent's hissing were so loud that they drowned out the crashing of the waves. The merchants, now hidden in the jungle, threw themselves to the ground and covered their ears with their hands. Clouds of blinding sand whirled up, darkening the sun. To the terrified merchants it seemed as if the world were coming to an end.

At last the sounds of battle died down. Once again the murmuring of the ocean could be heard, and the screeching of the gulls. As the air slowly cleared the merchants peered out fearfully from among the trees.

There, belly up, lay the long body of the serpent, bloody now, and crushed. The once hard, bright scales were dull and torn. The cold green eyes were faded and glazed. It was dead. Beside it, too, lay the two fearless friends, the lion and the elephant, alive, but dying. The serpent's venom had done its deadly work.

Later, the merchants built a great funeral pyre on the beach and, with all honors, consigned the bodies of the lion and the elephant to the flames.

And they wondered, "Why did two wild creatures give their lives to save us?" Indeed, they could not have imagined two more unlikely saviors—a mighty lion and a great bull elephant.

Such spontaneous and heroic compassion, the merchants concluded, would remain a mystery.

Commentary on page 217

THE DOE, THE HUNTER, AND THE GREAT STAG

Once, a great stag, leader of a herd, lived in the heart of a green forest. His doe was beautiful and graceful, with eyes dark as forest pools. The great stag and his wife, the doe, lived together in mutual respect and love.

One day, a hunter came into the forest and set a snare along one of the deer trails. Later, the great stag, leading his herd, stepped into the snare, which tightened around his leg just above the hoof. He tried to pull free but the noose only cut deeper. He tugged again, and the noose, cutting yet deeper, struck bone. With a cry, the great stag tumbled into the dust.

His herd, hearing his cry of alarm, turned and ran. But his wife, thinking only, "My husband is in danger!" leapt forward. There lay the great stag, his sides heaving, struggling to rise, one bloodied leg held by the tightened noose.

"Get up, my Lord!" cried the doe. "Use your great strength. Snap the snare! Quickly! Before the hunter arrives!"

But the great stag replied, "It is no use. It is beyond my strength. Run now! Run and be free!"

"No," said the doe. "I will not leave. I will find some way to free you." She licked the stag's face, and stood protectively beside him.

Soon the hunter could be heard rushing through the bushes. His spear blade, scraping against stones, sounded to the terrified doe like the screech of the bone-piercing winds that end an eon. The smell of death and dried blood struck her nostrils.

"Run!" cried the stag. "The hunter comes. He must not find you!"

But the doe only shook her delicate head from side to side. Her eyes were wide. She shivered and trembled. But, "I will not leave," was all she said.

The hunter's steps came closer. The leafy branches by the side of the trail swayed violently. They bent, then snapped and broke. Suddenly the hunter, gripping a spear in his hands, burst through the bushes before them.

"What's this?" he exclaimed. "Two deer with only one snare? I've never seen such a thing!"

But the doe rose bravely and walked towards the hunter. "Oh, Man-Who-Smells-of-Death-and-Blood," she said, "I have not been caught by your cruel snare. I stay of my own free will. It is my husband, leader of the herd, who is trapped. Let him go free, and I will stay in his stead. The whole herd will suffer if he dies."

The hunter was amazed. He looked from the doe to the helpless stag and back again. His face softened. He stabbed his spear point down into the earth.

"Lady," he said, "your words have touched my heart. I've never released a single creature from my snares before. But this day, you and your mate shall both go free. I am a hunter, it is true. But I'm also a man. And here I exercise my choice, and say you both shall live."

Leaving his spear, he approached the stag. Stooping down, he pulled open the noose with his calloused hands. "Arise, great stag," said the hunter, "and go freely with your doe. She has saved you both this day!"

The great stag rose painfully. Then, leaning against the doe's slender shoulder, he said, "Friend, virtue is a priceless jewel, and human or beast, it remains our only refuge in times of danger. You have done a noble deed this day. Let me repay you."

Digging with his antlers into the earth he uncovered a priceless gem. "Take this jewel," said the stag, "and buy your freedom. From this day on you shall never need to kill again. May you and your family live always in peace."

Then the great stag turned and, with the brave and faithful doe beside him, limped off, disappearing back into the forest depths.

The hunter watched them go. Soon he stood alone beneath the trees, the topmost branches tossing, the leaves fluttering and turning in the wind. Wild birds were singing freely all around. In his hands he held a single jewel, but it was, indeed, worth a fortune.

Commentary on page 218

THE BRAVE MERCHANT

Once, in days long gone by, when the Bodhisattva dwelt as a merchant in the ancient city of Benares, one of the solitary, nonteaching Buddhas entered the city. Walking silently, the Buddha went from house to house, gathering offerings for the midday meal. Arriving at the gate of the merchant's house, he stood in quiet concentration. Though his robes were ragged, he radiated both dignity and calm.

The merchant looked up from his work within the courtyard and, seeing the ragged stranger at his gate, suddenly thought, "Now there is someone at peace with himself and with all the world. It must one of the solitary Buddhas come from the mountains! I will make an offering to him for the sake of the Buddha-knowledge." Gathering some of the best food in the house, he hurried towards the sage who stood at ease, deeply absorbed, quietly waiting.

Suddenly, Mara, the Tempter, who opposes all goodness, appeared. "If this merchant makes his offering, his faith will increase a thousandfold," thought Mara. "Someday he, too, will find his way beyond my devices and power. I must stop him."

Then Mara made one of the great fiery hells to open at the merchant's feet. Flames leapt up, hiding the Buddha from the merchant's sight. Instead of the calling of birds and the noises of the street, the merchant now heard screams and groans. His heart beat wildly with terror and dread. Sweat dripped from every pore. But, mastering his terror, he thought, "This is Mara's doing. He seeks to overcome me.

Today we shall see who is stronger. Hell or no, I will make this offering. I am determined." And stepping forward, he fell into the flames.

Pillars of leaping flame beat against him. Red-hot iron walls rose straight up around him. Cauldrons of blood bubbled madly. Bloody figures crawled, writhing and screaming. Above the wild crackling of the flames and the mad howling of those in pain came voices, voices hard as iron, laughing and shouting, "This is the end, the end of all things!"

The merchant, his hair standing straight up on end, walked on. He walked on and on. Time stopped. Through blood and flame he walked forever.

As suddenly as they had appeared, the flames, screams, and demonic laughter ceased. Birds again sang sweetly and the sun shone down from a clear blue sky. Green-leaved trees again swayed in a gentle breeze. Men, women, and children strolled along the crowded streets just beyond the merchant's gate as before. It was over. The merchant had triumphed over the illusions of Mara. Though he had walked through a long tunnel of fire, he was entirely unscathed. Before him, once again, stood the solitary Buddha, his begging bowl held forward to receive the merchant's offering. In reality, hardly a minute had passed.

Flushed and triumphant, but trembling still, the merchant came forward and made his offering. The Buddha smiled, inclined his head toward the courageous merchant, and said, "Well done, noble merchant. Well done, indeed. Know, worthy merchant, that this life itself is also like a dream. Gains and losses pass swiftly by, even as the drifting clouds that pass silently overhead. But to those who walk on despite obstacles and fears, success comes at last, a triumph beyond all dreaming and doubt. Walk on, good merchant, walk on. In this dream of a life we shall surely meet again."

Then the solitary Buddha turned and walked from the city.

The brave merchant, sharing his wealth with others, walked on rightly through the many years of his life. And though Mara tried, he never did stop him.

Commentary on page 219

THE HARE'S SACRIFICE

O nce, the Buddha was born as a tenderhearted hare. One day he and his friends—an otter, a monkey, and a fox—decided that once a month they would observe a fast day. On this day, they would give the food that they themselves might have eaten to someone else, someone hungry and in need.

A month passes quickly in the forest. Trees bend and shift in the wind. By day clouds drift across the sun, and at night they race across the moon. Clear streams rush, carrying leaves and twigs and bugs down over the rocks and on to heaven knows where. Soon another fast day had arrived.

"I will be good," said the otter to himself scratching his stomach and fluffing up his wet fur. Slipping into the water, he swam across the shining lake. There, on the other shore, he found a fisherman's camp. Seven fish lay on the grass, strung in a row on a stick. "Is there anyone here?" called the otter quietly. There was no answer. "Well, these fish must have gotten lost," he decided. Taking the stick firmly between his teeth, he reentered the water and swam home. Just before he reached the shore, he suddenly remembered the fast day. "Someone is going to have a fine feast," he thought sadly, "but alas, it's not going to be me!" And feeling very righteous, he waddled out of the water, shook himself vigorously, and sat down in the sun to dry his fur and rest.

The monkey too, swinging in the trees, thought of the fast and resolved to be good. He would give his own meal to another. Hunting around, he found beautiful bananas and mangoes. "Why couldn't I have only found these yesterday?"

he couldn't help but think. "Well, today they shall be given to another." And setting them aside, he, too, rested in his tree feeling very righteous indeed.

The fox was trotting along, her sharp nose to the wind. Catching the scent of cooked foods, she bounded through the bushes until she came to a farmer's hut. "Ho, ho!" she thought to herself, "what, no one around? Why, look here, someone's left a pot of yoghurt on the ground and some bread baking on a spit." Slipping her head through the cord attached to the yoghurt pot and taking the spit of bread between her teeth, she trotted off, the plume of her tail waving with delight as she thought of the fine meal that lay ahead. She had not gone far when she remembered the fast day. Her tail drooped. "Oh, well," she sighed, "someone is going to eat well." Then, recovering her spirits, she trotted on feeling very righteous indeed.

The hare thought, "Today is the fast day. I'm tired of giving what grows of its own in the ground—carrots, cabbages, potatoes and such. I want to give more than that. But what do I have to offer?" He thought and thought, then he leapt up with delight. "I have it! This very day I shall offer my own body to someone in need. I shall give myself, give all!"

Up in the heavens Shakra's marble throne grew hot, a sign that somewhere on the earth someone was about to undertake a noble deed. "Aha," said the King of the Gods, "a little hare is about to take a big leap. I shall test him."

In less than an instant, the high god appeared in the hare's forest. Taking the form of an old beggar, he hobbled off, leaning on a staff, to where the otter was resting by the lake shore.

"Friend," said Shakra, King of the Gods, his voice weak and trembling now, as if with age, "can you spare a little food for me?"

"Of course," said the otter, "sit down right here. Rest." Running to his den, he dragged out five of the fish and lay them at the beggar's calloused feet. "Eat well," said the otter.

"Thank you for your kindness," said Shakra, his voice again full of vigor and strength. "I may be back for these." And off he went, leaving the astonished otter alone by the shore.

Next he came to the monkey. "Have you some food for a weary traveller?" he asked, extending a shaky hand.

"Of course. Sit down," chattered the monkey as he scrambled up a tree. In a moment, he returned carrying several bananas and a mango. "These are for you. Eat and enjoy them. They are fresh and ripe."

"Thank you," said Shakra, "you are very generous. I may be back for these." Striding off, he left the monkey scratching his head in confusion.

Next he approached the fox. "Help me!" he piteously cried. "I am old and very hungry. Have you any food?"

"Of course!" yelped the fox. "Lucky man, I've got just the thing!" Racing off, she returned with the pot of yoghurt and the spit of bread. She threw herself down grinning and panting, delighted with her own goodness. But, to her amazement, the old beggar rose and marched off into the twilight saying, "Thank you. I may be back!"

Then the god Shakra came to the little hare just as the moon was rising. "Friend," he groaned, "I have not eaten for many days. The roads have been hard and I am faint. Have you anything that I might eat?"

"Yes," said the hare, "I do. Just seat yourself and be patient, for tonight you shall have such a meal as I have never offered before!"

Gathering leaves and twigs, the little hare started a small blaze on the rocks of the forest floor. When the fire was burning fiercely, he shook himself to save any fleas that might yet be in his coat. Then, leaping high, he jumped straight into the flames! But what was this? The fire was cool! It was like ice. Not a hair or pore of his body was even singed!

"Come out from the flames, brave little hare," said a noble voice. And leaping out from the fire again, the little hare found himself facing one of the radiant gods. It was Shakra himself! The old beggar had vanished.

"What! What has happened?" exclaimed the little hare in astonishment.

"You, yourself, are the great event that has happened," answered Shakra, King of the Gods. "Your noble sacrifice shall be remembered for an entire eon. Look!" And reaching up

with a finger, he drew the hare's picture on the shining disk of
the moon. "There, noble hare. You shall not be forgotten for
as long as the moon shall shine in the sky. Now come with
me. Let me show you my home."

Bending down, the mighty god lifted the little wide-eyed
hare up into his arms. Then, soaring upward, they disappeared together into the vastness of the night sky.

The forest became very still. The flames of the fire died
down. A glowing log popped, shooting up a last burst of
sparks. The sparks whirled up, rising higher and higher, until
they too disappeared, lost at last against the brilliance of the
moon and stars.

The three friends—the otter, the monkey, and the fox—lived
on in harmony. Seated together, they would look up at the
moon and remember with amazement the day that the King
of the Gods himself had walked among them. And they would
recall their friend, the little hare, and his great sacrifice.

All that was long, long ago, but the hare in the moon shines
just as brightly today as he did when Shakra first put him up
there. If you don't believe me, why, just go out some night
and look! There he is—a sign for all to see that compassion is
the light that illumines our darkness.

Commentary on page 220

KING SIVI

Once, the Bodhisattva was a virtuous king named Sivi. He was wealthy and respected, and his kingdom was at peace. But he was not content.

One day he looked out through the window of his throne room, out over the streets of his city and over the tilled fields of his land. "What have I accomplished?" he sighed. "Life is short. Even the virtuous gods do not live forever. All that I have given—time, thought, wealth—seem trivial to me now. I have greater strength than I have yet shown. I want to accomplish more. I want to really help another. I want to give of myself."

Shakra, King of the Gods, heard this and thought, "King Sivi has led an exemplary life. The gates of the heavens will open to him when his earthly years end. Yet now he seeks to test his true strength. He seeks to advance further on the Path he himself chose long ago."

Then the King of the Gods transformed himself. Where but a moment before he had sat resplendent on his golden throne, clothed in flowing robes of gold and wearing a diadem of stars, now perched two birds: a dove and a hawk.

The hawk ruffled its feathers and glared with fierce, yellow eyes. The dove cooed, flapped its wings, and darted down down through the swirling clouds. The hawk launched itself in pursuit. Faster and faster and faster flew the little dove, and faster and faster and faster came the sharp-eyed hawk. Turning and twisting they dove down towards the earth, straight towards the palace of King Sivi.

The dove spied the open window, sped through it, and darting to the king's side, perched, shaking, on one arm of his throne.

"What is it, little bird?" asked the king kindly. "Can I help?"

"Oh, Great King," panted the little dove, "I am in danger. A fierce hawk is coming after me and wants to take my life."

"Don't worry," said King Sivi. "I will save you."

The hawk burst into the room. With a great flapping of its powerful wings, it too swiftly perched, gripping the throne's other arm with its curved claws.

"Great King," proclaimed the hawk. "My lawful prey sits by your side. I am weary with the chase. Let me claim my prize, and I will depart in peace."

"I cannot give you this dove," replied the king. "She came to me in danger, and I have promised to save her."

"That is all very well," said the hawk, "but what of my rights? I am a hunter, and doves are my food. You have robbed me of what is mine. Without food I shall starve. Where is the virtue in that?"

"I'll give you some other food," answered King Sivi. "Name what you will, and I will have it brought to you."

"Good King," said the hawk. "I need fresh-killed meat to live. Can you kill another creature so that I may live? Where would be the fairness in that? Consider. Give me the dove. It is the simplest way."

"It's true," thought the king to himself. "How could I kill another being to feed the hawk? That's no better than giving him the dove. Yet, if I save the dove, the hawk will starve. He's right. I have taken what is his. I must find some solution to this dilemma, or either the dove's blood or the hawk's will be on my hands. Each has an equal right to live. I must help them both, yet cause no harm to any other creature."

He sat still, deep in thought. Then he said, "I have a plan. The hawk shall eat, the dove shall go free, and no creature need be killed."

"What is your plan, O King?" asked the hawk suspiciously.

"I will give you a slice of my own flesh," answered King Sivi, "which shall equal the weight of the dove."

"If it is exactly equal," answered the hawk, "I shall be content."

"Bring my scales," called the king. A set of golden scales was carried in and set before the throne. The king's ministers begged, and his court—men and women alike—pleaded. "Great King, forbear. Do not jeopardize your royal life for the sake of a dove. You are a king and worth more than anyone or anything. Hawks kill doves. It is the way of nature. Let things be."

"I have given my word and I am determined," said King Sivi. "Besides," he added reassuringly, "how much can a little dove weigh?"

A jewelled knife was brought in upon a silken cushion. The dove was placed on one tray of the scale. King Sivi lifted the knife, bent down and sliced a piece of flesh from his thigh. A shudder ran through the crowd. Red blood ran from the wound, but not a groan escaped King Sivi's lips. He placed the piece of flesh on the scale's other tray. All watched. But the dove's side of the balance did not rise. So once again, King Sivi lifted up the knife and again he cut. But again, as before, the balance did not move. Then King Sivi cut and cut again. But no matter how much flesh he cut and piled opposite the dove, the balance would not move. The dove's side of the scale did not rise. King Sivi could do no more. At last he had his whole body placed upon the bloodied tray.

"Enough!" cried hawk and dove together with a single voice. The throne room was lit by a golden light. The birds were gone. In the center of the room now hovered Shakra, King of the Shining Gods. And beside him, whole and unharmed, stood King Sivi.

"Noble King," said the high god, "this day you have been tested as few have ever been. Your resolution to give, to do good, is indeed as hard as iron, as solid as a rock. Be well, Great King, for you have done well, indeed." Then Shakra, as is his way, vanished, leaving not a trace.

The kingdom rejoiced in the virtue of their king, and gifts of harmony, long life, and peace rained down upon all who dwelt in that land.

Years later, after King Sivi had grown quite old, he left this earth and went to live among the joyous gods. From their high realm, he could look out over the whole earth, out over cities, forests, and fields. He saw how men, women, and children labored and suffered without relief. He saw the burdens of beasts, and heard the cries of those that must eat and be eaten. He grew determined to return soon. Though much joy was given him in the heavens, how could that compare with having a world in which to do good?

Commentary on page 220

THE STORY OF A SNEEZE

Once, long ago, when Brahmadatta reigned in Benares, there dwelt in the city a Brahmin whose senses were so finely tuned that he could, just by sniffing, tell whether a sword would prove lucky or not. The king, getting wind of this, said, "Hire him!"

And so it was done.

Soon proclamations were sent throughout the land stating that all swordsmiths were to bring their new swords to the Brahmin for testing. Only blades he deemed lucky would be purchased by the king.

Too bad no one could sniff the Brahmin out, for if he was an honest man at the start, he didn't stay honest long. After a short time only those swords which were accompanied by gifts—gold, silver, jewelry, land, horses, fine cloth—met with his approval. He declared all other blades unlucky.

One honest swordsmith, outraged, vowed to repay the Brahmin in kind. He took a fine new sword, dropped freshly ground pepper into the scabbard, thrust the sword in, and set off for the palace.

He presented the sheathed sword, without any accompanying gift, to the Brahmin. The Brahmin unsheathed the blade, held it grandly to his nose, and with a flourish, sniffed: "Aaachoooo!" And with that, he slit the tip of his nose on the sword's fine, razorlike edge.

The king took pity on the Brahmin and had an ivory worker carve a cunningly real nose tip for him. After this he went back to his work of sword sniffing, but from then on, gift or no, he always told the truth.

Now, this king had a daughter as beautiful as sunlight on the river and as clever as the moon which floats perfect and full on even the smallest pond. He also had a brave and good-hearted cousin who lived at court and whom the king himself had raised from infancy. This cousin was now heir to the throne. Do you need to be told that when the daughter and the king's young cousin were both sixteen, they fell in love?

Brahmadatta went to his councilors. "Look," he said, "My heir has fallen head over heels in love with my jewel of a daughter and wants her as his wife. And she, in turn, has fallen in love with him. I say we should let them be wed. A finer pair cannot exist. It is a match made in heaven. What's more, in time they shall bring joy to all the realm, for their children will not only be smart, they'll be beauties as well. Yes. He shall be king, and she shall be queen. What do you think?"

And the councilors all said, "An excellent idea, O Brahmadatta. It will be just as you say." So it was agreed.

But after a while the king began to have second thoughts. "It's all very well that they want to marry. It's only natural at their age after all. Still, if he were to marry the daughter of some other king, and my daughter were to marry the heir of yet another, my royal line would continue through not just one, but two realms. And I'd have twice as many grandchildren. Hmmm. They are young, and love is, at their age, fickle. Certainly they will come to love whomever I choose for them, just as much as they seem to love each other now. At such times, wise minds, mature and rational minds, should prevail."

And calling again for his councilors, he said, "Look, I've been thinking. Follow me on this. If my heir, the prince, marries some other princess, and my daughter marries some other crown prince, our ties to two whole other kingdoms will be strengthened. Plus, I'll have twice as many grandchildren and heirs. Isn't that so? Shouldn't we make use of our opportunity? They are still children. Wise and mature minds should prevail."

And the councilors all agreed. "That is true. Exceptional thinking, O Great Brahmadatta," they proclaimed. "We agree. It should be exactly as you say."

"Well, then," said the king. "I think our duty is clear."

And so the young heir and the king's daughter were forced to remain apart.

But the prince plotted and planned. He bent his whole mind to the task of discovering some way that he and the princess might overcome the king's edict. But try as he might, he could come up with nothing. At last, in desperation, one night he went to the old woman whose hut stood at the forest's edge.

"Love," she cackled. "What would we not do for love?" Her eyes shone in the firelight, and her rings and necklaces glittered. "Tell me, my Prince," she said at last, "have you a bold heart? Would you dare to enter the grave for love?"

"For the princess's sake," he declared, "I would do anything. To have her as my own, I would descend into the deepest hells and face an army of demons."

"In that case," said the old woman, "I may have just the plan for you. I will tell the king that his lovely daughter, the princess, is in grave danger." The old woman paused and chuckled. "And that a demon king has become enamored of her. The only way to free her from this demon's love will be for me to take her to the graveyard where I will conjure the demon from her. The demon shall enter a fresh corpse, and the princess will be free."

"I don't understand," said the prince.

"You, my dear Prince," said the old woman, "shall be that corpse."

"I?"

"Yes, you. Only you shall be a warm corpse, a very warm corpse, indeed." The old woman chuckled. "Now listen well. You must bring with you to the graveyard a little bag of freshly ground pepper. You will lie unmoving on the ground, and I will set over you a small table draped with a cloth, hiding you from view. When I begin my incantation, you must sniff the pepper and . . ."

"Sniff the pepper?!"

"Yes, sniff the pepper. And don't interrupt! Now where was I?"

"You were speaking of pepper."

"Ah yes. Pepper. You must sniff the pepper so that you sneeze. Loudly. Then you must jump to your feet."

"Jump to my feet?!"

"Is there an echo? Just listen and listen well, or prince or no, this old woman shall leave you to your fate!"

"O Wise One! Please, I beg you. Do not abandon me in my time of need. I promise that I shall reward you greatly."

The old woman chuckled again. "Well, so be it. Now where was I?"

"In your wisdom," said the prince, "you said that I should jump to my feet . . ."

"Ah, yes. Now I will have let the guards know (for we shall have an escort of armed palace guards) that the corpse, once the demon king has taken possession of it, shall sneeze, rise to its feet, grab the nearest soldier, tear him to pieces and devour him. At that moment, the princess shall be free. Now, I guarantee you that when the soldiers hear that sneeze and see you rise to your feet as if from the dead, they will bolt like rabbits. Then you and the princess can run off and be wed."

"You are truly the wisest woman in all of India. I swear you shall live in luxury forever."

"My Prince," answered the old woman, "this old hut is luxury enough for me. I live here because I choose to. Now let me rest. This evening's talk has already proven too much excitement for these old bones."

The next day the old woman went to the king and told him the terrible news.

"How dreadful!" exclaimed the king, "yet how true. My daughter has seemed listless and moody of late. Do whatever is in your power, but free her from this demon king!"

"My Lord," said the old woman, "I shall. I have a plan." And the old wise woman revealed her device to him.

That night, the old woman and the princess, along with a company of armed men, set off to the graveyard. It was a hot, sticky night. A yellow moon floated like a jaundiced eye above the trees, and a pale mist rose up from the earth. Bats flitted in the moonlight and torches gleamed. Wild dogs howled in the distance like restless spirits.

The beautiful, dark-eyed princess and the old grey-haired woman, bent like a witch, walked together at the head of the column of soldiers. Moonlight gleamed on helmets, blades, and greaves. Leather belts creaked. Armor softly clanged.

They came to the burial hill. Bones, skulls, and scraps of flesh lay scattered all around. Though the night was hot, the air that rose from that barren ground was cool.

The princess shivered and drew her light robe around her. The soldiers whispered uneasily among themselves.

"This," said the old woman, "is the place we seek."

The prince had been lying atop the hill waiting for the princess, the wise woman, and the soldiers to arrive. The cold, clayey dampness of the cemetery had worked into his bones. Yet, cold as he was, he sweated with a strange heat. Fires seemed to burn beneath him. Sweat gathered at the base of his skull, the small of his back, his ankles and knees. Strange voices laughed and moaned. Scaled creatures, covered with blood, with snakes for hair, danced from out of the shadows between the trees. His hair stood up on end with the snapping of every twig and the rustling of every leaf. One thought filled his mind: run. "Run!"

But the prince would not run. He lay in the silence, and exerting his will, fought to master the wild pounding of his heart and the mad whirling of his thoughts. "Let fear come," he said, "let whatever will come. I await my princess and shall not stir from this spot until my task is done and she is mine."

At last, he heard the tread of sandaled feet, muttering voices, clattering armor. His ordeal was over. He had triumphed over fear.

The old woman approached. "Ah," she crooned. "A fresh corpse, still slick with the sheen of fever and death. Bring the table." A soldier hastily brought the low table and the cloth. The old woman placed the table over the prince and draped the cloth over the table, hiding him from view. Then she began her incantation.

Beneath the table the prince drew a bag of pepper from his robe. He opened the bag, sniffed, and . . . "AAAAA-CHOOOOO!" He leapt to his feet, tossing the flimsy table aside. He heard such a scream like that of a banshee from hell—the old woman playing her part. Then, what a sight met his eyes! Swords, spears, helmets littered the ground. Screaming soldiers fled wildly down the hill in every direction.

"AACHOOO!"

"Enough sneezing," laughed the old woman. "Take your bride, for you have won her, and be off with you."

And the prince and princess descended the hill and ran off, laughing, into the night.

Before long the king learned the truth. "Well," he said, "I always did say they'd make a fine couple. If they had wit and spirit enough to devise this plan and to carry it off, they deserve their good fortune. They have proved their mettle, though I suspect," he added, looking now at the old woman, "that they had some help. Still, who would not rejoice in such a pair after all. Yes, we shall welcome them back. In time, they shall be crowned king and queen, as I myself originally planned."

And all the councilors said, "Excellent thinking. Yes, most excellent, O Great Brahmadatta!"

So the prince and princess returned to the palace, and in time, wisely ruled the land.

One day years later, not long after the prince had become king, he was walking in the garden with the Brahmin, the one with the famous blade-sniffing nose. It was a hot, very hot day. The sun burned down and, as it did, softened the wax that held the Brahmin's ivory nose tip in place. The nose tip drooped, and before the Brahmin could grab it, fell off. The Brahmin, ashamed, stood with his hands before his face.

But the young king bent down, picked up the nose tip and handed it back. "Don't worry," he said, "it's nothing of which you need be ashamed. You may have made a mistake, but you learned a hard lesson well. Your honesty is highly regarded these days. Yet how remarkable it is after all," he said, pausing to reflect. "Just think. A single sneeze lost you a nose and made you a better man, and with just one single sneeze, I myself won a kingdom and a bride. How the simplest things can alter our destinies! Truly, who can measure the effects of even a single sneeze!"

When the wise old woman heard that, she laughed. "So, that young fool of a prince has learned a thing or two after all!"

Commentary on page 221

PREACHER OF PATIENCE

Long ago the Buddha was a sage, a long-haired, dark-bearded rishi who dwelt alone in the mountains and forests seeking Truth.

At one time he entered a vast park, like a small forest, where he dwelt peacefully, striving alone in concentrated calm for greater wisdom.

A king, surrounded by his five hundred wives, consorts and dancing girls, seeking relief from the duties of his station, came into this park. The female musicians played. The dancers danced. The king ate, drank, and at last, growing tired, lay down and slept.

His women, finding their lord now asleep, ceased their entertainment and, being both curious and delighted with the park's beauty, wandered off to explore the beautiful set-ting. Tiny silver bells on their anklets and bracelets jingled as they walked. Their voices murmured and rose in soft laughter. As they moved through the park, they themselves made a gentle and pleasant music. After a time, they came upon the sage seated in deep contemplation beneath a great tree.

Surrounding the sage, they asked, "Who are you? Why have you come to this forest? Why do you sit here so sternly and so alone?"

The sage ceased his meditation and answered, "I am a wandering hermit. I dwell alone far from all frivolities and distractions, for my mind is set on wisdom. And you?"

"We are the women of the king," they answered. "Our lord sleeps now, and being free from the need to entertain or comfort him, we are delighting in the beauties of this park. But what is wisdom?"

Then the sage, seeing that their minds were ripe for teaching, began to discourse to them on the perfections of character and the transcendental insight that frees one from sorrow.

The women seated themselves gracefully before the sage and quietly listened. A great peace settled upon them, and all grew aware of a joy far beyond the delights of the palace.

As the day wore on, the king awoke and found himself alone, his women gone. Irritated at their desertion, he girded on his sword and set out in search of them.

Their trail was not hard to follow. Here he found a scarf draped over a bush, there a golden ball. Here was a silver comb, there a drum or tambourine.

Deeper into the forest he followed their path.

Then he heard a voice speaking, a man's voice, steady and clear. Hastening forward, he found all his women seated before a naked, matted-haired ascetic. And their faces glowed with delight.

"What is this?" he roared. "You desert your king to disport yourselves in sin with a filthy beggar?"

"No, no, my Lord," said the women. "This man is a great rishi, a wandering hermit. Far from all distractions, he devotedly walks the path of Wisdom. He has given us valuable teaching."

"Ha!" shouted the king. "I know his sort. I know what he has in mind! Valuable teaching indeed! What sort of 'teaching' has he given you? Tell me!"

"He has taught us of Patience, Lord," they answered. "He has taught us how to attain an even mind, a mind that endures all troubles."

Then the king, drawing his sword, strode towards the sage.

"The sage raised one hand, the delicate fingers slender as lotus stems. Raising his dark eyes, he looked straight at the king now walking towards him, sword upraised. "Patience, my friend," he said steadily, "patience."

"Patience!" yelled the king, "patience! Let us see your patience, you great liar."

And swinging his sword, he lopped off the fingers of the sage's upraised hand. No blood, only a milk-like substance flowed from the wound.

The sage did not change his expression. Once again in his clear, firm voice, like a parent speaking to a wayward child, he intoned the word, "Patience."

But the king was infuriated. "Patience!" he screamed, "patience! Here's my patience for you, you seducer of my royal women!"

And swinging his sword, he cut off the sage's arm, crying, "So, are you still patient now, you rogue!"

But the sage, his dark eyes fixed firmly on the king, calmly replied, "Oh, King, one must always have patience."

Hearing this, the king became like a maddened bull. He stamped upon the earth in a fury and tore his garments in a rage. The sweat was running from him. His robes were loosened and disheveled, his face puffy, red with anger and heat.

"Still it's patience, is it! You'll sing the same dreary song forever, it seems. Well, I'll make you speak the truth. I'll make you sing a different tune." And swearing all the louder, he once more swung his sword, cutting off the sage's other arm.

Not a thought of anger or fear, loss, regret, or self-concern arose in the sage's mind. No pain disturbed the deep calm of his patient, all-enduring, steadfast Mind.

Once again he looked upon the raging king, and with deep compassion spoke a single word: "Patience." Then he added, "Patience, great King, frees a man from all sorrows."

"Patience," stormed the king, the eyes starting from his head, the veins swelling thickly, "patience! You stealer of the royal women, you foul derider of the royal dignity, you filthy opposer of the royal will, I'll give you patience! I'll send you to your eternal patience! My power is greater than yours. The patience I'll give you is final and it is real!"

And with a last swing of his sword he cut off the sage's head. The sage's body remained upright, seated gracefully still. With a kick, the king knocked it over to the ground.

"Now we shall have true patience," he laughed madly. "My patience has won! We'll never hear that word 'patience' again!"

But a voice rang out over the forest speaking one word, "Patience," and the ground opened up at the king's feet. Flames shot up, and he was swallowed by the earth itself, which had opened in horror at his deed.

Commentary on page 222

THE BLACK HOUND

Shakra, King of the Gods, arose from his golden throne and peered down towards the earth. The sun's light glinted off shining seas and shone on pearl-like clouds. Snow-capped mountains gleamed. There were continents of many colors. It was beautiful, yet Shakra felt uneasy.

His luminous senses expanded down through the many heavens to embrace the earth. He felt the heat of war. He heard the bawling of calves, the yelping of dogs, the cawing of crows. He heard children crying. He heard voices shouting in anger. He heard the weeping of the hungry, the lonely, the poor. Tears fell from his eyes, showering the earth like meteors.

"Something must be done!" said Shakra. And he changed himself into a forester with a great horn bow. By his side stood a black hound. The hound's fur was tangled. Its eyes glowed with crimson fire. Its teeth were like fangs. Its mouth and lolling tongue were red as blood.

Shakra and his hound leapt, plummeting down down down from among the shining stars. At last they alighted on the earth beside a splendid city.

"Who are you, stranger?" called out an astonished soldier from atop the city's walls.

"I am a forester and this," said Shakra, "is my hound."

The black hound opened its jaws. The soldier on the walls grew dizzy with terror. It was as if he was peering down into a great cauldron of fire and blood. Smoke curled from the hound's throat. Its jaws opened wide, wider still . . .

"Bar the gates!" shouted the soldier. "Bar them now!"

But Shakra and his hound leapt over the barred gates. The people of the city fled in every direction, like waves flowing along a beach. The hound bounded after them, herding the people like sheep. Men, women, and children screamed in terror.

"Hold!" called Shakra. "Do not move!" The people stood still. "My hound is hungry. My hound shall feed."

The king of the city, quaking with fear, cried, "Quick! Bring food for the hound! Bring it at once!"

Wagons soon rolled into the market loaded with meat, bread, corn, fruit and grain. The hound gobbled it all down in a single gulp.

"My hound shall feed!" cried Shakra.

Again, the wagons rolled. Again, the hound gobbled the food down with one gulp. Then it howled such a cry of anguish, like a howl from the belly of hell.

The people fell to the ground and covered their ears in their fright. Shakra, the forester, plucked his great bow's string. Its sound was like that of the crashing thunder on a stormy night.

"He is still hungry!" cried Shakra. "Feed my hound!"

The king wrung his hands and wept. "He has eaten all we have. There is nothing more!"

"Then," said Shakra, "my hound shall feed on grasses and mountains, on birds and beasts. He shall devour the rocks and gnaw the sun and moon. My hound shall feed on you!"

"No!" cried the people. "Have mercy! We beg you to spare us! Spare our world!"

"Cease war," said Shakra. "Feed the poor. Care for the sick, the homeless, the orphaned, the old. Teach your children kindness and courage. Respect the earth and all its creatures. Only then shall I leash my hound."

Then Shakra grew huge and blazed with light, brighter and brighter. The black hound leapt up, curling like smoke, as together they rose up into the air, higher and higher.

Down below, in the streets of the city, men and women looked up into the skies with dismay. They reached out their hands to one another and vowed to change their lives, vowed to do as the mighty forester had decreed.

From up above, Shakra looked down from his golden throne and smiled. He wiped his brow with a radiant arm. The countless stars blazed with light, and the darkness between them slumbered like a dog by the fire.

Commentary on page 223

THE HUNGRY TIGRESS

Once, long, long ago, the Buddha came to life as a noble prince named Mahasattva, in a land where the country of Nepal exists today.

One day, when he was grown, he went walking in a wild forest with his two older brothers. The land was dry and the leaves brittle. The sky seemed alight with flames.

Suddenly they saw a tigress. The brothers turned to flee but the tigress stumbled and fell. She was starving and her cubs were starving too. She eyed her cubs miserably, and in that dark glance, the prince sensed long months of hunger and pain. He saw, too, that unless she found food soon, she might even be driven to devour her own cubs. He was moved to compassion by the extreme hardness of their lives. "What after all is this life for?" he thought.

Stepping forward, he calmly removed his outer garments and lay down before her. Tearing his skin with a stone, he let the starving tigress smell the blood. Mahasattva's brothers fled.

Hungrily, the tigress devoured the prince's body and chewed the bones. She and her cubs lived on, and for many years, the forest was filled with a golden light.

Centuries later a mighty king raised a pillar of carved stone on this spot, and pilgrims still go there to make offerings even today.

Deeds of compassion live forever.

Commentary on page 223

GREAT KING GOODNESS

O nce, long ago, when Brahmadatta reigned in Benares, the Buddha came to life as the child of the queen. They named him Silava, or "Goodness." Prince Goodness he was called. When he was sixteen, his father, the king, died, and he became king in his place—King Goodness.

His first act as king was to have six platforms built from which to distribute gifts, one at each of the city's four gates— north, south, east, and west; one at the city's center; and one at the palace gates. From each of these he regularly distributed money, medicines, food, silks, and jewels to all those who came.

He regarded all the people with such loving kindness that he felt towards each one of them as a parent feels towards a beloved only child.

Now, at one time, it was discovered that a certain minister of King Goodness had taken for himself money set aside by the king for the poor. This man, the king also learned, mistreated all who tried to question him about it, using not only harsh words but dealing out blows as well. King Goodness spoke to the minister and reasoned with him, but the minister simply denied it all. "I have done no wrong!" he exclaimed, "and will not remain here to be mistreated!" Gathering his wealth, he left the kingdom and crossed the borders into the neighboring land of Kosala. And there he rose in influence and power until he was that king's advisor.

One day the minister said to the King of Kosala, "Sire, the city of Benares is like a ripe honeycomb, easy in the taking. Its wealth is great. Its king is feeble. Send your soldiers into the city. Take the palace, the treasury, all. The king has no force to withstand you. His goodness has made him weak."

But the King of Kosala was suspicious. "You have left Benares only recently yourself," he said. "You are a spy for King Goodness! Yes, I see it all now! This is a ruse to destroy me. Upon entering the city, my forces will be ambushed. You are conspiring with King Goodness!"

"No, Sire, no!" exclaimed the minister. "Never."

"Really," said the king. "Do you take me for such a naive simpleton? I can see it all, I tell you! And I think that perhaps a little torture will bring out the truth for all to see. Guards!"

"Sire!" exclaimed the minister. "Please, wait! If you doubt me, just send a raiding party across the border. Let them attack an outlying village of King Goodness's realm. Then see what he will do!"

So a raiding part was sent. After robbing, beating, burning and looting, they were at last captured by King Goodness's soldiers, brought to Benares, and set before the king.

"My children," asked King Goodness, "why have you done such terrible things? Why have you robbed and beaten others? Why have you burned their homes?"

"We were hungry!" they said. "We needed money, and we were paid to do it."

"My children," said King Goodness, "if you need food, money, clothing, whatever, come to me in the future and I will give it to you. You need not harm others. Such actions only harm yourselves." And giving gifts to the astonished men, he set them free.

"As you see, Sire," said the evil-hearted minister when those men had returned, "Benares is a honeycomb, a ripe plum. The king is intoxicated with his own goodness. He has no power to resist. Attack, my Lord, and take the kingdom from the hands of this weakling."

"Wait," said the King of Kosala, "not so fast. We shall try this again." So another raiding party was sent closer yet to the capital. Again violence was done. And again, these men were captured and brought before King Goodness.

"My children," he asked, "why have you done these things?"

And again the men said, "Why, we needed money, and were paid to do it!"

Then King Goodness again said, "Come to me in the future and I will help you. But do not harm others. By such actions you grievously harm yourselves." And giving them gifts, he allowed these men, too, to return to their homes unharmed.

"You see, Sire," said the minister. "Didn't I tell you! He is a weakling—and a fool. Attack!"

"Wait," said the king, suspicious still. "Third time tells all."

So yet a third group of men was sent, and this time they struck in the heart of the kingdom, on the very streets of Benares. Yet once again, even they returned telling the same tale. They too had been given gifts by King Goodness and released.

Satisfied at last that King Goodness was, indeed, a thoroughly good king, the King of Kosala raised his army, mounted his war elephant, and set off to capture the ripe, golden honeycomb that was Benares.

That afternoon, as King Goodness sat upon his throne with its legs carved like those of an antelope, he turned to his bodyguard of one thousand champions standing there. Each of those men was an unbeaten warrior, loyal, strong, and disciplined. And King Goodness said, "My children. It is war. I can feel it. You must be prepared." And those one thousand champions shouted, "Give us the order, Lord, and we will destroy any army. We will drive them back, take their king captive, and secure our borders."

But King Goodness said, "No violence, my children. None. Let them enter the kingdom. Let them enter the city. Let them enter the palace and yes, even come into the throne room itself. But you must be prepared. No one shall lift a hand in violence. Is that understood?"

And those mighty warriors, so strong in their discipline and their dedication to that great, good king, all, to a man, answered, "Yes."

Then the army of the King of Kosala entered the land and none opposed them. They marched into the city of Benares. No army of warriors stopped them. They mounted the steps of the palace and shattered the great bronze doors. Still no weapon was raised against them. They marched into the marble throne room of the great King Goodness. There sat King Goodness on his golden throne, surrounded by his one thousand champions. "Remember, no violence, my children," cautioned the king. "No thoughts of anger or hatred. Let thoughts of charity and love alone fill your hearts." And even as the men of Kosala laid rough hands upon him, he cautioned his champions, over and over, "No violence, my children. None." And so great was the discipline of those one thousand champions that not even one broke forth in anger to destroy the enemy host.

Then the great King Goodness and his one thousand champions were all brought to the graveyard. Their weapons were taken from them and all were buried up to the neck in the earth. The ground was stamped down around them. And, as the sun set, they were abandoned there.

Darkness fell. The night grew chill. Towards midnight furtive shapes gathered, pacing nervously in the shadows. The jackals had come to devour fresh corpses. As they slunk forward, King Goodness said to his men, "Let your hearts be filled only with love and charity, my children. More powerful than any weapon is the desire for goodness."

When the jackals came close, the king and his men gave a great shout. At once the jackals turned and fled in terror. But, after a time, when nothing more happened, they returned and drew closer again. Then once more King Goodness and his men gave a great shout. And once more the jackals fled in fear. But, again, finding no one giving chase, they once more crept near. Then, for the third time, the king and his men raised their cry. But this time the jackal leader barked, "These are only prisoners, condemned men, trapped and helpless. Let us go forward and devour them."

And this time they came on and did not turn away.

King Goodness could see the jackal leader padding forward. Ears erect, it stopped, sniffed the air cautiously, then came on again. In the brightness of the moon's light its eyes glinted and its teeth gleamed. Then King Goodness raised his head, exposing his throat, as if seeking a quick and easy death. The jackal king, sniffing cautiously, came closer still. Then, seeing no danger, it lunged forward. But before its teeth could grip, King Goodness grabbed the fur of the jackal's throat with his own teeth and held tight. Terrified, the jackal king lunged this way and that, struggling to break free. It pulled and tugged desperately back and forth and from side to side, moving the king as it did so and loosening the earth around him. The wild scrabbling of its claws dug up and loosened the soil even more.

At last the jackal king broke free and ran off, howling, into the night, followed by his pack.

Then King Goodness, rocking back and forth in the loosened soil, broke the hold of the earth which had been stamped down around him. He worked his arms free, and at last climbed up out of the burial ground, free. Then he worked to free his companions. As each man was released, he, too, worked to free others, so in a short time all one thousand men were again free.

Now, as it should happen, a corpse had been left lying in that graveyard extending across the territory of two goblins. Each goblin claimed the greater portion of that corpse as its own. Their argument grew more heated, worse and worse. Then, at the point of coming to blows, one of these two goblins said, "In this graveyard stands King Goodness, a truly righteous man. Let us bring the corpse to him. He will divide it fairly for us." And to this the other goblin agreed.

Dragging the corpse by a foot, they approached King Goodness and asked for his help. "Certainly," said the king. "But I am, as you see, covered with dirt. I must bathe first."

Then, just like that, with their magical powers the goblins made the king's own golden bath, filled with scented water, appear. Straight from the palace where that usurper king slept, they brought it magically through the air. When King Goodness was clean and refreshed, the goblins brought his own robes to him, the very robes which had been laid out for that usurping King of Kosala. They brought him perfumes in a golden casket and garlands of fresh flowers laid out on ivory fans. Then the goblins asked if there was anything else he might require. "Well," said King Goodness, "I am hungry." And just like that, at once, fresh-cooked rice flavored with the choicest curries and the finest spices and herbs lay on a golden plate before him. The goblins also brought his own golden cup, filled with rose-scented water, for him to drink, straight from the usurper's table. Then King Goodness, well satisfied, had but one more request. "My sword," he said, "rests by the pillow of my bed. Bring it and I will now fulfill your request."

At once the great sword appeared. Then, King Goodness set the corpse upright and with a single stroke split it perfectly. The goblins were overjoyed! The king washed the blade and girded on his sword.

The goblins ate their fill, and when they were done, glad of heart and filled with gratitude, they asked King Goodness if there was not something else they might yet do for him.

"If you would set me in my bedchamber where the usurper lies and also bring my men into the palace, I would be well satisfied," said King Goodness.

In an instant it was done.

King Goodness stood once again in his own bedchamber and looked down upon the sleeping form of that usurper, the King of Kosala. Then, raising his sword, he struck the sleeping king upon his side with the flat of the blade. The King of Kosala awoke and saw, by the light of the lamp burning there, his enemy, King Goodness—or his ghost—standing beside him sword in hand. And the King of Kosala was terrified! Summoning his courage he asked, "Are you man or ghost?"

"Man," answered King Goodness, "even as you are."

"How did you enter? It is impossible," said the King of Kosala. "The gates are guarded. The doors are barred. The halls patrolled. What's more, you were left as food for the jackals. Yet you stand here sword in hand, robed in splendor."

Then King Goodness told the whole story in all its detail.

Then the heart of the King of Kosala was moved and he cried aloud, "Sir, this is wondrous! I called myself a man, was blessed with a man's shape, with a man's heart and mind. Yet, for all that, I did not know the worth of your goodness, while even these blood-drinkers, these eaters of carrion flesh knew it! I will never plot against you again! I swear it!"

Then he swore an oath of friendship with King Goodness, swore it on his own sword, and he begged, too, for the king's forgiveness. Then he had King Goodness lie down in safety upon his own bed of state, while he stood by the doorway, guarding the great king from danger.

When the morning came, the King of Kosala had the drum sounded and gathered all his men. Then, in full sight of his army and of all the people, he announced, "I thought I was a great king and that this man here, the King of Benares, was a weakling and a fool. But in one night, all is changed. My only concern was for power; my only recourse violence and war. But King Goodness is far greater. The forces of heaven and of earth are on his side! That is greatness indeed!" Then, turning to King Goodness he said, "Great King, rule in peace. My men and I shall keep watch over your borders. I will use my might to protect your realm as well as my own." And passing sentence on the treacherous minister, he departed with his army of men and his war elephants, back to his own land.

Seated in splendor upon his golden throne with legs carved like those of an antelope, beneath a great white parasol, King Goodness looked with joy upon his people and upon his one thousand mighty men. "If I had not remained true," he said to himself, "if I had not persevered fearlessly in goodness, both the people of my own kingdom as well as those of the kingdom of Kosala would have suffered greatly. At this moment what joy arises in me! How could any victory gained through violence or war compare with it!"

And speaking from his heart, he said to the assembled people, "Never doubt it. Effort in goodness will be rewarded. Even if you don't see how it may work out, persist in goodness. The fruit of such perseverance is sweet indeed!"

Commentary on page 227

THE NAGA KING

Long ago, when Anga was King of Anga and Magadha
King of Magadha, the two warring kingdoms were separated by the Campa River. The great Naga King, Campeyya,
lived with his sixteen thousand subjects beneath the surface
of that river.

In the fighting between the kingdoms of Anga and Magadha, sometimes the King of Magadha won part of the Anga
kingdom, and sometimes the King of Anga took part of
Magadha. One day, the King of Magadha, having been wor-
sted in battle, fled on horseback, pursued by the warriors of
Anga. He came to the river, which was running high. Behind him rode the enemy seeking his life. "Better to die in
the river than be vanquished by foes," he said, and urging his
horse forward, he plunged into the swirling water.

The serpent king, Campeyya, had built a magnificent jewelled pavilion on the river bottom. The river bed was covered with gold and silver grains fine as sand. Flame-bright
trees of branching coral all hung with jewels—diamonds,
rubies, emeralds, pearls—grew all around.

That day the serpent king, Campeyya, was relaxing in
splendor in his jewelled pavilion. Musicians played upon
instruments of crystal and gold. Naga maidens danced, swaying and turning. Suddenly the music stopped. The maidens
grew still. Looking up, Campeyya, King of the Nagas, saw a
man on horseback plunge into the river, and after struggling
in the current, come drifting slowly down towards them. The
serpent king saw nobility in the face of that man and felt
an immediate liking for him. Extending his protection over

horse and rider, he allowed both to arrive safely on the river bottom. Rising from his throne, the great Naga King offered the stranger his own seat saying, "Fear nothing, friend. I have only your welfare in mind. Tell me who you are, and why you have entered my realm." Then the King of Magadha told him his troubles. The serpent king, Campeyya, said, "Great King, do not worry. I shall make you master of both kingdoms."

For six days the King of Magadha remained beneath the surface of the river as the guest of the Naga King. On the seventh day, he rose up again from the river's depths, and with the serpent king's protection still upon him, overcame the King of Anga. So at last the constant warring ceased and, as the Naga King had promised, the King of Magadha now ruled both kingdoms in peace. From that time on there was great friendship between the human king and his friend and benefactor, the serpent king.

To celebrate their friendship, the new king built a pavilion of gold and precious jewels on the riverbank. Each year he offered tribute there to the serpent king. And each year the serpent king, surrounded by a great host of naga people, took human form and came out of the river to receive the offered gifts.

At this time, the Bodhisattva was the eldest son of a poor family. Each year he stood in the crowd that gathered to view the alms-giving and the return of the Naga King. One year, upon seeing the Naga King's great wealth and splendor, the desire to also live such a life arose within him. Shortly thereafter, still in this condition of desire, he became ill and died. Now, as it so happens, at the same time the Naga King, Campeyya, also died. As the Bodhisattva had led a virtuous and charitable life, his mind-born desire was realized, and he came to life as the new king of the nagas of the river Campa.

When the Bodhisattva opened his eyes and saw his great glittering body stretched out along a golden couch, he thought, "I have been a man and had stored up as many good deeds as grains of rice in a granary. Yet now I have become a mighty serpent. Though I have gained riches, I have been foolish. I have lost the path of virtue." And though as he looked around him he saw only splendor and magnificence, he was filled sorrow.

Then the naga maiden, Sumana, seeing the Bodhisattva in this serpent form, cried with joy, "A great god, Shakra himself it must be, has taken life among us. Rejoice in our great king, in his power and beauty!" Then all the nagas came, and, bowing before the Bodhisattva, played such music in his honor as he had never before heard, not even in a dream. So beautiful was this music and so great their joy that his sorrow was dispersed. Putting off his serpent form, he sat on his throne in garments of splendor.

Choosing the maiden, Sumana, as his wife, the Bodhisattva ruled in wisdom. One day he thought, "Though I now live in magnificence as a serpent king, I am still far from ultimate Truth. Better to be a man, even a man such as I was without wealth or power, and master the ways of Truth, than dwell in luxury on the river bottom. This is not the true freedom. I must discipline myself and regain a human state." Then in order to regain a human birth, from that time on, he fasted for one day each week to discipline himself and to increase his virtue.

But he found this too easy and sought a greater challenge. Then he decided that each month he would leave the river and go into the human world. There, for the time of the half-moon, he would maintain vows of fasting and nonviolence. No matter what might happen to him, he would not raise his great strength or magical power against another.

So on the appointed day he left the river, and taking the form of a hooded serpent with a body like pure silver, lay coiled on an ant heap by the roadside. "Let those who want my skin take it," he said. "Let those who wish to find a dancing serpent to display for money in the towns, find me. Let the ants bite all they wish. Though my power is great I will harm no living thing." And lowering his hood, he lay coiled meekly in the dust.

But people passing by who saw the Great Being lying there on the ant heap didn't harm him. Instead, they offered flowers and perfumes. And after a time, the village people, seeing him return regularly to the ant heap each midmonth, built a cloth pavilion over him, spread smooth sand for him to lay on, and continued to make offerings. In comfort, once more the Bodhisattva easily kept his vows.

One day Sumana, his wife, said to him, "My Lord, the world of men is filled with treachery and danger. While you are there, far from home, let me have some way of knowing if you are well or in distress."

Then the Bodhisattva led Sumana to a clear pool of water in their garden beneath the river and said, "O Sumana, look into this clear pool. If anyone should strike me, the water will become cloudy. If a winged garuda carries me off in its claws, the water will disappear. If a snake charmer seizes me, this clear water will turn to blood. Now you shall know how I fare though I am far away." Then Sumana was content. Shortly after this, the Bodhisattva again left the river to make his way to the anthill.

At this time, a Brahmin was returning from the city of Takkasila, where he had gone to learn a powerful charm. Passing through that village, he heard of the great serpent and thought, "I will see if my charm works on him. If it does, I will use it to make him obey me. I shall gain riches by making him dance in the villages and towns."

The Brahmin gathered the necessary herbs, and repeating his charm, approached the Great Being.

As soon as the Bodhisattva heard that charm his ears seemed as if pierced with splinters. His head ached as if he had been clubbed. Never had he known such pain. Lifting his head and flicking his tongue in and out, he raised his hood. But when he saw the Brahmin snake charmer standing near, he thought, "Even my slightest breath could shatter his body. He does not know my power. Yet I have made my vows and will not harm him." And lowering his hood, he let his smooth, scaled head sink down once again onto the dusty earth.

The Brahmin chewed a special herb and spit it onto the great serpent's head. Immediately a fiery blister arose. Repeating his mantric charm, the Brahmin smeared his hands with the herb, took hold of the Bodhisattva's body, and stretched him out full-length on the ground. With a forked stick he pinned the Great Being's head, and with a club he beat him. He spit more of the herb upon the Bodhisattva's mouth so that it filled with blood. "Snake," he said, "you are now in my power. Do as I say, or you shall suffer much worse!"

Then the Brahmin took hold of the serpent king and, twisting his body and causing him great pain, pushed him into a basket of reeds. Carrying him to the next village, he again used the charm to make the great Naga King perform.

The crowd went wild, tossing jewels and coins. Though it was just a rural village, the Brahmin collected a thousand rupees. Why? Because the dance of the snake king was like the dance of no snake they had ever seen. Spreading his hood, the Great Being moved his body with such grace and such speed that his movements seemed to form circles, squares, lotus flowers in the air. He moved his head so that one, ten, a hundred, a thousand hooded heads appeared; one, ten, a hundred, a thousand flickering tongues.

At first, the Brahmin had planned to release the snake when he had earned a thousand rupees. But now, seeing how easily he might become truly rich, he thought, "If I can gather such wealth in a village, what could I do in a town or even at some royal court?" And he bought a cart, loaded the snake king in his basket on the cart and drove on, followed by an admiring crowd. From town to town he went, gathering much money, heading all the while towards the palace of King Uggasena, who reigned then in Benares.

For all this time the snake king refused to eat. The Brahmin killed frogs for him, but the Great Being thought, "If I eat these frogs and ease my hunger, he will kill more. I cannot allow it. I have taken vows." And he would not eat. Then fried cakes and honey were given to him. But he thought, "If I am tempted and eat what he offers, I will never be free. I shall be in this basket until I die." So again he did not eat.

Sumana, the snake king's wife, grew daily more concerned. Her lord had not returned. At last, fearful of what she might find, she went to the clear pool and peered into its depths. The pool was like a pool of blood! Then she knew that her lord had been captured by a snake charmer! At once she set out to find him. Arriving at the ant heap, she saw it was deserted. But in the dust of the bare ground she saw the marks of a struggle. Taking the form of a beautiful woman, like a radiant goddess, she set off through the air. Alighting in the fields outside a nearby village, she heard talk of the serpent's miraculous dance and of the snake charmer's journey to Benares. Weeping now, she flew towards Benares and the palace of the king.

By this time the Brahmin had arrived at the palace of King Uggasena. All the necessary preparations had been made for the serpent king's dance. Galleries had been built, and crowds had gathered. The king was already seated in expectation on a dais covered with fine carpets and cushions of silk. The courtyard had been spread with white sand and a fine carpet had been placed in its center. Then the Brahmin carried a jeweled basket to the carpet, took off the lid, and charmed the snake king forth. The Great Being began to dance, forming circles, squares, and lotus flowers with his twining body, making one, ten, a hundred, a thousand hooded heads appear. The crowd was ecstatic. Thousands of kerchiefs waved in the air, and jewels fell like rain all around the dancing serpent king.

But slowly the snake king grew strangely quiet and ceased his magical dance. The crowd called, "Dance, royal serpent! Dance! You have won our hearts!" The king called, "Why have you stopped, great snake? Dance on. You shall be well rewarded." But the serpent king, his length held erect, only gazed solemnly up into the sky. Then the crowd looked upward, as did the Brahmin and the king. And all were filled with wonder. High overhead, standing all alone in the bright air, was a beautiful, shining woman. A golden light radiated from her. And she was weeping. It was Sumana, who had found her lord at last. Then tears fell from the Great Being's eyes too, and feeling shamed, he crawled into the basket where he lay hidden from sight.

Then King Uggasena called, "Surely you are a goddess. Not human, at any rate, is your shining beauty. Tell me who you are and why you weep. Is it for rage or for sorrow?"

"I am no goddess," answered Sumana, "but a Naga Queen. I weep for rage and for sorrow. My great lord, whose power, like that of Shakra, King of the Gods, is fierce as fire, whose single breath might destroy a province or turn your city to cinders, now dances harmlessly before you. Such is his love of goodness, and so great his vowed restraint, he will not strike to gain his freedom. His body is bruised and blistered; his sides bony and thin. Yet, beneath the Campa River,

sixteen thousand nagas call him king. This snake charmer
has taken a great lord for his own profit. He does not know
what he has done. But you, O King, desirous of merit, will
you not set my great lord free?"

And hovering in the air high overhead she recited this
verse:

> "Justly, gently set him free,
> Buy, Great King, a serpent's liberty.
> Giving gold and cattle, jewels and rings
> will win great stores of merit for thee."

The king thought and replied:

> "Justly now and gently see
> I'll buy this serpent's liberty.
> With gold and cattle, jewels and rings
> To win vast stores of merit for me."

And King Uggasena, turning to the Brahmin, offered him
the finest bull of his herds, one hundred of his finest cows,
one hundred coffers filled with gold and with gems, and a
golden throne in the form of a flax flower set with silken
cushions of blue. "Release this holy naga lord," he said, "and
all this shall be yours."

"No need, Great King," said the Brahmin. "I release the
naga lord willingly." And he offered this verse:

> "I want no gifts, great majesty,
> But release this serpent willingly.
> Naga Lord, please pardon me.
> This deed will to my merit be."

Then he bowed before the Great Being, who still lay coiled
in the basket. Then the serpent king came forth and crept
into a flower where he put off his serpent shape and reap-
peared in the form of a young man arrayed in robes of shining gold. There he stood, handsome as a god, and Sumana,
descending from the skies, stood beside him.

Indeed, all those who had come that day thinking to just
see a serpent dance found themselves well rewarded!

After that, King Uggasena travelled with the Bodhisattva
and Sumana in great splendor to the river Campa. "One
request I make before we part, Great One," he said. "Allow
me to see your palace beneath the waters. Let me enter your
realm."

Then King Uggasena and all his retinue descended with
the Bodhisattva and Sumana to the river bottom. Uggasena
had never seen such magnificence, and, great king though he
was, he was awed. "Why, Great Being," he asked, "did you
leave such unearthly magnificence to lie on an ant heap by a
dusty roadside?"

"This vast treasure is nothing compared with the treasure
of human birth," answered the Bodhisattva. "Through human birth, Full Enlightenment may be realized. It is for this
I would labor. As to this treasure, take it. I renounce it all.
Hills of pearl, groves of flame-colored coral trees, clusters
of jewelled fruit—diamonds, emeralds, rubies, sapphires—
mountains of gold, lakes of silver. Take what you will and
use it for good." Then he had the nagas of his realm fill
countless coffers with treasure for the King Uggasena, who
returned, rich beyond measure and strengthened in virtue, to
his own kingdom.

The king had been given so much gold, however, that as
he travelled home, the excess, spilling continuously from his
overladen treasure carts, stained the earth. And that is why
the ground extending from the shores of the Campa River
to the ancient city of Benares remains golden-colored to this
day.

Those who know this tale, when seeing the golden earth,
remember the treasure of their own humanity and dedicate
themselves to virtue. So it is said.

Commentary on page 227

SECTION III

LATER STORIES

MOST LOVELY FUGEN

About three hundred years ago, in Japan, there lived a
Buddhist priest named Shoku Shonin. For many years
he had been a devotee of the Bodhisattva Samantabhadra,
or Fugen, the Bodhisattva of Wise and Compassionate Action. Day and night, Shoku Shonin focused his mind on the
Bodhisattva. Day and night, he recited verses from the sutras
which promised Fugen's protection. Shoku Shonin had only
one wish. He wanted to see Fugen.

One day as Shoku walked through the streets of a local village, he happened to overhear two merchants talking about
a woman who lived in the town of Kanzaki, several days'
walk distant. This beautiful woman, they said, attracted large
crowds each evening by dancing while dressed as the Bodhisattva Fugen. Shoku was outraged.

That night he had a dream. He heard a voice that said, "Go
to Kanzaki and watch her dance."

"Foolishness!" proclaimed Shoku upon awakening. "Devil's
promptings will never move me." And he didn't go.

The next night the dream voice came again. "Go to Kanzaki and watch her dance!"

"Never!" said Shoku.

The third night the same dream came again. "Watch her
dance," said the voice. And that morning when Shoku awoke
he said to himself, "Perhaps I am called to end the sacrilege."

So he tied on his straw sandals, set the wide, deep bowl of
his monk's travelling hat upon his head, and, with his ringed
staff in his hand, set off along the roads to Kanzaki.

After two days of brisk walking, he entered the town. It was early evening. The sky was just beginning to darken. A few stars glittered faintly overhead. A crowd had already gathered. Torches were lit. Then as the sky grew dark, as if by magic the woman appeared on a small stage which had been set up in the courtyard. She was breathtakingly beautiful, and she was dressed in the flowing, Indian-style robes and necklaces which in paintings and sculptures adorn the Bodhisattva Fugen. Keeping time with a small hand drum, she began to dance. Her jewels sparked in the torchlight and all the men, except for the priest Shoku Shonin, entered into a trance of delight.

Shoku Shonin's rage grew. It was blasphemy! But gradually, an inexplicable change overtook even him. He grew calm and a deep peace spread through all his limbs, rising from the soles of his feet up through the crown of his head. The night sky shimmered, and the ground seemed to drop away beneath his feet. What did he care? The dance! The dance! Such joy radiated through the entire universe from this woman's dance. The stars were dancing, the earth was dancing. His eyes seemed to penetrate the darkness, and it seemed as if out in the night the trees, the animals in their holes, the people of the town were all somehow moving to, were all breathing in time with, were all part of this wonderful dance. The beating of his own heart, the rush of air in and out of his lungs, the ticking of his pulse were themselves rhythmic elements in the perfect miracle of the dance.

A ray of golden light shot from between the arched brows of the dancing woman. Dazzled, Shoku Shonin closed his eyes. When he opened them, there, before him, on the little platform in the courtyard, he saw not the woman but the radiant figure of the Bodhisattva Fugen, seated on a great six-tusked white elephant, golden beams of light shooting all around.

Tears of joy trickled down Shoku Shonin's old face. His lifelong dream had been fulfilled. For how long he stood there gazing, drinking in the scene before him, he never knew. When he came to himself at last, the stage was bare. The torches had burned low. The last of the men were leaving. Coins and favors littered the dancing platform.

Shoku turned and stumbled out into the street. As he left the village behind he heard a faint tinkling, as if of little silver bells. There before him stood the dancer in the robes of Fugen. "Tell no one," she said, "of what you alone have seen this night. Go in peace, old friend." And she was gone. A faint scent, as if of some heavenly incense, lingered on the night air. Then that, too, was gone, blown away on the wind.

In a daze, Shoku started walking again. Two days later he discovered that he had arrived back at his own temple. Of his two-day journey on the roads, he remembered nothing.

Shoku told no one of his strange experience. But years later, just before his death, he put his palms together and related the whole incident to a brother monk. Then, as a fragrant perfume mysteriously wafted on the air, Shoku Shonin peacefully died.

Commentary on page 229

THE DOG'S TOOTH

Once, as a Tibetan trader was preparing to leave on his travels, his mother asked if he would bring her a relic from India, the land of the Buddha. "I am too old myself for such a pilgrimage now," she said.

The son assured her that he would find a holy relic. But months later when he returned, he was dismayed to discover that he had forgotten all about his mother's request. He apologized to her and vowed that next time he would not be remiss.

But when he returned from that next trip, he was once again ashamed to find that, what with all his travelling, his buying and selling, his mother's request had slipped his mind. He was determined to never be so forgetful again, and made up his mind to find his mother an especially holy relic when next he travelled to India.

The trader set off once more, and spent busy months buying and selling. At last, quite pleased with his efforts, he started off leading a train of pack ponies, heading for the mountains of Tibet and home. In time, the trail left the hot plains behind and wound higher and higher into the mountains. Just as he was coming through the final pass that led to his village, he remembered—and it struck him like a thunderbolt!—he had forgotten his mother's relic this third time, too!

At that moment he happened to notice a dog's skull lying by the roadside. The jawbone, with several brownish teeth still attached, was lying nearby. The trader jumped down from his horse and pried loose one small, brownish tooth from the jawbone. After polishing the tooth on his sleeve, he wrapped it in a piece of the fine brocade cloth he had just recently purchased.

When he arrived at his home he gave the tooth to his mother, telling her that it was an especially sacred relic, a tooth of Sariputra, one of the Buddha's greatest disciples.

Beside herself with joy his mother placed the dog's tooth on the altar, prostrating herself before it again and again.

The next morning, the son left to begin selling his goods— spices, silks, brocade cloth, and herbs from India—promising to be back within the month. "She'll be happy," he thought. "Later I can find a genuine tooth-relic to replace the dog's tooth. Yes, all is well."

Weeks passed. One evening, just before nightfall, the son returned. His trading had again been successful. But what was this? There were crowds in the courtyard of his house! He slid off his horse, hurriedly tied the ponies, and hurried inside.

Many people were also inside, neighbors, and lamas, and strangers—pilgrims, by the look of them. His mother was beaming. "My son!" she cried upon seeing him enter. Then, taking his hands in hers, she said but one other word: "look!"

He looked. There on the altar was a small brownish tooth, lying on the piece of brocade in which he had wrapped the dog's tooth. Beams of light emanated from the tooth and rippled through the crowded room. The trader had never, in all his travels, seen anything like it. It was clearly a most holy relic, undoubtedly genuine.

"Mother," he asked, "where did you find such a sacred relic?"

"Foolish son," she answered. "Modest child! This is the holy tooth of the Buddha's own disciple, Sariputra, which you yourself gave me!"

The trader went closer and looked again. It was indeed the dog's tooth after all. Of this he could have no doubt. Yet, even as he looked, golden beams of light leapt from the tooth and, shining through the open window, seemed for an instant to touch the distant stars.

Spontaneously, the trader prostrated himself before the tooth.

So great was the power of that old woman's faith that, deluded as she was, she had, indeed, turned a dog's tooth into a holy relic.

Commentary on page 229

A Legend of Avalokitesvara

The Bodhisattva Avalokitesvara looked down into the many hells and saw that they were filled with countless suffering beings. A great vow spontaneously arose in his heart. "I will liberate all beings from their sufferings in the lower realms," he announced. Then, through the countless ages how he labored, descending into hell after hell, emptying hell after hell. At last the unimaginable task was actually done. The hells were empty. All living things had been freed from suffering.

The great Bodhisattva ceased his eons of heroic exertion. Wiping the diamonds of sweat from his brow, he looked down into the now empty, silent hells. And he smiled. Here and there a curling wisp of smoke rose up. Now and then, in some vast cavern far below, faint echoes sounded as a loose brick slid from a pile of rubble. But the raging fires had been quenched, and the great iron cauldrons were quiet. Sweet silence flowed through the dark halls. Even the raging demons were gone—the horse-headed, tiger-faced, horned and fanged ones. They too, in the end, had been released by the mighty efforts of the Compassionate One.

But what was this? Suddenly there came a wailing scream, then another. Flames leapt, smoke whirled, blood-filled cauldrons bubbled madly. Whips cracked, chains clanged, demons roared. The radiant smile faded from the Bodhisattva's face. In less than an instant, all was exactly as before. The hells were again completely filled.

The heart of the Bodhisattva Avalokitesvara filled with sorrow. His head broke into eleven heads. His arms shattered into a thousand arms. With his eleven heads the Bodhisattva could look in every direction to see the sufferings of every being. With one thousand arms he could reach into any realm to save those in need.

Rolling up his one thousand sleeves, the great Bodhisattva settled down once more to the unending task.

Commentary on page 230

STILSON'S LEAP

On a gray day, late in November 1941, a squadron of
Spitfires was flying back across the English Channel.
The sky was low with few breaks in the clouds. They had
broken up a formation of enemy bombers. While most were
low on fuel and many of the planes were pocked with bullet
holes, if luck held all would make it back safely to the base.

Suddenly flames leapt from the commanding officer's plane.
The whirling propeller slowed, then froze. Trailing dark
smoke, the damaged aircraft began hurtling toward the sea.

The cockpit canopy slid back and the CO tumbled out.
His parachute opened, and the others, circling, watched him
drift slowly down through the wind and silence toward the
ocean, which splashed and foamed, tilting yawningly below.
His burning plane, continuing its long, smoking arch, hit the
waves and quickly sank.

The others saw him, too, hit the sea, sink, then—supported
by his life vest—rise up and swim away from the entangling
parachute lines. He waved them off, but awkwardly, as if injured. Despite his signal, they continued circling, though fuel
was now dangerously low. They agreed to wait until he was
in his life raft before they left.

The raft never surfaced. Without it he would never survive
in that cold water until the rescue launch arrived.

Meanwhile, they radioed his position over and over.

The acting squadron leader knew there was nothing more
he could do. Peering through the perspex canopy from the
tiny cockpit, the heater going full blast, he flew down low,
right over where the CO was struggling in the cold waves.

It was now his responsibility to bring the squadron home. Cursing the day, he gave the order that they all return to base.

One pilot, named Stilson, ignored the order. Instead he gained altitude. His plexiglas canopy slid back, the graceful green and brown camouflage–painted fighter plane arched over and Stilson tumbled out, falling free. His chute blossomed behind him. Then he, too, floated down towards the foaming sea. The sun broke through the clouds as his empty plane ploughed into the sea a mile away, kicked up a long plume of rainbowed spray, then sank and was gone.

The others saw Stilson float down, strike the choppy, glinting surface of the Channel, sink, then come frothing up into the sunlight. They saw him cut loose from the shroud lines and kick free of the billowing, sinking chute. They saw his inflated raft pop up to the surface, saw him pull himself in and paddle over to where the CO was still struggling feebly in the bitterly cold water. They saw him haul the CO into his own tiny raft. On their next pass, their last, the other pilots saw both men bobbing in the tiny raft together. Then the clouds closed in again, obscuring all.

The others all made it back safely, filled out their reports, and waited. But no word came. In the morning, the sky was peaceful and clear and they flew out over a bright, blue, calm, sparkling sea.

But no traces of either man were ever found.

Commentary on page 231

DIGIT

Digit yawned, showing his long canines, and swung to his feet. Powerful muscles rolled beneath his shaggy black hair. Hands, strong enough to tear a leopard in half or to snap a four-inch bamboo stem, now gently pulled a single leaf from an overhanging branch. Resting on the knuckles of one broad hand, he rolled the leaf and placed it between pursed lips. Teeth, with which he could rip logs apart, now delicately separated the fleshy leaf from its stalk. Chewing thoughtfully, Digit sat down again, leaned back against the bole of the tree, and crossed his arms on his chest. His deep-set brown eyes took in every shadow, every movement, every minute flash of light reflecting off the green, misted leaves.

The early-morning mists burned away and the twisted, moss-covered branches, wide as velvet armchairs, glowed serenely in the golden light. The rich odors of moist earth and rotting vegetation filled the air.

The Old Man, the group's mature silverback, now walked calmly, with a rolling, four-legged, sailor's gait, across the glade. The others slowly rose from their nests, shimmied, slid and swung down from the trees, and began to follow. Digit let them pass, then, rising to his feet, responsible and alert, took up his guard's position at the rear.

The Old Man led them on, thrashing through the thick vegetation, rustling the long grasses as they went. Not a gorilla could be seen. Only the shaking of the tops of the slender, tasseled grass stalks and the deep, contented belch-grunting of their feeding marked their path.

The Old Man led them on at a leisurely pace through thickets of tender young bamboo and patches of wild celery and blackberries, eating as they went. The family moved steadily ahead, rustling the bushes, splitting the limbs of trees to strip out the pith, nibbling berries, and selecting the tastiest leaves with a connoisseur's eye. They came to an old banana tree. The broad, dark green leaves, shot with streaks of yellow-gold, gleamed in the midmorning light.

The silverbacked Old Man strolled up to the tree, reached up with both great, black-furred fists, and calmly took hold of a main stem. Then, without visible effort, he slowly, almost lazily, pulled. With a terrific, slow motion rrrrrrrrrip, a whole section of the fibrous bole tore evenly away. Pale yellowish strands of tough woody fiber, strips of hard, mottled bark, years of accumulated dirt and debris rained down onto his massive shoulders and high, crested head. Contentedly, he began digging out the soft white pith.

One by one the whole family joined in. After a few minutes only a stump of the tree remained.

The day grew warmer. The family moved on, nibbling and browsing. The sun shone down, casting deep shadows beneath the trees as the Old Man led them to an open glade high up on the mountainside. Just beyond the glade stood a crested ridge making a kind of wide bowl open to the sky. Soon all the gorilla family was stretched out in the sunshine there—the silverback, the few mature males, the adolescents, females, and babies. Some lay on the earth among the long grasses, others were perched up in the branches of the trees.

Digit sat up, sleepy and dreaming, his silvery back propped against the bole of a tree. His hands lay cupped, open and relaxed, on the earth beside him. The sunlight streamed down into his palms, warming the skin, the bones. He felt absently at the ridge of scar which encircled his right wrist and disappeared into the root of the badly twisted third finger—his bracelet of memory left long ago by a poacher's wire snare. The Old Man, using his great teeth, had freed Digit from the trap that day. The hand had been mangled. Digit did not forget.

Digit rubbed his scarred hand. He looked up. Immense white clouds drifted slowly, high overhead, in the clear blue

sky. He looked around. The shaggy bodies of his family lay
slumbering in the glade. He watched the ants carrying bits
of leaf and particles of food among gigantic-seeming stems
and stalks. Slowly his own eyes grew heavy and closed. His
crested head nodded forward, and in another moment he,
too, was asleep.

He had a dream. He dreamed he was a hawk floating motionless, high in the air, rocking, balanced on long pinions.
The wind blew freely all around. Down below on an endless,
dusty plain—a plain red as rust, red as dried blood—gigantic
animals stirred into life. Taking shape out of the dust, they
stretched, yawned, and began to move.

The wind came soughing through the trees. Leaves fluttered like hands, and Digit heard a voice calling, "Digit!
Digit!"

"Here I am," he answered. "Who calls?" But the voice on
the wind kept calling and calling.

Now a great dog, spotted like a leopard, leapt into the sky
and gnawed the sun. Crimson drops sizzled and fell. Wherever one touched the earth a dark red flower sprang up,
nodding and bending its heavy, sweet-smelling blossom on a
slender stem.

A bolt of lightning snaked across a star-filled sky. The
surface of a still pond rippled, the water dark and viscous.
Many voices began speaking but what they said—or who
they were—he could not tell. Then, "Digit," a single voice
began again. "Digit!"

Digit awoke with a start. It was midafternoon. Shadows
stretched like fingers across the darkening glade. He rose
to his feet, rested his great bulk on his knuckles, and sniffed
the air. All seemed peaceful, yet he grabbed the bushes and
shook them grumpily. The sun shone brightly overhead, but
it was as if he could feel storm clouds gathering somewhere
nearby. He grunted in annoyance, slapped his tense chest,
pok! pok! pok! The sound rang out. As his family awoke,
Digit set off through the glade towards the trees. A wind
came up. The leaves fluttered on the branches like hands.

Digit stopped, alert and poised, resting on all fours. The
long grasses and bushes on the ridge before him trembled.

He rose angrily to his feet. He tore up fistfuls of vegetation, flinging them towards the sky, a pungent fear-warning odor rising around him.

Five poachers, wearing torn T-shirts and greasy khaki shorts, burst through the bushes, their wiry dogs bounding before them.

A terrible, roaring scream burst from Digit's throat. At once his family rose, then, barking and screaming, hurried off. Digit wanted to run too, but he would never abandon his post to let the poachers pass—never.

The startled poachers paused. Then, as their dogs raced forward snapping and snarling, they lifted their heavy spears.

Digit stood his ground and became huge, monstrous in his fear and rage. His knotted muscles stood out like ropes. Every hair stood up stiff and erect. Screaming, he hurled his great fists at them like clubs. He reached out towards the frenzied dogs to gather them to him and save his family forever.

Five spears tore into his chest. Digit stood still, almost puzzled, like a man struck by lightning on a cloudless day. Only this lightning bolt illumined every pebble, stone, and leaf in this world and in every other, etching them all into his brain with an intense, neon blue electric flame. Each fleeting emotion and flickering thought were scored forever onto the red plain of his heart. Time froze. NOW!NOW!NOW! clanged a giant bell whose tolling split the sky. And Digit's useless body, its heart stopped in mid-beat, toppled forward upon the earth.

But Digit was ascending a ladder of light. He climbed as agilely as he had climbed the great trees of the forest, moments, days, years, lifetimes ago. Up and up he went. Higher and higher, his great arms moving effortlessly.

Though the sun was just setting and it was still light, somehow the stars were also already out, shining in the velvety blackness directly overhead. Great petals of incandescent flame leapt from the setting sun. Each distant star, Digit now saw, also gave off its own stream of light, like petals or like tongues of flame—rose, amethyst, icy blue, blood red. There was a humming like the music which rises up off sunbaked rocks at midday. It was like the sound of many voices, too.

Down below, Digit could see the poachers hacking with their sharp-bladed pangas at a great, black, shaggy corpse. They chopped off the crested head, the hands and feet, while the dogs snapped and snarled and worried the shaggy trunk.

"How strange," thought Digit, rising higher and higher. Now he saw his family, sheltered safely once more beneath the green forest leaves. He saw wild mountains spread below. He saw cities, too, filled with women, children, and men. He saw blue, foaming seas.

"Go on, Digit," said a kindly voice. "Don't stop." And Digit, light as a feather, light as a green forest leaf, went on rising higher and higher into the great, starry, African night.

Commentary on page 234

KOGI, THE PRIEST

The whale skeleton:
I kneel to pray in it, as
in a temple.
                —Sen Akira, "Three Whale Haiku"

This is the story of Kogi, the Priest. His given name was Eizo, and as a child he loved the sea. He grew up in a fishing port and the sea, waves, and beaches filled his childhood. As a child, he was something of a dreamer. He could sit and watch the waves rolling in and back out again, the seabirds circling overhead for hours.

When he was a young man, the war was raging in the Pacific, and he joined the navy. They made him a gunner and taught him to shoot and to kill. He fought and killed.

When the war ended, he learned of opportunities in the whaling fleets and signed on as a harpooner, his gunner's experience standing him in good stead. Then, for the next seven years, he worked the whaling fleets, killing the great whales—the blues, the fins, the rights, the sperm. But in the seventh year of that slaughter, his story—that is, the story of Kogi, the Priest—suddenly begins. It was as if his life ended, then started over. This is how it happened.

On this day Eizo stood, as he always did when whales were ahead, behind the heavy, swivel-mounted cannon. A cold, gusting, twenty-five-knot wind blew against his face and chest as he squinted out into the grey, heaving sea. The sun was setting below the rim of clouds, but there was still time to make the kill. A small pod of sperm whales was not far ahead. Soon they would be close enough. The ship was gaining on them. He could make out the whales' ridged backs sliding through the sea. He could see the foam beating around them. Yet, for all their panicked speed they seemed to move effortlessly, like great birds flying.

Eizo released the catch on the cannon. The two-hundred-pound explosive harpoon was already loaded. Gripping the cannon's polished handles, he slowly swung the massive device to sight on the whales ahead. Steady. Steeeaddy. Closer. Closer. NOW! With a sudden, terrible, thunderous, explosive blast, both sea and sky were hidden behind a screen of black smoke. The air stank of gunpowder. The inch-thick line flew out, uncoiling rapidly. It was a hit! Then, in a few seconds, from ahead came a second but now muffled Boom!—the harpoon head exploding. The line twisted as the agonized whale writhed, rolling in the bloodied sea.

Though men were shouting all around him, Eizo hardly heard. The cannon had been reloaded, and once again he sighted along its heavy barrel. Again he grew ready, tense as the line. A dark shape rolled before him. Again the cannon roared. Sea and sky were hidden behind a screen of smoke. The air stank of gunpowder. The inch-thick line flew out uncoiling. It was a hit! A good shot. But as the air cleared he saw that the whale was smaller than he had thought. An adolescent calf. They'd be lucky to make the limit on it. But there was nothing he could do. The harpoon head exploded, and with a spray of blood, that whale died.

He paused as the crew raced around him, reloading the cannon with a third harpoon. Once more he steadied his legs and took aim. Then, what was this? The great bull sperm whale had turned in the water and was now swimming back directly towards the prow of the ship! Foam rose up in white crests like breakers before it, as on it came.

Time slowed. The clouds parted as the sun shone down upon a blue and sparkling sea. Eizo's vision grew telescopic, preternaturally clear. He could see the pale mottled patches around the whale's jaw and mouth as the bull's great square head lifted from the rippling, bubbling water and planed on the waves like the prow of a fast-moving ship. He saw how its wet, rubbery skin shaded from a glossy jet black to the softest iron gray. He saw the delicate, pale pink lining of the inside of the whale's open mouth. He saw the ivory teeth set like pegs in the narrow lower jaw, glistening in the silvery white foam as the bright blue-green of the sea flared like flames.

As the whale approached, its wet, inky skin flashed redly in the dying sun and the thousands of wrinkles and scars criss-crossing its length seemed to run with blood. Water droplets sparkled along its immense body like diamonds, emeralds, rubies, pearls. The whale, rearing through the waves, seemed to Eizo like one of the great Naga Kings, who, he remembered, according to Buddhist legend of old, dwell in jeweled palaces beneath the rivers, lakes, and seas.

The sound of water pouring into deep rocky pools filled Eizo's ears. Then a voice, thunderous as surf, spoke: "Eizo," it said. "Do not kill. Never, never kill! Never kill again!" It was the voice of the sperm whale.

"Am I mad?" thought Eizo. "What is happening? I must be insane." He stood as if frozen, shaking and trembling, sweat streaming from every pore. The ship rose and suddenly fell. He lurched and grabbed for support. His hand caught at the gun. Boom! the cannon fired as he, slipping on the wet deck, fell with a crash against the iron floor. A crimson spear tore through his brain as he sank down into darkness and knew no more.

He was flying, soaring, rising weightlessly through an emerald sea. A thin, swirling, pearl and silver curtain danced above his head. He arched and rose towards it, poured through it into bright sunlight, air, and warmth. His pleasure burst into breath, a vast whooshing exhalation and slow drawing in in in of breath. His hands and arms were gone. He had two great flippers at his sides. He had no face or nose or hair, only a great, square featureless head projecting smoothly forward, eyes set far back on either side, a long, narrow, toothed jaw hanging directly below. His body was sixty feet long, weighed sixty tons, and ended in a great fluked tail. He was a sperm whale.

Terror gripped him. He felt as if he were lost in a nightmare, caught between worlds, trapped as a panicked mind in a weirdly alien body. A swirling green world surrounded him, extending endlessly in all directions except above.

Whistles, squeaks, raspings, and hissings came at him, penetrating his huge body as if it were glass. He breathed slowly,
and slowly, slowly the fear left him. He hung weightlessly
in a vast green world, breathing, listening to the waves lap-
ping against the shoreline of his own huge body. The ocean
was alive with squeakings, twitterings, raspings, but now he
understood that many of those haunting, resonant calls were
the calls of his own kind.

The surface of the sea was like a carpet of jewels, the light
pouring down thick and slow, shifting and disappearing
down and down into the darkening haze. The sun burned
upon his back. Eizo turned his fins, arched his ridged spine,
and pushed down with his flukes. His whole immense bulk
hurtled ripplingly down into the cool depths of the sea.
Slowly, steadily, the light green of the sea darkened. Emerald green became pine green, became dark as evergreen.
The darkest of all greens was tinged with purple, became
black, became inky-black, became absolute BLACK. Still, he
plunged on and on, down and down and down into unending darkness and cold. The weight of one mile of ocean
pressed upon him. His arching ribs bent. His lungs collapsed. He grew long and sinuous as a grinning serpent.
The air hummed in the cavities of his body like bees trapped
in a bottle. He hunted breathless and without physical sight
along the icy bottom of the world.

But in sound, he could See. He could See, with his Mind,
the images formed by the echoes of his own voice cascading
back through the icy darkness. He glided over an undersea
world of mountains, caverns and canyons, sound-visioning it
all with luminous clarity.

Then, "There! ITS movement!" He was irresistibly drawn.
His fifteen-foot-long toothed lower jaw swung open. He sent
out a great stunning burst of high-pitched sound, and turning
his sixty-foot body in a final gliding push, slammed into the
body of the immense squid.

Though the squid was stunned, already hurt and dazed, its
ten long, cold, powerful arms writhed around him. Its strong
suckers gripped at his two-foot-thick skin. Its beak sliced
and tore. Gripping with his toothed jaw and pushing with
all his strength, he swam up through a mile of sea as those
tentacles, thick as trees, strangled and frantically squeezed,

the squid's great, staring, unlidded, foot-wide eye pressed up against his own. Up he rose, his jaw clamped upon the struggling squid, unerringly following the beacon of sound that led to his pod.

Gradually, light and warmth and color returned. When he broke the surface again in a great burst of clotted breath, the squid was dead. He had been a mile under the sea without air or warmth or light for over an hour.

He tore at the squid, gulping it down in chunks, breathing through the single nostril on his head in long, sweet, easy breaths, then swam on protectively behind his females and calves. In the vast, languid emptiness of the glittering afternoon sea, there was neither house, nor tree, nor flower, nor bird, nor object of any kind. He had nothing, nothing, not even hands to grasp a single thing, and yet, he had never before dreamed of such contentment. He felt richer than a king. Had there ever really been another life? If so, it was faint, half-remembered. He had awakened from it as from yesterday's dream.

The falling sun touched the waves. White, dolphinlike clouds leapt overhead. The whales blew, breathing together, and flew, weightless as birds, over the hidden terrain of the ocean floor far below. Their ridged backs and broad, wrinkled heads ringed with fleecy foam shone like ebony in the slanting sun. The water tingled electrically between them and rang like glass chimes. On and on they swam, their backs arching and rising, their flukes bending and rippling through the cold, green sea.

Slam! Bang! Slam! Bang! Something beat loudly against the surface of the sea behind them. The whales anxiously quickened their pace. But Slam! Bang! Slam! Bang! On it came quicker yet, like iron footsteps striding after them. Then Eizo, the whale, was filled with a sudden and terrible dread. It was if he remembered something of this from somewhere before. He rolled his eyes back—and there was the catcher ship, once his own ship, its black iron hull streaked with rust like dried blood, smashing through the waves just behind. And he could see that the cannon was loaded.

BLAM! the cannon roared. A cow was hit. She screamed so high no man could hear. Then, BOOM, the harpoon head exploded and she died, her blood staining the sea. The chase went on. Again the cannon roared. And now, amidst the smoke and sudden, terrible noise, an adolescent calf was thrashing wildly in an agony of pain and fear. Then a great protective determination awoke in Eizo's whale-heart. He turned in the sea and swam directly on, on towards the oncoming ship. Waves broke and foamed against his mountainous brow. "Do not kill!" he roared. "Never kill! Never kill again!" He could see men he once knew standing high up near the point of the iron prow pointing down at him.

"Don't kill!" he repeated in a thunderous voice, his great toothed jaw open wide.

Boom! A blinding flash and a sharp and terrible pain drove him down into the sea. He gathered his immense strength, rose, and swam on, once more straight at the oncoming ship. "Do not kill . . ." he began again, when, with a muffled roar, sea and sky ripped, and in one horrible burst, tore completely apart. Eizo's scream was lost in the thunder. And he knew no more.

He floated up to consciousness like a drowning man given up by a repentant sea. He lay in a narrow bunk. A single dim, wall-mounted ship's lamp burned above him. He was covered with sweat and every muscle and bone in his body ached. But he was alive. And he was a man once more. He flexed his fingers and stared at them in amazement. He touched his own hands, arms, head, felt hair, a nose—a nose!—in astonished disbelief.

He rose dizzily and looked in the mirror. A thin, haunted, sweat-shining human face peered back at him. His own face. And, yet, something else too. He was a man and had dreamed he was a whale. Or was he a whale, even now, dreaming that he was a man?

He showered slowly and dressed. Weak, and trembling with the effort, he climbed the spiralling metal stairs to the deck. Clang, clang, clang, his steps echoed hollowly as he rose, lurching with the ship's movement. He pushed the iron door open.

He was on the pulsing iron deck of the factory ship. The deck ran red with blood. Mountainous slabs of gleaming, dark purplish meat, reeking entrails, glistening blubber towered above him. A sperm whale's long lower jaw, the white teeth bright, lay gleaming in the sun. The bodies of three sperm whales, a female, an adolescent calf, and a great bull, lay stretched before him. They were being rendered down into so much bone and meat and oil. One of those huge dismembered bodies, he knew, had just recently been his own.

Saws whined, hoses hissed, chains clanked, dark, oily smoke curled across the decks, and great iron cauldrons bubbled madly. Wrapped in black rubber aprons and high open-top boots, men were shouting, hacking, and chopping with powerful saws and knives, while winched steel cables screamed and massive iron hooks swung just over their heads. It was a scene from hell.

"I won't kill," said Eizo. "Never again." And he returned to his cabin below deck.

Eizo lay in his narrow bunk. Once again he saw the clear, sparkling sea of his childhood. He recalled a summer night, long ago. "I have heard it said," his mother was saying, "that the Lord Buddha gave his highest teachings into the care of the nagas. Deep down in their jewelled palaces beneath the seas, they guard this treasure of Perfect Wisdom. They keep it safely until the day we shall be ready to receive our inheritance."

The memory passed. In his mind's eye he now saw, swimming in silent procession before him, the hundreds of whales he himself had slain. They spouted red blood and swam in a crimson sea, white birds fluttering and calling all around them.

Eizo relived his own brief life as a whale. Dream or no, the memory was sharp and clear. The instinctive courage and wild joy of his whale life flooded him. He saw again the vast, elusive beauty of the sea. And alone in his narrow bunk, he could not help but weep bitterly.

Eizo remained to himself through the rest of the voyage. He refused to return to his position at the gun. When the ship at last neared port he reemerged from his room with his head shaved like that of a Buddhist monk's. When the ship docked, he collected his pay and left. He sought out a Buddhist temple he knew of that stood near the shore. It was an old place, with few believers still supporting it. The abbot, a lean-faced, serious man, lived there training three or four black-robed novices and several senior monks.

Eizo entered the temple with his sea bags slung over his shoulder and asked to be admitted to the abbot. The monks eyed him curiously, with his shaved head and seaman's clothes. But he was announced to the abbot and admitted. The tide was already coming in on the beach below when, several hours later, he emerged clothed in the black robes of a Buddhist monk. And his name was Kogi—a name he took from an old folktale about a Buddhist priest who dreamed he was a fish and who, upon awakening, found indications that his dream had indeed been true.

All that was years ago. The sea rolls on as it has since earliest times. The whales that survive still live their vast, unknown lives. And whalers still kill.

Kogi is the abbot of that little temple now. Some of the whalers have been going there to talk with him. Some have left the fleets and have started their lives over. It has not been easy for them or for their families, but they persist, slowly finding their way into lives that do not require that they kill. Kogi's strange experience and his life have come to mean a lot to them. Behind the temple, on a hillside overlooking the sea, is a small burial plot covered with stone markers, memorials, and tablets. Some have on them the names of deceased whalers. Most are inscribed with the numbers and species of the whales these men have slain.

Kogi has said of his own experience: "Not to kill but to cherish all life is the essence of the Buddha's teaching. Some come to understand this through formal periods of meditation. Some find it as petals blossom, or as petals fall. Some see it in the stone lying in the dust of the roadside. Mothers have told me they hear it in the cries of their newborn. These words came to me from the mouth of a bull sperm whale. It does not matter where or how one hears. But having heard, one should follow the import to the best of one's abilities. There are no more important words on this or on any other world."

On the altar in that temple by the sea is a figure of the Buddha flanked by the Bodhisattvas Monjushri—Bodhisattva of Wisdom—and Samantabhadra—Bodhisattva of Compassionate Action. These figures were all carved by Kogi from logs which washed up on the beach below the temple. Though these large carvings are rough and simple, they radiate honesty and power. Kogi's Buddha sits, as is customary, on a carved lotus throne. But his Monjushri and Samantabhadra are unique. Monjushri, with his delusion-cutting sword, typically sits on the back of a fierce lion. Samantabhadra should sit on an elephant's back. But Kogi's Samantabhadra sits on the back of a diving blue whale, and his Monjushri is on the back of a great, open-jawed sperm whale.

The ex-whalers appreciate that. And so, perhaps, do the whales.

Commentary on page 235

SECTION IV

COMMENTARIES

COMMENTARIES

1. Introduction

Accepting the idea of rebirth or rebecoming on which the jatakas depend can prove awkward for contemporary Westerners. Rebirth is not exactly the same as reincarnation, though there are similarities. Reincarnation implies that there is some fixed entity, some individual being or soul that is reborn. Rebirth, however, suggests that there is no fixed entity, being, or soul; and yet, simultaneously, no energy—physical, mental, emotional, or spiritual—no effort, including one's moral exertions, can ever be wasted or lost. Nothing we do consciously is without its consequences. Rebirth holds that each effort of will, each action following from each thought, gives rise in turn to future thoughts, future actions and efforts. This causal conditioning is what creates, and is at the same time a manifestation of, our life in time and space. This is the world of relativity and of the workings of karma, or cause and effect on the moral plane. Ultimately, the doctrine of rebirth insists that there is no limited "doer" behind these deeds. In reality there is only Self, or Buddha-Nature (the Absolute, the Void, Emptiness). And yet, paradoxically, this Absolute Self-Nature is not separate from our conditioned, causal existence.

The Buddhist teaching of rebirth also holds that our bodies are the crystallization, the physical manifestation of our past thoughts. After the final disintegration of this body-mind, a new body-mind will arise out of the subtle workings of the karma we ourselves have created and are now creating by the way we live and think in this present life. The being we will be in our next birth stands upon the shoulders of who we are now. The present moment is the birthing ground of all future selves.

So those who feel that there is no rebirth, and that we are only here on this earth once, are also right. The specific "I," the person with the unique biography, personality, upbringing, family, possessions, etc. that we are now will never be again. This lifetime, then, is a one-time-only experience and needs to be cherished as such, even as it also needs to be respected as the vehicle through which we establish our future beings.

There is no way, according to this teaching, to simply coast comfortably to some beneficial future existence. Ineluctably, such coasting, while not necessarily harmful in itself, will tend continually to create less than ideal consequences. The message is thoroughly practical: we need to live wisely in this present life, this present moment. Buddhist teaching and training suggest that out of the specific thoughts, decisions, and actions of this present life, this present moment, will arise new existences entirely appropriate to all that has gone before. This process began in the endless past and will extend into the endless future.

A thorough, lucid, and contemporary examination of the Buddhist vision of karma and rebirth can be found in The Zen of Living and Dying by Roshi Philip Kapleau.

SECTION I

2. Beginnings

References to this little-known jataka (Subhasa Jataka) appear, in several differing versions, in The Sanskrit Buddhist Literature of Nepal by R. Mitra, published in Calcutta in 1882. I have not come across any versions in the Pali Jataka literature—or elsewhere. Still, it remains an interesting story. There is a psychological acuity to this brief tale, with its images of elephant training giving rise in the king's mind to a desire for freedom from his own half-realized life. And it marks the conscious beginning of the Buddha-to-be's religious career. The training path of the Bodhisattva (literally "wisdom-being") will now extend, according to traditional sources, through four inconceivable periods: a total of four times $3x10^{51}$ x $320x10^6$ years, or four times nine hundred sixty thousand million billion billion billion billion years—an unimaginably long, and so for all ordinary purposes endless, period of time. In the cosmic, mythic language of the Indian imagination, we are being told that this is an eternal, time-transcending effort. And because this is so, it is not an exertion which one makes in the future. It is the exertion one makes now.

The twelfth-century Zen Master Dogen, one of the greatest of all the Japanese Zen Masters, described this Path as one of "sustained exertion," and added that "to attempt to avoid exertion is an impossible evasion, for the attempt itself is exertion." To quote Dogen more fully:

> The great way of the Buddha . . . involves the highest form
> of exertion, which goes on unceasingly in cycles from the
> first dawning of religious truth. . . . It is sustained exer-

tion proceeding without lapse from cycle to cycle. . . . It is through the sustained exertions of the Buddhas and Patriarchs that our own exertions are made possible, that we are able to reach the high road of Truth. In exactly the same way it is through our own exertions that the exertions of the Buddhas are made possible, that the Buddhas attain the high road of Truth. Thus it is through our exertions that these benefits circulate in cycles to others, and it is only due to this that the Buddhas and Patriarchs come and go, . . . attaining the Buddha-mind and achieving Buddhahood, ceaselessly and without end. This exertion too sustains the sun, the moon, and the stars; it sustains the earth and sky, body and mind, object and subject, the four elements and the five compounds.

This sustained exertion is not something which people of the world naturally love or desire, yet it is the last refuge of all. . . . (de Bary, The Buddhist Tradition, 369)

Elsewhere in this same section Dogen wrote: "The exertion which brings the exertion of others into realization is our exertion right at this moment."

It is traditionally said that Shakyamuni himself, having completed this entire process and perfected himself to the fullest, is still "only halfway there." From the Buddhist point of view, spiritual development is limitless.

In considering the beginning of this vast and profound process as presented in this jataka, the twelfth-century Japanese Buddhist monk-poet Saigyo has an appropriate verse:

The mind for truth
Begins, like a stream, shallow
At first, but then
Adds more and more depth
While gaining greater clarity.

(LaFleur, tr., Mirror for the Moon, 47)

Yasutani Roshi, a Japanese Zen Master of modern times whose teachings have had a tremendous effect on the development of American Zen, has said, "Man fancies himself to be the most highly-evolved organism in the universe, but in the view of Buddhism, he stands midway between an amoeba and a Buddha" (Kapleau, Three Pillars of Zen, 157)

The jataka itself is part of the Bodhisattva Avadana, a collection of Buddhist tales and legends purportedly told by the Buddha for the edification of his disciples while in residence at Sravasti near the water tank of Anavatapta. Avadana is a general term applying to a vast body of traditional "noble-giving" literature, i.e. to stories of the Buddha and other great Buddhist figures and their exertions and sacrifices in this and earlier lives.

One traditional appellation for a buddha is jina, or "conqueror." This is so because a buddha is one who has conquered all egoistic delusions, all greed, anger, ignorance and selfishness of even the subtlest sort. Most fundamentally, a buddha has "conquered" the delusion that self and other are separate, that a discrete and separate self independently exists. The wisdom and compassion which are inherent to our True, or Buddha-Nature can then flow forth.

Buddha is a Sanskrit term or title meaning simply "awakened." According to Buddhist teaching, there have been many buddhas already on this earth, and endless buddhas—that is, fully awakened, fully spiritually developed, wise and compassionate beings—even now exist throughout the endless sentient worlds of our limitless universe. And there will be countless more yet. The Buddha is the historical person, born Siddhartha Gautama, who with a complete experience of Enlightenment became the Awakened One, the Buddha of our historical time.

The traditional, deeply mythic view is that Prince Siddhartha, who was born in northern India some 2,500 years ago and then attained Enlightenment, must have actually begun working towards the realization of such an incredibly lofty condition in the far distant past. The depth of both his realization and character, it was believed, could not be the result of just one lifetime of effort.

Myth, of course, is not simply another kind of literal reality so much as it is a way of saying something truer than mere facts can admit, while still abiding by the conventions of ordinary language. It is not real, but it is true. As Melville says in Moby Dick, "It's not down in any map; true places never are" (79). Mythic perception puts us intimately in touch with a powerful and suggestive kind of truth.

In The Power of Myth, Joseph Campbell states that "the basic theme of all mythology [is] that there is an invisible plane supporting the visible one" (71). Myth suggests this truth, gives us an experience or a flash of insight into it by mobilizing our deep intuitive and imaginative powers. Mythic thinking unites us with a deeper level of experiencing and being. The truth of myth does not efface personal, psychological, or literal levels of reality but embraces all of them.

It is, perhaps, in the nature of things that stories and myths can easily degenerate into dogma, and the mythic then becomes bound to the literal. When this happens, a tale's liberating power—its essential appeal to the imagination and spirit—is lost and its creative force entombed. Mythic thinking, when allowed to function freely, tends to open the mind to what is highest, and restores us to the deep, creative wellsprings of wish and dream.

This brief, artless little tale manages to open suggestive vistas onto the depths of human character and personality.

3. Sumedha Meets Dipankara Buddha

The legend of the meeting of the hermit Sumedha—the historical Buddha of our world cycle in an earlier birth—and the Buddha of that distant time, Dipankara, is a key moment of the jataka tradition. It comprises the major event in The Nidana-Katha, "The Story of the Lineage," the traditional introduction to the Pali Jataka.

Set in the inconceivably distant past, the story reveals a crucial moment in the Bodhisattva's career. Having already attained a high degree of self-mastery, he now gives up the idea of personal liberation and aligns his future destinies with the welfare and liberation of all living things. Not until he has attained the ability to aid all beings will he himself enter Nirvana, and not until all are freed will he cease working for the welfare of others. (See "The Legend of Avalokitesvara." Also "The Brave Little Parrot," who, free from the flames, could have flown to safety, but the plight of others still suffering and in danger prompts him to act. Also the story of "The Banyan Deer," who risks his personal freedom and the freedom of his herd to plead for the liberation of others.) As it will obviously require an inconceivably vast period of time before all beings, down to the last blade of grass, have attained full liberation, this vow of renunciation suggests a limitless dedication, a dedication without end. The jatakas (in both the written and oral traditions) are essentially a very small part of the record of all the subsequent lives of Sumedha, from this moment of decision to his historical birth as Siddhartha Gautama and the attainment of Buddhahood. These vows underlie and define the Path of the Bodhisattva.

The desire to fulfill this selfless and heroic vow to liberate all beings is at the heart of Mahayana (literally "Great Vehicle"—the vehicle capable of carrying all beings to Liberation) Buddhism. In Zen monasteries and training centers throughout the world, four vows are chanted at the conclusion of all formal periods of seated meditation (zazen). One contemporary translation of these four Bodhisattva vows (as used at the Rochester Zen Center and its affiliates) goes like this:

> All beings without number I vow to liberate.
> Endless blind passions I vow to uproot.
> Dharma gates without measure I vow to penetrate.
> The great Way of Buddha I vow to attain.

It is such a set of vows which spontaneously arises in the heart of Sumedha.

Buddhist cosmology holds that, on this earth, there have been many buddhas—some sources say seven, others twenty-four—including the historical Shakyamuni Buddha. The next—several million years from now—will be the Buddha Maitreya, who presently meditates in the Tusita Heavens on skillful ways to save all beings. The buddha just prior to Shakyamuni but many ages after Dipankara is said to have been the Buddha Kashyapa. A curious travellers' tale is related by the famous seventh-century Chinese Buddhist pilgrim Hiuan Tsang concerning this previous, non-historical Buddha:

> At a distance of two hundred li to the West the traveler comes to a mountain that is enveloped in clouds and vapors. Its sides rise extremely high. They appear to be on the point of collapse and remain as it were in a state of suspension. A number of years ago the thunder roared and a piece of the mountain fell away. In the caves which were thus exposed sat a religious with eyes closed. He was as tall as a giant; his body was wasted and his beard and unkempt hair fell down to his shoulders and obscured his face. He was seen by some hunters or woodcutters who ran to inform the king. The king hurried to the spot and, the news having spread, he was soon joined there by the entire populace. A monk explained what had to be done: "The man who has entered a state of ecstasy can remain in this condition for an indefinite period. His body is supported through mystical power and escapes destruction and death. Exhausted as he is by his long fast, were he to emerge from the state of ecstasy abruptly he would die in the very instant and his body might crumble to dust. First his limbs must be moistened with butter and oil to make them supple again, then the gong can be struck to wake him." This was done, and when the saint heard the gong he at last opened his eyes and looked around him. Then, after a long pause, he asked those present: "You who are so small in stature, who are you?" Receiving a reply from one of the monks who was standing around he asked for news of his master, Buddha Kasyapa, Sakyamuni's predecessor who had passed away hundreds of thousands of years before. The monk replied, "Long, long since did he enter the great Nirvana." "Hearing these words," Hiuan Tsang goes on, "the saint closed his eyes like a man in despair; then suddenly he asked, 'And has Sakyamuni appeared in the world?' 'He was incarnate,' they replied, 'he gave guidance to the age, and he entered Nirvana in his turn.' At these words the sage lowered his head. Then he lifted his flowing hair with one hand and rose majestically into the air. By a divine miracle he was transformed into a fiery sphere which consumed his body and let the calcined bones fall back to the earth. The king of the country had a stupa erected to him in the heart of the mountains." (Grousset, In the Footsteps of the Buddha, 218-9)

When Sumedha returned to his isolated hermitage his exertions would have probably included long periods of one-pointed meditation as well as contemplation of the paramitas or perfections. Often ten such perfections are identified, but in the Mahayana there is a more concise formulation: 1) dana, or charity; 2) sila, or morality; 3) ksanti, or patience; 4) virya, or strength; 5) dhyana, or contemplation; 6) prajna, or intuitive wisdom. These perfect qualities of character express the nature of a buddha, our nature. Their full realization, however, requires long and dedicated training. To master them and escape the limitations of a cloistered virtue, Sumedha would not remain in isolation. The jatakas show his subsequent exertion in the world, working through countless lifetimes to master these innate perfections.

A kalpa has been described as that period of time in which a deva (in essence, a god or angelic being) descending just once every hundred years from the highest heavens and lightly brushing the top of a mountain with the sheerest cloth would have worn the mountain completely down. Modern science—geology and astronomy—give us other ways of measuring time on this eonian scale, but certainly none so poetic.

For more on devas, see commentary for "Leaving Home."

4. The Birth of the Buddha

Legends of the Buddha's birth, like those of the births of other great religious figures, include miraculous elements. One wonders: does this say more about the person who has been so born, or about the workings of the human mind in attempting to explain the birth of a child whose destiny proves remarkable? As with all symbolism, there is the implicit tension of trying to put into words what there are no words for. The result is a language of myth. So, while these miraculous events need not be taken literally, neither should they be viewed as untrue. Profound truths are expressed in this image-language of another order. Maya's dream and all the other miraculous elements (the Buddha's walking and talking at birth; the appearance of devas and devic music, etc.) have their traditional root in the first, most seminal, and perhaps finest biography of the Buddha, The Buddhacarita, or "Acts of the Buddha," of the first-century Indian poet Asvaghosha.

One of the most brilliant of the luminous T'ang era (eighth-ninth centuries) Chinese Zen masters, Unmon, is said to have exclaimed about those miracles: "If I had been there I would have cut him up and fed his flesh to the dogs!" Harsh-sounding and irreverent words, perhaps. Yet I think a piece, at least, of Unmon's intent is clear enough: "Let's not get hypnotized by soothing words and nice ideas! Do not ignore this miraculous ordinary moment in your own life!"

The Buddha's sounding of the "lion's roar" is a traditional expression signifying that the utterances of a buddha, filled with the energy and conviction that flow from deep Understanding, have great power. Like the lion's roar that stuns lesser beasts, the words of a buddha, coming as they do from such Knowing, transcend speculation. A buddha's words are majestic in their Truth.

The birth takes place countless lifetimes—four asenkheya kalpas and one hundred thousand world cycles (births and dissolutions of the world)—after Sumedha's meeting with Dipankara Buddha. It fulfills the prediction of birth made then.

5. Leaving Home

The Buddha's leaving home brings history and legend together. Joseph Campbell calls the Buddha's home-leaving "the most celebrated example of the call to adventure in the literature of the world" (Hero with a Thousand Faces, 56). The prince Siddhartha did leave home 2,500 years ago to seek and to find Enlightenment. The mythic imagination, however, was obviously deeply at work in the tradition which followed, finding, as is its way, the universal in the particular. In this story of one person we find the story of all. At some point each of us does awaken from naive innocence to see the cruelties and imponderable injustices of life. And all, too, do eventually leave the security of home to find his or her own way. That in such a few days the prince would literally for the very first time see sickness, aging, and death is probably unlikely. That he for the first time actually SAW them—that is, took them in and was struck, not just intellectually but in the guts—is true, even likely, enough. So my Zen teacher, Roshi Kapleau, would often say. Robert Aitken Roshi states, "If it could be shown that Shakyamuni never lived, the myth of his life would be our guide. In fact it is better to acknowledge at the outset that myths and archetypes guide us, just as they do every religious person. The myth of the Buddha is my own myth" (Taking the Path of Zen, 7).

The gods who guide Channa's speech, and who in some versions of the Buddha's leaving home take the form of the old man, the sick man, the dead man and the homeless truth seeker (in some versions a hermit or monk), are the devas of higher-than-earthly realms and are part of traditional Buddhist cosmology.

According to Buddhist thought there are six realms: hell realms, hungry ghostly realms, animal realms, human realms, realms of the asuras or warring spirits, and highest of all, realms of the blissful devas or gods. These six realms are arranged like a kind of Ferris wheel, with hells and their denizens at the very bottom, heavens and the devas at the top. Two of these realms are ordinarily visible to us: human and animal realms. The six realms may be viewed mythically or psychologically—or both. Mythologies of cultures throughout the world reveal something of this same archetypal pattern of possible realities. Certainly it is not hard to accept the psychological reality of one's own daily wandering through these six realms of being. Hateful, demonic thoughts give way to greedy, ghostly ones, which may in turn be replaced by clouded, animalistic thinking, which then inexplicably brightens into kind, considerate, even godlike perceptions of the world and those around us, only to be supplanted by ordinary, selfish, human ideas—or worse, a fall again into paranoid and hellish thought realms—and so on.

Devas, gods or beings of higher realms, exist, according to Buddhist thought, in many levels and varieties. Some of these higher-than-human beings dwell in realms of great sensual delight, others manifest a very pure spirituality. They generally lead lives of great freedom and pleasure, lives of wish fulfillment won through positive karma of the past. But it is no ultimate condition, and when their good karma is exhausted, it is said, such beings may fall into realms of terrible anguish and suffering. In Buddhism, the human realm is considered most advantageous—even more so than life in any of the heavens. It is from the human realm, through the vehicle of a human body and mind (which are seen as very hard to attain, in terms of rebirth), that one may gain enlightenment. (See "The Naga King.")

In each of these realms, even in the lowest of the hells, are said to be buddhas and bodhisattvas resolved out of their great, selfless compassion to help all suffering, beings—an expression of the universal compassion underlying all transitory states of existence. (See "Most Lovely Fugen" and "A Legend of Avalokitesvara.")

In Buddhism, no one is condemned eternally to heaven or hell or to any state in between. All such states are causally created by one's own thoughts and actions, i.e. karma, and as one's karma changes, the realm in which one resides must also change. Viewed mythically, beings are reborn in one realm after having died—their karma exhausted—in another. Viewed psychologically, we move from states of suffering and inadequacy to conditions of great confidence and security, and vice versa, in the course of a lifetime, as well as in the course of a day, an hour, an instant. In the jatakas we see the Buddha himself moving, spiritually evolving, through his experiences in different realms—human, animal, or deva. Sometimes in Buddhist tales and legends, other realms—hungry ghostly, warring spirit, and demonic—or beings may appear. These various mythological types, of course, also appear throughout the traditional literatures of the world.

Devas appear often in the jatakas, and in Buddhist tales and legends in general. In this collection see also "Sumedha Meets Dipankara Buddha," "Birth of the Buddha," "The Brave Little Parrot." For appearances by Shakra, King of the Gods, see "The Steadfast Parrot," "The Hare's Sacrifice," "The Black Hound," "King Sivi."

An especially clear examination of the six realms (and of the wheel of rebirth formed by the six realms) appears in The Three Jewels by Sangharakshita.

6. Enlightenment

The Buddha's struggle for Enlightenment is at the center of all Buddhist religious teaching, practice, literature, and art. The intense efforts of one person reveal the potential open to all. Myth and history, symbolic, spiritual, and actual experience are blended in all the accounts which have come down to us. This version, like most, draws much from Asvaghosha's classic first-century work, The Buddhacarita, or "Acts of the Buddha." I originally wrote this version for use at the Zen Center in Rochester, New York, back in 1972. Its annual oral presentation has become part of the ceremonial calendar of the year.

The twelfth-century Japanese Zen Master Dogen, in his writing on exertion (see notes for "Beginnings"), says of the Buddha himself:

> Shakyamuni Buddha began his exertions deep in the mountains. . . . At the age of thirty he labored to achieve the Enlightenment which embraced all sentient beings. Until the age of eighty he labored in the forests and monasteries, without any thought of returning to his royal palace or of sharing in the wealth of his kingdom. Not once did he put on a new robe; not once did he exchange his bowl for another. . . . His whole life was one long exertion . . . a life that knew nothing but sustained exertion. (de Bary, The Buddhist Tradition, 370-1)

The Buddha, then, is clearly seen not as a divinity, but as completely human. Even so, as "the state of a Buddha is one of the highest possible perfection, it seems self-evident to Buddhists that an enormous amount of preparation over many lives is needed to reach it" (Conze, Buddhist Scriptures, 20). The Buddha's Enlightenment reveals the stored and storied meaning of the jatakas; it is both first and last cause.

While the bibliography contains many different versions of the Buddha's life and Enlightenment, one of the most dramatic for contemporary readers will be found in Beyer's strong and poetic rendering of Asvaghosha's Buddhacarita in The Buddhist Experience. Sangharakshita's Three Jewels also contains a well-balanced, intelligent, and useful brief account of the Buddha's entire life and his Enlightenment. A more recent work, The Awakened One: A Life of the Buddha by Sherab Chodzin Kohn, also does an excellent job of telling the entire story of the Buddha's legendary life.

The earth's response to the Buddha's touch as he is questioned by Mara (the Buddhist devil or tempter) just prior to enlightenment is, in essence, the record of all those past lives partially recorded in the jatakas. The scene of the approach of Mara's hosts—his daughters of desire, his monsters of anger and hatred—is the kind of temptation scene familiar to religions and cultures worldwide.

There is something deeply suggestive, not threatening, yet eerie and almost uncanny, about the Naga King. The previous buddha, Kashyapa (see commentary for "Sumedha Meets Dipankara Buddha"), had attained Buddhahood and passed into Nirvana (see "Parinirvana" and commentary) many long ages ago. Yet, to the Naga King, it is as if only a single day had passed. The long row of identical buddhas' begging bowls resting quietly in his submarine chambers seems to raise a curtain in our minds. Suddenly we are looking upon staggering vistas of time, and the hairs prickle along our necks. The mysterious Naga King gives us a wonderfully mythic perspective on the phenomenon of time.

For more on nagas (but no more, alas, on Kala Naga Raja, the wonderfully ancient and mysterious Black Snake King), see "Parinirvana," "The Naga King," and "Kogi, the Priest" tales and commentaries.

The obeisance of Mara's elephant, "Mountain-Girded," in the Enlightenment account interestingly prefigures the later submission of the maddened elephant, Nalagiri (see "Nalagiri").

For more on Mara, the Tempter, see "The Brave Merchant" story and commentary.

7. The Story of Angulimala, the Robber

The events of this story are said to have occurred during the Buddha's historical lifetime. The conversion of the murderous robber Angulimala remains one of the most poignant of traditional Buddhist tales, perhaps, in part, because it touches the myth of each person's life. Who does not at one time or another find themselves on a wrong road? Dante hits the myth on the head:

> Midway in our life's journey, I went astray
> from the straight road and woke to find myself
> alone in a dark wood
>
> . . . .
>
> How I came to it I cannot rightly say,
> so drugged and loose with sleep had I become
> when I first wandered there from the True Way.
>
> (Inferno, Canto I, 1-3, 10-12)

Angulimala may not know how he ends up on his dark road either, but the jataka tradition itself would have us know. Angulimala, the robber, the tradition says, was in an earlier life the sticky-haired monster converted many world cycles in the past by the Buddha in his life as Prince Five-Weapons. (Jataka no. 55. See "Prince Five-Weapons.") In the Sutano Jataka (No. 398), he who is to become Angulimala is identified, in a birth after that of the sticky-haired monster, as a yakka (yaksha), or flesh-eating (sometimes man-eating) spirit or demon who is converted by the Buddha—at that time a good and kindly youth—to the ways of virtue. In the Maha Sutasoma Jataka (No. 537), the being who is to be Angulimala is identified by the Buddha as having evolved still further, having attained the condition of a human king. This king, through no fault of his own, is given unbeknownst to him the cooked flesh of a dead man to eat. Unfortunately, a karmic memory of his delight in the taste of human flesh when he was a yaksha is awakened. He delights in the taste again and becomes a cannibal. He is saved from this wrong action by the Buddha, who is at that time a prince named Sutasoma (so named for his childhood love of pressed soma juice).

The very complete, traditional version of the story of Angulimala, which appears in An Anthology of Sinhalese Literature up to 1815 by Christopher Reynolds, is of particular merit and was a major source for this retelling.

In essence, the story of Angulimala is a kind of karma-tale. Because Ahimsaka goes so far wrong, he must necessarily undergo a dreadful purgation if he is to free himself from the effects of his own delusive actions. No one can do it for him, not even the Buddha. He must reap what he has sown. But he does it willingly, consciously. The great Tibetan poet and mystic-saint, Milarepa, says something similar about the path of his own life:

> I started by accepting and understanding the Doctrine of Karma long before I grasped that of the Void: that's why I felt so deeply about [the] evil I had done . . . with the destruction of so many lives and so much property. I knew that by Karmic Law, I would go down to the plane of Hell when I died. That's why I held so firmly to my Guru through thick and thin and persevered so rigorously in meditation. I had to. (Jivaka, The Life of Milarepa, 134)

The sinner who becomes a saint is not that unusual a story, after all.

Interestingly, the story of Angulimala also makes clear that the innocent boy, Ahimsaka, takes his first step on the road towards becoming the robber Angulimala when he fails to trust his own intuition, reason, and judgement. The Buddha is said to have emphasized that each person must decide on the merit of the Teachings for his or her own self. I have heard his words quoted by various Buddhist teachers like this: "Do not do something because your teacher tells you to do it, nor even because I tell you to do it. Do it only if, after examining and reflecting, you find that it accords with your own deepest intelligence and Reason."

An often-quoted interchange between the Buddha and Sariputra, one of his most advanced and devoted disciples, expresses this spirit of reasonableness clearly:

> "Lord," said Sariputra, "such faith have I in the Blessed One that I think there has never been, nor will ever be, nor is there now any other who is greater or wiser than the Blessed One as regards the higher wisdom."

The Buddha replied, "Grand and bold are the words of your mouth, Sariputra. You have burst forth into a very song of ecstasy! Surely you have known all the Blessed Ones who in the long ages of the past have been Buddhas?"

"Not so, O Lord!" said Sariputra.

And the Lord continued, "You have then perceived all those who in the long ages of the future shall be holy Buddhas."

"Not so, O Lord!"

"Then surely, O Sariputra, you must now know me truly and have penetrated the depths of my mind."

"Not even that, O Lord."

"You do not know the minds of the Buddhas of the past or of the future. You do not even truly know my mind. Why then, Sariputra, are your words so grand and bold? Great, indeed, is your faith, Sariputra," concluded the Blessed One, "but take heed that it be well grounded." (adapted from Paul Carus, The Gospel of Buddha, 221-2)

Since ancient times, however, near-total devotion to and reliance on one's spiritual teacher or guru has been a strong component of Indian religious tradition. There is no doubt the method has produced powerful results. On the other hand, the possibilities for wrongdoing can also be extreme. Perhaps at the time of the Buddha this story served as a comment on a teaching tradition which, even then, must have had a long history. The emphasis on personal experience and personal accountability is one of the significant ways in which the Buddha's teaching diverged from the older spiritual traditions of ancient India, and in part may help to account for the spiritual revolution it engendered. Later on, the flowering of Chinese Zen Buddhism's independent and lively genius was to extend this revitalization of spiritual practice and training further.

One thousand is essentially an unimaginable number of people to kill, beyond the range of literal possibility. This is in keeping with the often cosmic scale of the Indian imagination.

The story also reinforces some of the words that tradition ascribes to the Buddha at the time of his Parinirvana. At that time, just before his entrance into Nirvana, it is said that he stated, "Salvation cannot come from the mere sight of me. It demands strenuous effort in actual spiritual practice."

8. Nalagiri, the Elephant

Two of the Buddha's cousins appear as archetypes throughout Buddhist literature. One, named Ananda, was renowned for his loyal, gentle, generous, and sensitive nature as well as for his extraordinary intelligence and memory. He was, for many years, the Buddha's attendant. It is through Ananda that the sutras (essentially, the teachings of the Buddha himself) have come down to us. Tradition holds that he was there, heard the Buddha's discourses, remembered them perfectly, and then passed them on orally. The traditional opening words of each sutra, "Thus have I heard," are a reminder of Ananda and this oral transmission and experience. Many stories bring to life the close and intimate ties said to have existed between the Buddha and Ananda. In this collection see "Parinirvana," and commentaries for "Great Joy, the Ox," "Shakra's Black Hound," and "The Hungry Tigress."

The other cousin, Devadatta, was infamous for evil and wrongdoing. So driven was he by his own selfishness that he attempted the Buddha's murder not just once but on several occasions. In "Nalagiri, the Elephant" both Ananda and Devadatta appear. They coexist in many other jatakas as well, Devadatta always doing evil—acting selfishly, cruelly, etc.—and Ananda always doing good or learning to do so. In the endless future, however, as tradition asserts that all things are ultimately destined for liberation and Buddhahood, even Devadatta, after condemning himself through his own evil actions to countless lifetimes in the lowest hells, will rise, his negative karma expiated at last, and attain Perfection. In the many stories which include Devadatta (in this collection see "The Falcon and the Quail," "The Lion, the Elephant and the Merchants' Cries," "The Golden Deer," "The Blue Bear," "The Preacher of Patience"), he is seen as the unconverted and unrepentant evildoer, the one still completely addicted to the poisons of selfishness, anger, and greed. In many ways Ananda and Devadatta are the Buddhist version of the "good and evil twins" —a mythic pattern common to many traditions. Yet, in this version, the pattern ultimately serves to reveal the profound idealism of the Mahayana vision. Even Devadatta, the one who embodies the most spiritually retrograde elements of the cosmos, is assured of Buddhahood. But obviously it will take an incalculably, unimaginably long time!

Stories abound of the power of sages over wild animals. In Empty Cloud, the autobiography of Zen Master Hsu Yun, one of the greatest of the twentieth-century Chinese Zen Masters, several such incidents are related. In one, a tiger enters the meditation hall and peacefully receives the precepts—much to the consternation of the monks. There are other, considerably older Chinese stories of certain great but eccentric Zen Masters, sometimes portrayed in Zen paintings fast asleep, completely at ease, with their heads cradled on the side of a sleeping tiger. And there is the Zen Master of T'ang era China whose two attendants, it is said, were not humans but tigers named "Big Emptiness" and "Little Emptiness," emptiness (i.e., empty of all limiting concepts, especially the concept of a separate selfhood) being a Zen expression for True Nature.

As miraculous as this tale is, the Buddha is certainly not alone in this territory. St. Francis of Assisi, for one, would certainly have appreciated the tale.

The most complete version of this tale can be found in Reynolds's Anthology of Sinhalese Buddhist Literature. There is also a good, brief recounting in Coomaraswamy's Buddha and the Gospel of Buddhism. Many accounts of the life of the Buddha include a retelling of this famous incident as well.

9. Kisa Gotami

A famous, beautifully direct teaching story. One traditional appellation for the Buddha was "The Great Physician," as his teachings healed the sicknesses of the unexamined life in the world. In the well-known Zen Ox-Herding pictures (attributed to the twelfth-century Chinese Zen Master, Kuo-an Shyih-yuan), which demonstrate the successive stages of spiritual development in Zen, the greatest sage is shown, in the tenth and final picture of the series, as not holding aloof from life but rather mingling freely and unselfconsciously with all people. The verse to that illustration includes these lines: "Without resorting to magical powers/withered trees he swiftly brings to bloom." The implication is that the fully enlightened person, without self-consciously trying, naturally helps others realize their own innate potential.

10. Parinirvana

After forty-five years of teaching, the Buddha entered Nirvana. The moment is revealed as a powerful and fitting cullumination of an active and generous life. Usually we see the Buddha lying on his right side on a stone couch between twin Sala trees. He is teaching until the end, considerate of the needs of those around him, confident in the reality of his teaching, surrounded by monks and nuns, laypeople, nagas (great serpent-beings), devas (godlike beings), and animals, spiritually very strong yet simultaneously old and physically weak. Many carvings and painted scrolls depict this moment in all its beauty and intensity. Seventeen centuries later the Buddhist monk-poet Saigyo, viewing blossoms, wrote this verse:

> I saw in Yoshino's
> Billows of Blossoms that long-ago
> Time of Great Passing
> When the Sala trees surrounding Him
> Suddenly turned as white as cranes.

> (LaFleur, tr., Mirror for the Moon, 91)

Though almost two thousand years had passed, Saigyo looks at blossoms and sees the Parinirvana. The moment of the Buddha's Parinirvana is unrivaled—except for the Enlightenment itself—in the depth of feeling it evokes, the impression it has made on the Buddhist imagination.

The two events—Enlightenment and the Parinirvana—complement each other. With Enlightenment, the Buddha breaks through to Permanence, the substratum of all existences, and what is eternal and abiding is brought dramatically to the fore. At the time of his Parinirvana, the passing of all things, the impermanence of all created forms is given preeminence and becomes, in effect, his final, eloquent teaching. The Enlightenment and the Parinirvana, permanence and impermanence, taken together reveal the essence of the Buddha's life-as-teaching.

In Foundations of Tibetan Mysticism, Lama Govinda, speaking about the Buddha's life and teaching career, writes:

> Those who keep aloof from the contacts of life, miss the opportunities of sacrifice, of self-negation, of relinquishing hard-earned gains, of giving up what was dear or what seemed desirable, of service to others, and of the trials of strength in the temptations and ordeals of life. Again: to help others and to help oneself go hand in hand. The one cannot be without the other.
>
> However we should not force our good deeds upon others from a sense of moral superiority, but act spontaneously from that natural kind of selflessness which flows from the knowledge of the solidarity of all life and from the indescribable experience of oneness, gained in meditation, and experience whose universal character was expressed . . . in the general religious attitude of the Mahayana.
>
> It was this knowledge of solidarity . . . which, however imperfect in its first dawning, led the Buddha in his former existences upon the path of enlightenment, and which made him renounce his own immediate liberation (when meeting the Buddha of a previous world-age), in order to gain perfect Buddhahood through the experiences and sufferings of countless rebirths in the practice of the Bodhisattva virtues, which would enable him to reach the highest aim, not only for himself, but for the benefit of innumerable other beings as well.
>
> It was this knowledge which made the Buddha return from the Tree of Enlightenment in order to proclaim his Gospel of Light, according to which the faculty of enlightenment (bodhicitta) is inherent in every living being. Whenever this faculty becomes a conscious force in any being, a Bodhisattva is born. To awaken this consciousness was the life's task of the Buddha. It was this that caused him to take upon himself the hardships of a wandering life, for forty long years, instead of enjoying for himself the happiness of liberation. (43)

The appellation Tathagata (literally, He-Who-Is-Thus-Come) is a traditional title of the Buddha. It implies a condition of total Presence in which time and space, past and future have been thoroughly transcended.

Nirvana literally means "extinguished," or "blown out," or according to some sources, "cooled down," implying that all causes leading to limited existence (i.e., greed, anger and ignorance) have, like a candle's flame, been at last extinguished. It may also suggest the complete stilling (hence "blowing out") of breath which is said to occur in deep meditation. A full buddha, Buddhist tradition holds, being freed not just from all limited existence but from even the subtle causes leading to limited, self-centered existence, does not die but enters fully into Nirvana. The death of such a one is a Parinirvana—an entrance into Nirvana.

This version of the Buddha's Parinirvana is drawn from Coomaraswamy's Buddha and the Gospel of Buddhism as well as from Asvaghosha's classic Buddhacarita as it appears in Conze's Buddhist Scriptures. The Parinirvana moments themselves are mostly quoted, with some adaptation and editing, from Conze.

SECTION II

11. *Give It All You've Got* (Vanupatha Jataka, No. 2)

An encouraging, straightforward jataka of perseverance and steadfastness. One can easily see from this jataka the ease with which these tales have been used in teaching—by the Buddha, to whom they are traditionally ascribed, but also by Buddhist teachers, preachers, and wandering storytellers ever since. The traditional opening and closing of each jataka is ascribed to the Buddha and establishes a context in the present for the tale of the past. The opening for this jataka tale essentially goes like this:

Once a young monk came before the Buddha and said that he could not go on, that the training was too difficult. "I am like a dry well, O World Honored One. I have tried and tried and cannot go on. It is pointless. There is no water down at the bottom of this well shaft. I feel I should quit and return, still unenlightened, to my home."

The Buddha replied. "This is not the first time you and I have spoken in this way. What you did in an earlier birth you can do again now. Let me tell you an old story."

And a version of its closing is as follows:

"Now, long ago," said the Buddha, "ages past, you were that youth, strong but without full confidence in your own strength, and I was the merchant who encouraged you to go on and try once more to split the rock. Son," he added, "the rock of ego is hard to crack. But you can do it. Give it one more shot and give it all you've got!" And the young monk, heartened, returned to his practice with vigor and achieved a breakthrough into Truth.

12. The Brave Lion and the Foolish Rabbit (Daddabha Jataka, No. 322)

Much kinder than the later European tale of "Henny-Penny" or "Chicken Little," this jataka, often known as "The Flight of the Beasts," dramatizes the strength and purpose of compassion. In Western European versions of this tale, the powerful animal is a fox who uses his strength to shamelessly take advantage of the other animals—whom he gobbles up. It is a cautionary fable. But in this story, the brave lion uses his strength and courage to help those endangered by their delusive fears. One can't help but wonder about the differing effects on the psyches of children who grow up exposed to one or the other version of this universal tale.

While ostensibly simply a tale about rumors and "groundless" fears, the central image remains a potent image of impermanence and of the dissolution of all corporeal and solid-seeming things in the experience of death. The Tibetan Book of the Dead lists the sensation of the earth crumbling beneath one's feet as a potential experience in the death process. The anxiety which this charming little story faces quite head-on, then, is not negligible. In one sense the message of the buddhas—indeed, the whole point of Buddhist training—can be summed up in a word: fearlessness. This should not be understood as a rigid or aggressive attitude toward an external and threatening universe. Rather, it implies a simple readiness to live, growing out of an understanding of the inseparability of oneself and the universe.

Yasutani Roshi says:

> When you truly understand . . . [the] fundamental principle you will not be anxious about your life or your death. You will then attain a steadfast mind and be happy in your daily life. Even though heaven and earth were turned upside down, you would have no fear. Even if an atomic or hydrogen bomb were exploded you would not quake in terror. (quoted in Kapleau, Three Pillars of Zen, 80)

Laughing ultimately at all fears, even fears of death itself, this simple jataka reveals its deeply Buddhistic vision and roots.

The Buddha is traditionally known as "the lion among men." In accounts of the Buddha's birth he sounds "the lion's roar" (see "Birth of the Buddha" and commentary). In "Enlightenment" he strides like a lion towards the Bo-tree—i.e., his stride is confident, fearless, royal. In the story of "The Lion, the Elephant, and the Merchants' Cries," the Buddha is once again born as a lion, the king of beasts. My own oral performance–derived retelling of this story has been published as the children's book, Foolish Rabbit's Big Mistake (see bibliography).

13. The Quail and the Falcon (Sakunagghi Jataka, No. 168)

Tales in which the small and weak triumph over the big, strong, and proud are among the most universal and timeless of all story types. Such tales express the essence of all the more complex stories of good versus evil and may, it has been conjectured, be deeply rooted in the structure of the human psyche—an effect, perhaps, of our evolutionary roots. Millions of years ago, after all, we were small, weak, and almost helpless creatures surrounded by truly huge, powerful, and dangerous animals—animals much bigger and tougher than any now living. Cleverness, the connection of mental agility with goodness, as well as an abiding faith in the triumph of the small over the large (and a tendency to root for the underdog) may be our psychological inheritance from these ancient times.

This little jataka also bears a remarkable resemblance to the classic Hopi tale, "Field Mouse Goes to War." In that Native American tale a tiny mouse destroys an attacking hawk by the same essentially nonviolent, non-aggressive stratagem: at the last moment he leaps aside and lets the hawk destroy itself. Why should a Hopi and a Buddhist story have such a clear similarity? The archetypal view is that the minds of peoples all around the world are so similar that essentially similar story patterns will emerge, given the right conditions, in every culture and every period of time. Just as people everywhere are recognizable as human (two eyes, a head, a nose and mouth, arms, legs, etc.), so, too, there is a human shape to the mind. Or, just as trees of one type will bring forth identical buds and leaves, so too the mind brings forth its archetypes in dream and story. The other view, that of cultural dissemination, suggests that in the depths of history there have been cultural exchanges now unknown to us. Other factors such as environment and its affects on the mind may also come into play. Perhaps the truth includes combinations of all possibilities.

What is the underlying "ground" that saves the little quail in this jataka? In Buddhist terms it might be the ground of being—unlimited, unconditioned Mind itself. From this Ground we can face all dangers. In the Pali Jataka the Buddha comments on the tale he has just told of the falcon and the quail, interpreting it more specifically for monks: "O Brethren, when people leave their own station Mara finds a door, . . . What is foreign ground, Brethren, and what is the wrong place for a brother? I mean the Five Pleasures of Sense. What are these Five? The Lust of the Eye . . . [and so on]. This, Brethren, is the wrong place for a brother" (Cowell, The Jataka, vol. 2, 41).

This brief, Aesop-like animal fable also recalls the well-known African-American story, "Brer Rabbit and the Briar Patch." Having tricked Brer Fox into tossing him back into the briar patch, the ever-resourceful Brer Rabbit escapes once more, singing out, "Born and bred in the briar patch Brer Fox! Born and bred in the briar patch!" For more jataka connections with Brer Rabbit see "Prince Five-Weapons."

In this story Devadatta is traditionally seen as the falcon.

14. The Steadfast Parrot (Mahasuka Jataka, No. 429)

Often the jatakas embody Buddhist ethics, showing believers how to live properly in the world, while simultaneously showing the future, historical Buddha defining his own personal Path. In this beautiful and simple jataka we can see these combined processes at work. Both the necessary qualities of any fledgling bodhisattva, as well as the resolute mind the historical Buddha himself must display to win complete enlightenment and Buddhahood in the Siddhartha birth, are revealed. This testing of the paramitas is consciously undertaken in the jatakas at least as early as the Sumedha birth (see "Sumedha Meets Dipankara Buddha"). In addition, one of the fundamental story patterns of the jataka tradition is established—that of the testing of the Bodhisattva's mettle by Shakra, King of the Gods. (See also "The Hare's Sacrifice," "King Sivi.")

15. Prince Five-Weapons (Pancavudha Jataka, No. 55)

This lively jataka seems to be an early version of the well-known Tar Baby story. Burlingame, in his Buddhist Parables, identifies the story as such. If so, the roots of this familiar, and seemingly childish, story pattern are deeply metaphysical. Even when we are completely stuck in the fives senses, there is yet a deeper, transcendental aspect to our nature.

This particular version grew out of my years of telling it, and its oral flavor owes a great debt to the many children (and adults) with whom I've had the chance to share it. Like "The Brave Lion and the Foolish Little Rabbit," "Great Joy, the Ox," and to a lesser extent "The Monkey and the Crocodile," "The Wise Quail," "The Brave Little Parrot" and "The Banyan Deer," "Prince Five-Weapons" is a story that I have often told. I hope other adults will continue to pass on these tales, and others like them, to children today. Storytelling is a potent tool for counteracting the negative effects of TV. Through stories, language is charged with deep feeling and the tales really live, emerging in our own minds, in our own images, in ways uniquely alive for each of us. We are empowered by our own vision through the oral telling. What's more, the experience is social, not private. The context of oral telling should be always kept in mind when thinking about the jatakas in general, but this group of stories bears the clearest stamp of such telling. Perhaps of all the stories in this book, they are the ones that work most naturally (but by no means exclusively) as children's tales.

Cowell describes the tale essentially as one of a defeated hero who nonetheless triumphs and subdues his adversary through fearlessness. Joseph Campbell writes in Hero with a Thousand Faces:

> As a symbol of the world to which the five senses glue us, and which cannot be pressed aside by the actions of the physical organs, Sticky-hair was subdued only when the Future Buddha, no longer protected by the five weapons or his momentary name and physical character, resorted to the unnamed, invisible sixth: the divine thunderbolt of the knowledge of the transcendent principle, which is beyond the phenomenal realm of names and forms. Therewith the situation changed. He was no longer caught, but released; for that which he now remembered himself to be is ever free. The force of the monster of phenomenality was dispelled, and he was rendered self-denying. Self-denying, he became divine—a spirit entitled to receive offerings—as is the world itself when known, not as final, but as a mere name and form of all that which transcends, yet is immanent within, all names and forms. . . .
>
> As the rising smoke of an offering through the sun door, so goes the hero, released from ego, through the walls of the world—leaving ego stuck to Sticky-hair and passing on. (88-9)

See, too, the note for the story "Angulimala" for how this brief jataka connects with that much more complex tale.

Recently, in telling both this story and that of "The Brave Little Parrot," I have experimented with changing the lead character from hero to heroine. Princess Five-Weapons and a female parrot reveal interesting new possibilities in both tone and atmosphere for these narratives. New incidents, too, have emerged. The "dark side" of the jataka tradition has been its emphatically patriarchal mentality— perhaps the legacy of an almost exclusively monastic transmission. Should we assume the Buddha could be reborn as any sort of animal but never as a woman or in feminine form? The denigration of the feminine damages us all. Each tradition contains outdated orthodoxies waiting to be re-awakened to life. Traditions create, and must ceaselessly recreate, themselves through the lives, needs, and experiences of their current practitioners.

16. The Wise Quail (Sammodamana Jataka, No. 33)

The theme of harmony, of working together for the common good, is clearly stated in this parable-like tale.

17. The Monkey and the Crocodile (Sumsumara Jataka, No. 208; also Vanara Jataka, No. 342)

A humorous and clever jataka, much like an Aesop's fable, that has long functioned in the West as a popular children's story—and one not without its depth. What is a tender heart? the story asks, and where does it reside? Is it the physical heart that hangs like a red fruit among the branching veins of the body? If not, then what is it, and where is it to be found?

In this tale, likely to have been recycled from older Indian sources, the monkey is the Buddha and the crocodile, Devadatta.

There are a number of jatakas in which the Buddha appears as a monkey. In the most famous of these (Mahakapi Jataka, No. 407; also in Aryasura's Jatakamala), the Buddha is a heroic and self-sacrificing Monkey King. With his own body he forms a bridge so that his tribe can escape from the hunters who are waiting below. In the Pali version, one monkey—Devadatta in an earlier birth—jealous of the Monkey King's power, stamps upon his back as he is crossing. The Monkey King, badly injured, falls. The human king runs to him and learns a lesson in kingship. Repentant, he buries the body of the Monkey King with great honors, and inlaying the skull of the Monkey King with gold, sets it up upon a spear as a royal reminder of wisdom and goodness. In the Jatakamala, the story of the Great Ape focuses on the duties of kingship. No Devadatta monkey appears and the Monkey King survives the trauma of having been a bridge for his people. The human king learns a much-needed lesson in the duties of his office and harmony is restored.

In this collection, there is an echo of the monkey calling out "Who calls?" to the crocodile when Digit, the gorilla who sacrifices himself for the welfare of his family-group, answers the voice in his dream with essentially the same words (see "Digit"). The story of Digit is an original tale of my own which I have used as an example of a modern jataka; in it, Digit's noble self-sacrifice recalls the beautiful traditional tale, "The Monkey King." My retelling of the Jatakamala Monkey King story has appeared as a picture book entitled The Monkey Bridge (see bibliography).

18. Great Joy, the Ox (Nandivisala Jataka, No. 28)

In the Pali Jataka, in the introduction to this tale, the Buddha interestingly reveals, "Ananda was the Brahmin of those days and I myself Nanda-Visala [the ox]." So in some lifetimes, the animal might be the Buddha while his disciples are "already" human. The universe of the jatakas is clearly not progressively straightforward or linear. In it, evolution may mean something other than going from a less to a more complex form. Great Joy's resolute stand under the shouts, the hurled clods of mud, sticks, and stones prefigures the Buddha's steadfastness during the time of his temptation by the forces of Mara, just prior to his great Enlightenment. Ground has been laid for future success. The evolution revealed in the tale is spiritual.

The tale itself is also a clear little demonstration of the importance of kindness, and of the kind of teaching that encourages, sustains, and offers respect. In addition, one should know that in Asia, the ox often symbolizes True Mind—that which works patiently for the sake of all, and patiently bears the difficulties of the world.

We may brush aside such simple folktales as childish. Yet how many adults have really grasped—that is, can live by—the lesson implicit in the tale. "A child of three may already know it, but a man of seventy can still find it hard to put into practice," as a traditional Zen anecdote puts it. (See commentary for "King Sivi.")

19. The Golden Goose (Suvannahamsa Jataka, No. 136)

To kill the goose that lays the golden egg is an image we all know well from the Grimm brothers' tales. Though no goose is killed in this story (which may well be the source of the later Western European tale), and no golden eggs are laid, the plucking of the goose symbolizes this kind of impatient greed well enough.

In this version of the tale, I found it interesting to allow the mother to grow through her error. Rather than ending the story at her low point of failure or with the goose's departure, by continuing the story one finds that error itself may be the precursor of wisdom. It all depends on where one ends, or how far one goes with the story. Stories are ways of exploring and presenting possibilities. As Blake says, "If a fool would persist in his folly he would become wise."

20. The Brave Little Parrot

Another classic animal birth jataka. In the original, the bird may actually be a quail. Some liberties have been taken with this story, too. In its original form, a god makes rain fall from the clouds, rather than spontaneously bursting into tears as in this version. The bodhisattvic vision, however, remains clear. A bird that could fly to safety from the burning forest does not leave, but rather, risks its own life in order to attempt an impossible task: the liberation from danger of all others. (In the Lotus Sutra the Buddha uses the image of a "house on fire" to stand for this world, and in the famous and dramatic Fire Sermon, he describes all things as burning—on fire with the flames of greed, anger, and ignorance.) The story suggests that wholeheartedly offering to the world what we can—even if it is only a few drops of water—can have tremendous effect. A fine teaching for us today, living, as we literally do, in a world on fire.

A beautiful legend about Avalokitesvara (Kwan-Yin in Chinese; Kannon, Japanese; the name meaning variously, "He Who Looks Down from On High" or "He Who Hears the Cries of the World"), the Bodhisattva of Compassion, expresses a related idea. Having worked extremely hard to empty the hells (and there are many in Buddhist tradition, as there are many heavens), the Bodhisattva's labors seemed at last done. After centuries of unending work he had at last saved all beings from suffering. But, to his great dismay, when he looked down into those hells he saw that they were once again already full!

His head split into eleven heads. His arms shattered into a thousand arms and in the palm of each hand was an opened eye of wisdom. With many hands and arms he started up again. The spontaneous response of the Bodhisattva of Great Compassion is not to turn away in defeat from the overwhelming task of universal liberation, but to continue, beyond all limit or comprehension (see "The Legend of Avalokitesvara" and its commentary).

The little parrot, too, does not consciously know how he can possibly succeed. But he does not turn back. And his spontaneous, selfless, seemingly hopeless activity becomes successful. (See "Great King Goodness." Also "Prince Five-Weapons," who, though defeated, still triumphs.)

In my picture book version of "The Brave Little Parrot" (see bibliography), I have made the little parrot female. The compassionate, heroic nature of the little bird struck me as a deep expression of the Eternal Feminine. Too many jatakas cling to an entrenched, patriarchal world view. Such changes encourage subtle and necessary shifts in consciousness. The process of story-exploration and the recasting of materials goes on today.

21. The Banyan Deer (Nigrodhamiga Jataka, No. 12; also Nandiyami - ga-Jataka, No. 385; also in *The Jatakastava, or Praise of the Buddha's Former Births*)

A beautiful and classic jataka which is part of the Pali canon, but which also gained great favor in the Mahayana tradition. Indeed, like the story of "The Hungry Tigress," it is one of the pillars of the jataka vision. An unshakable willingness to risk oneself for the sake of others—growing out of a clear perception of the interrelation of all living things—forms the core of the tale and give it its strong bodhisattvic flavor. It is one of the finest teaching tales of the tradition, deceptively simple yet revealing much. While "there can be no peace for any unless there is peace for all" can be a complex concept to express and to prove, this ancient tale negotiates the territory with grace. In the end it dramatizes the Great Vow itself—to save the many beings. The king learns to truly liberate all beings from the entrapments of his own greed, anger, and ignorance. It is a perfect paradigm of Buddhist teaching and aspiration.

Similar stories, sayings, and injunctions can be found in all religious traditions. One of the most poignant and powerful remains the Talmudic precept: "To save one soul is to save the whole world." What makes the Buddhist vision unique, and allies it as well with our contemporary, ecologically alert worldview, is that these spiritual principles are expressed among not just human beings, but animals, too. Indeed, in many cases, the animal is teacher to the human character (see "Great Joy, the Ox," "The Blue Bear," and their commentaries).

The Golden Deer jataka absorbs this Banyan Deer tale-type, seeming to take its lofty pattern for granted, and then plays with it, setting it in a new and more sophisticated story context. But they are clearly related tales (see "The Golden Deer," story and commentary).

Tradition proclaims Devadatta to be the leader of the other herd. He is the deer king who chooses strict justice over mercy.

22. The Blue Bear of the Mountains

"The Blue Bear" is a straightforward and classic jataka. One source for the tale exists in an English translation from the Indo-Scythian text (Khotanese) of The Jatakastava, or "Praise of the Buddha's Former Births." In the three-paragraph summation of this jataka which appears there, the Buddha is presented as a noble, blue-furred bear who saves a hunter from freezing in the snows. The hunter then betrays him to those who would kill him. In response to his own evil the betrayer's hands then fall off. A scene from this jataka exists in the famous paintings of the Ajanta caves of India. Generally, in this type of jataka, the Bodhisattva as an animal demonstrates great, selfless compassion and saves a man from danger. But the Bodhisattva-animal is then ungratefully betrayed by the very man he saves. A king then recognizes and honors the wise beast's true worth. Many lessons are woven into this simple and oft-repeated pattern.

A variety of such stories and their permutations are scattered throughout the Pali Jataka. One such tale which appears both in the Pali Jataka (Mahakapi Jataka, No. 516—not to be confused with Mahakapi Jataka, No. 407, the story of the Monkey King) and in The Jatakamala of Aryasura, where it is titled "The Great Ape," tells of a monkey who helps a man escape from a deep pit. Once out, the man, thinking only of his own hunger, tries to kill the monkey with a rock in order to eat its flesh. But the wise monkey escapes the fatal blow, and in the Jatakamala version, then teaches the evildoer another lesson in charity and compassion. Eventually the man feels such burning remorse for his selfish act that his body breaks out in a fearsome leprosy. In time, he is seen by a king who, enquiring about the cause of his illness, learns from him of the necessary effects of both good and evil actions. (For another tale in which a transformation of character is brought about through suffering the consequences of wrongdoing, see "The Golden Goose".) In the Pali version, the wrongdoer is identified as Devadatta in an earlier birth, and at the end of that tale, the ground opens up and swallows the evildoer—as in the tale "The Preacher of Patience."

See "The Golden Deer" for another version of this same jataka type. In both "The Golden Deer" and "The Blue Bear" jatakas, Devadatta is the man who fails in these past lives to recognize the responsibilities of gratitude. The Buddha is, of course, the wise beast. One interesting implication of this story type is that an animal may be more spiritually developed, more "human" than a human being. This is so, too, in the story of "Great Joy, the Ox." In "Great King Goodness," a somewhat similar recognition by the King of Kosala—that the blood-drinking goblins have been more sensitive and perceptive, more human than he—prompts his conversion.

23. The Golden Deer (Ruru Jataka, No. 482; also in Aryasura's Jatakamala and the Jatakastava)

This tale seems to draw from its much more well-known cousin jataka, "The Banyan Deer" (in its liberation motif), as well as from "The Blue Bear" (in its depiction of the animal savior who is then betrayed). This is a normal part of the oral tradition: motifs and incidents wandering naturally back and forth across story lines which are not hard and fast, but are as permeable in the mind and imagination as a cell wall. What is so interesting about this story (the version here is based on the Cowell translation of the Pali text), in addition to its motif of universal liberation, is the very realistic dilemma the tale poses. Instead of simply giving us a happy ending, the implications of the Golden Deer's request and the human king's promise are explored. The king's vow is tested and the deer themselves must learn the responsibility that comes from a promise kept. A most interesting story, and one whose underlying jataka-pattern is hauntingly similar to the following actual newspaper account which appeared in 1987, Gannett Newspapers, Rochester, N.Y.

> Six more bodies recovered in river after bus accident. The Associated Press and Reuters.
> COMFORT, Texas — Searchers found six more bodies in the churning waters of the Guadalupe River yesterday, bringing the death toll to eight after a church camp bus and van tried to skirt the swollen river and were washed away.
> Two people were still missing late yesterday after the seventh, unidentified victim was found 18 miles downstream and an eighth victim was found two miles downstream. Helicopters scoured the river while National Guardsmen and scuba divers searched the banks.
> One frightened teenager hurled down the churning flood waters said he owed his life to a ride aboard a swimming deer that guided him to safety.
> "The deer just came up under me and I held on tight," said Chris Ray, 17.

This tragic yet remarkable little news article uncannily echoes such traditional jatakas as "The Golden Deer" and "The Blue Bear." Real life and the jataka perception can, it seems, come eerily close.

We are comfortable thinking that stories are pretendings, or that they are "just" symbolic, mentally created events. But perhaps they are true. Perhaps the imagination is a power truer, more real than we had thought. One of the great writer-storytellers of our time, Nobel Prize–winner Isaac Bashevis Singer, has mused that perhaps the stories we write and tell and seem to create are actually events that do take place, at some level, on some world, in some dimension of the universe. The brain, he suggests, can create nothing new and the universe is so vast that truth cannot be bound to what is simply currently understood or acceptable. The truth admits of many possibilities—some as yet undreamed, some unacknowledged. (See also "The Brave Little Parrot," "The Blue Bear," "The Lion, the Elephant and the Merchant's Cries," "Digit," "Stilson's Leap," "Kogi, the Priest.")

The action-motivating desire of the queen to hear the teachings of the Golden Deer is an interesting echo of the crocodile-wife's misplaced desire—in the tale "The Monkey and the Crocodile"—for the wise monkey's "tender heart."

Verses, such as those spoken by the Golden Deer to the king, are traditional to the Pali jatakas and may comprise the oldest and most canonical stratum of the tale.

Interestingly, a friend from India told me that the king's proclamation granting freedom from the hunt remains on display in one of the old palaces to this day. And that some form of this covenant of peace between humans and animals still seemed to exist in the surrounding countryside when he was a child.

24. The Lion, the Elephant, and the Merchants' Cries

The Nepalese Bodhisattvavadana-Kalpalata, a storehouse of legends from the fifth century, is partly a sequel to and partly a poetic amplification of (according to Mitra) the Bodhisattva Avadana, which is called "a tree of yielding whatever is wanted of it" (kalpalata). In it we learn:

> One evening the Lord was conversing familiarly with all his Bhikshus at the Jetavana grove. The conversation turned on an inquiry about the origin of philanthropy. Is it a natural propensity, the result of accumulated deeds or merit, or of constant practice? The Lord said, "even ferocious animals, like lions are susceptible to that feeling. For instance, a company of merchants were on the point of being devoured by a large venomous serpent, on the seashore. They screamed aloud at the prospect of instant death; their screams were heard by a lion and an elephant. They fell from a high hill on the serpent and crushed him to death. But they themselves lost their lives from the poisonous breath of the dying reptile. I am that lion, Sariputra [one of the Buddha's great disciples] is the elephant, and Devadatta is the reptile." (Mitra, Nepalese Buddhist Literature, 78)

Why should a lion, a flesh eater, help men? Why should a bear or a deer come to the aid of those in distress? Why should a dolphin rise from the depths of the sea and carry an exhausted swimmer to shore or a dog break down a locked door to pull a sleeping child from smoke and fire? Such things occur regularly in the jataka-world. And they also happen in real life. (See "Blue Bear," "Golden Deer," "Brave Little Parrot," "Banyan Deer" and their commentaries. Also "Stilson's Leap," "Digit," "Kogi, the Priest.")

Mention of this jataka also appears in the verses of The Jatakastava, or "Praise of the Buddha's Former Births":

> The merchants, surrounded by a serpent, in great distress, whom you saw then in a forest, in your compassion, as the lion king you called your friend, the elephant. You roared together with him; you offered up your life.
> Upon the elephant you mounted; standing on the top of his head with your claws you surely split his forehead by your clutching it. The merchants escaped, they all found life. You however, lost it with your beloved friend. (stroth 155-6)

25. The Doe, the Stag and the Hunter (Suvannamiga Jataka, No. 359)

A sensitive and interesting jataka. It is unclear from the tale itself which deer was the Buddha in an earlier birth. The most admirable and decisive character in the story is the doe. It is she who manifests the compassionate and heroic bodhisattva mind. However, the traditional introduction and conclusion, which form "the tale of the present" in which past life roles are identified, tells us that this story was told by the Buddha while in residence at Jetavana about "a maiden of gentle birth in Savatthi" (Cowell, The Jataka, vol. 3, 120). She had married into a family with heretical views, but by inviting Buddhist Elders regularly to her new home had effected a change of heart in her husband and in-laws. Eventually both she and her husband, we are told, attained enlightenment. The introduction to the tale in the Pali Jataka relates that the Buddha, overhearing the monks discussing this case, said, "'Brethren, not now only, did she set her husband free from the bonds of passion. Formerly too she freed even sages of old from the bonds of death.' And with these words he held his peace, but being pressed by them he related a story of the past" (ibid, 121). Once the tale is told, the conclusion is as follows: "The Master here ended his lesson and identified the Birth: At that time Channa was the hunter, the female novice was the doe, and I myself was the royal stag" (ibid, 123).

Channa was the name of the Buddha's charioteer when, as the prince Siddhartha, he was first moved to leave his home (see "Leaving Home"). Perhaps by this time, he, like many other of the Buddha's former acquaintances, had become a monk. Cowell's note to this simply identifies Channa as "a Brother who was suspended for siding with heretics" (ibid, 123). It is unclear. But what is also unclear is whether patriarchal elements in the tradition have found it harder to acknowledge that the Buddha might have had female past lives than animal ones.

26. The Brave Merchant (Khadirangara Jataka, No. 40; also Jataka-mala)

Another of the testing jatakas. In this one, however, it is not Shakra in disguise, but Mara himself who tries the Bodhisattva's resolution and courage. That the Buddha as a merchant was able to overcome the challenge of Mara sets the stage for his final defeat of Mara just prior to Enlightenment. Interestingly, the Vimalakirti Sutra states that:

> the Maras who play the devil in innumerable universes of the ten directions are all Bodhisattvas dwelling in the inconceivable liberation, who are playing the devil in order to develop living beings through their skill in liberative technique. . . .
> . . . only one who is . . . a bodhisattva can harass another bodhisattva, and only a bodhisattva can tolerate the harassment of another bodhisattva. (Thurman, The Holy Teaching of Vimalakirti, 55-6)

Compassion can, it seems, take many forms.

The "solitary Buddha" in this jataka refers to one who attains enlightenment on his or her own (usually, it is said, through an understanding of the interrelation of cause and effect), and not under the guidance of a Teacher. Such a person remains alone, perfecting his or her initial accomplishment and not teaching others. Traditionally such a one is termed a pratyekabuddha (Sanskrit) or paccekabuddha (Pali). However, the great Mahayana Buddhist text, The Lotus Sutra, says this is an illusion. In reality, there is only one Path—the Path of the Bodhisattva, who, realizing Truth, continues with his or her own spiritual development even while working for the welfare of others. As the very idea of an isolated self is an illusion, pratyekabuddhas are really bodhisattvas in disguise (Hurvitz, trans., Scripture of the Lotus Blossom, xix-xx).

In the Jatakamala there is a much more involved version of this dramatic tale, and much of the testing takes place in discussions between Mara and the merchant before the crucial deed itself—the walking through flames—is begun. The oral style of the Pali Jataka and the consciously literary style of the Jatakamala can be con-trasted easily in these two versions. The emphasis on narrative is replaced by a testing through discourse in the later version. One might also profitably compare versions of "The Golden Deer" in both collections, as well as versions of "The Monkey King" (Mahakapi Jataka, No. 407) and "The Great Ape" (Mahakapi Jataka, No. 516) for similar discoveries.

27. The Hare's Sacrifice (Sasa Jataka, No. 316; also Jatakamala and verses of the Jatakastava)

Another of the classic and most widely known jataka tales. The famous nineteenth-century Zen monk-poet Ryokan wrote a beautiful and tender verse version of this jataka which concludes:

> From that time till now
> the story's been told,
> this tale
> of how the rabbit
> came to be
> in the moon,
> and even I
> when I hear it
> find the tears
> soaking the sleeve of my robe.

> (Watson, trans., Ryokan: Zen Monk-Poet of Japan, 49)

In Ryokan's version, based on a version of the tale found in the Konjaku Monogatari, a collection of Japanese stories compiled around 1100, the hare dies from his sacrifice and it is his dead body that is "laid to rest/in the palace of the moon" (ibid, 48).

28. King Sivi

This story is not found in the Pali Jataka in this form but is carried forward in the Mahayana tradition. (In the Pali Jataka's story number 499, a King Sivi gives his eyes away and then is restored by Shakra. This story also appears in the Jatakamala.) This does not mean that this jataka and others like it (most notably "The Hungry Tigress") are any less authentic than those in the Pali canon, which were themselves, after all, not committed to writing until almost a thousand years after the time of the Buddha. It does mean that such jatakas might have been carried on longer orally or that they remained within the Sanskrit literary tradition rather than becoming part of the jataka tradition as canonized in the Pali texts.

This particular version is based on a brief recounting I heard over twenty years ago. A complete translation of a Tibetan text of this jataka does appear in Beyer, The Buddhist Experience: Sources and Interpretations. Also, in Burlingame's Buddhist Parables there is a full translation of the tale as it appears in Aryasura's poetic Sanskrit work, the Sutralamkara. In these versions, as in the story of Rupavati (see commentary, "The Hungry Tigress"), it is not until Sivi is asked by Shakra if during or after his sacrifice he experienced any regret—and he answers that he experienced none whatsoever, only the great joy of doing good—that he is restored.

The tale of King Sivi—the weighing of his flesh, and the flight and confrontation of the falcon and dove—appears among the magnificent ninth-century stone carvings of Borobudur, Indonesia, where many jatakas and avadanas are recorded in exquisite detail. For all its ten-derheartedness, the story of King Sivi is remarkably unsentimental. Its ecologically sound view of the equal rights of predator and prey makes especially clear sense today. Indeed, its grasp of deep ecology seems nothing less than prescient.

The conclusion of this version of the story—"How could that com-pare with having a world in which to do good?"—may seem paltry. After all, simply "to do good" suggests the vague aspiration of a childish mind. It must be taken in its traditional context. The so-called Three General Resolutions of Buddhism, which along with the Precepts form the foundation of Buddhist action and life, are:

> To do good
> To avoid evil
> To liberate all sentient beings.

There is an interesting Zen story from China about these resolutions. A governor of a province, who was also a noted poet and a Zen lay-man, came to the famous Zen Master Dorin or "Birds-Nest"—so called because of his habit of meditating up in a tree—and asked, "What is the highest teaching of Buddhism?" Dorin answered, "To do good and avoid evil." The governor responded, "Even a child of three knows that." "Yes," replied the Zen Master, "but a man of seventy can still find it hard to put into practice."

29. The Story of a Sneeze (Asilakkhana Jataka, No. 126)

This traditional but relatively little-known jataka is both humor-ous and sophisticated. Yet, even in this comic and entertaining tale one senses, as in the story of "Great Joy, the Ox," something of the tradition's interest in showing the Buddha-to-be's constant efforts to strengthen character and will, as well as the insight he will need in his final quest for Enlightenment. The prince's triumph over his fears while lying in wait in the charnel ground especially prefigures some of Siddhartha Gautama's austerities.

There is a fairy-tale–like quality to this jataka, too, with its king and prince, princess and wise old woman. And there is all the richness of the Indian style of storytelling, with the pepper and the sneeze being woven in throughout in unexpected ways.

The conclusion, in which the pattern is completed (the Brahmin returns to the tale and the two sneezes are compared) and the prince is brought to a deeper appreciation of the mystery of even the simplest things, suggests that the original teller was quite conscious of his or her aim in handling the basic story material.

Many of the Pali jatakas open with lines to the effect that the events of the story occurred when Brahmadatta reigned in Benares. Benares (or Varanasi) is said to be the oldest continuously inhabited city on the earth. Perhaps, even in the Buddha's time, such an opening immediately suggested something of antiquity and functioned like "once upon a time" to suspend disbelief and establish a conventional and timeless space in which the tale could then unfold.

30. Preacher of Patience (Khantivada Jataka [Sanskrit Kshanti Jataka], No. 313; also *Jatakamala,* and the brief verses of the *Jatakastava*)

A brief yet remarkable jataka. Not an enjoyable tale, and one, like "The Hungry Tigress" and "King Sivi," likely to seem bizarre to Western readers. Yet these jatakas, in their very extremity, make their lessons all the more clear. Patience means real patience; compassion means real compassion—to the limit of all possible testing. Like cubism in painting, these stories distort ordinary reality enough to make their meaning, not merely their surfaces, come through. Like "The Hungry Tigress," "Preacher of Patience" offers neither solace nor the wish fulfillment of magical intervention or restoration. These two tales are the strongest "stuff" of the jatakas. Two of my own attempts at creating modern jatakas—"Stilson's Leap" and "Digit" (in which we metaphysically go "back stage" behind the curtain of death)—are also like this.

For similar tales, but ones which turn on a final, magical restoration— as if at the end of the tragedy of King Lear the dead Cordelia were to begin to breathe—see "The Hare's Sacrifice" and "King Sivi." Such tales with their sudden happy endings are, of course, no less true than "Preacher of Patience" and "The Hungry Tigress." They emphasize a different perspective—not realistic, but certainly no less Real. Actually, each of these two ways of ending a story has its own underlying and quite formal conventions.

Myth and legend, as it has been said, reveal a truth too great to be limited by mere fact. The patterns of both sorts of tales are examples of mythic thinking and perception. In literature, these two types of tales underlie the respective visions of comedy and romance on one hand, and tragedy on the other. They are two different, but actually quite interconnected, even complementary, ways of looking at the real facts of ordinary life. They are what William Blake termed Innocence and Experience, "the two contrary states of the human soul." Happy endings and painful ones are each equally conventional and equally valid, and each is originally based on a perception of Truth.

There may also be the suggestion of a very ancient and universal tradition of religious experience lying behind this jataka. Mircea Eliade, in his classic work, Shamanism: Archaic Techniques of Ecstasy, reveals that a ritual death and a symbolic or hallucinatory experience of dismemberment are traditional aspects of the neophyte shaman's initiation. The shamanic tradition, built on an ecstatic experience of death and rebirth, extends back into Paleolithic times. It may also underlie the yogic traditions of ancient India. So, something of a very archaic inner, visionary experience may have been captured in this jataka, which presents the dismemberment of the yogi-sage as occurring in literal, albeit non-historical, space and time.

Mention of this jataka is made in the famous Diamond Sutra.

31. The Black Hound (Maha-Kanha Jataka, No. 469)

The principle dramatized here is that bodhisattvas can take any form in order to be of aid to suffering mankind—even acting in ways that might, at first glance, seem quite contrary to what one would expect. In time, however, deep, underlying compassion and wisdom are revealed. The Bodhisattva has in this tale attained the state of the high god Shakra, who appears often in the jatakas to test those on the path of virtue. Buddhism does not deny the existence of gods. It merely emphasizes that such lofty beings are also subject to suffering the cycles of cause and effect. (See "The Steadfast Parrot," "The Hare's Sacrifice," "King Sivi." Also, "Most Lovely Fugen" and "A Legend of Avalokitesvara.")

The black hound is a transformation of Shakra's charioteer, the god Matali. The Buddha declares at the conclusion of this jataka that at that time—i.e., in the ancient, mythic days of the previous world cycle, the time of the Buddha Kashyapa when the events of this jataka are said to have occurred—he had been Shakra, and Ananda, Matali.

This is a powerful and resonant jataka. In this retelling, I aimed for the sparest presentation possible. Such a tale, like the story of "The Hungry Tigress" which follows, should, I think, be allowed to speak for itself.

32. The Hungry Tigress

"The Hungry Tigress" is perhaps the classic jataka. Significantly, Aryasura placed it first in his classic Jatakamala. His telling is quite elegant, literary, and philosophic. Yet in this jataka, the profound mystery of compassion, arising from a deep experience of Oneness, is upheld without explanation, wavering, or sugarcoating. For those new to the jatakas it can be a very strange story—"Why should a human being give his or her life for an animal?" It goes against the ingrained hierarchies of Western tradition in which human beings are allowed to dominate.

Still, "The Hungry Tigress" is also a uniquely relevant tale for our times. As we daily grow more deeply aware of our intrinsic responsibilities to the well-being of nonhuman life—tigers, trees, butterflies, whales, and plants—we may find this twenty-five-hundred-year-old religious drama speaking more clearly to us. In it, compassionate self-sacrifice for the sake of another being—not simply another human being—and the universality of suffering are vigorously upheld.

This is, in part, what makes the jataka tradition so interesting, even unique. The tales dramatize Equality and give life to an awareness of the ultimate worth of each living thing—even of something which may directly threaten our own self-interest and safety. ("Tyger Tyger burning bright," chanted Blake—"Did he who make the Lamb make thee?") In this fundamental realm, not only does each thing have its necessary and meaningful place in the Whole, each thing is the Whole, the center of the Universe itself. How have, how do, and how shall we humans live with this? As natural habitats disappear and tiger (and other animal) populations are threatened, we can only find our-selves considering once again the deep message of this ancient tale.

Which is not to recommend that we should literally offer our bodies to tigers! As this, and all jatakas, are literary forms, we can see in this story of the prince and the starving tigress an artistic effort to express, through story patterning, a universal language. Through that language of image and action, the heart's desire is given shape. Our deepest aspirations, normally impossible to reveal except perhaps in times of great emotion or of great focused purpose, are called forth.

So, what does the mind of a bodhisattva look like? What does pure compassion look like? Feel like? What is a love that is not stained by likes and dislikes, appearances, desires, or self-interest? How deep does our kindness, our sense of kindred go? By its very extremity, this jataka throws its light here.

The tale of the prince Mahasattva (Great Being) and the hungry tigress does not appear in the canonical Pali collection of 547 jatakas and their verses, but only finds its way into written record with the rise of the Mahayana where it gained tremendous popularity over the centuries. In Nepal today a tree is said to mark the spot where this jataka occurred. Devout pilgrims still go there to festoon the tree with scarves, prayer flags, and locks of pilgrims' hair as offerings to the Buddha. The pillar referred to in this story and in "The Banyan Deer" are the pillars of the great third-century-B.C. Indian king Ashoka, who, after years of triumphant and bloody conquest, renounced all violence and war and made a dramatic conversion to Buddhism. After that, one of his meritorious acts was to erect carved pillars on the sites of the great events of the Buddha's legendary, as well as historical, life. He helped promulgate ethical and socially conscious policies, whose edicts he also had carved on stone pillars.

In the Nepalese jataka tradition, there is much supplementary material on the tigress and her cubs, as well as on the contexts of this brief but powerful jataka. The Sanku and Sandhidatta Avadana which follows is from the Bodhisattva Avadana, as is the Subhasa Jataka (see commentary, "Beginnings"):

Sanku and Sandhidatta, two brothers, lost their father Arthadatta, a merchant of Rajagriha, when they were very young. Their mother brought them up with great difficulty, and, when they grew up, employed them in pilfering. The thieves were detected by the vigilant police of Ajatasatru [the king] and sentenced capitally. At the place of their execution the Buddha interposed in their favor, rescued them from the gallows, and carried them to his hermitage, where soon they rose to the exalted rank of Arhat.

The Lord said, "In one of their former existences, they were the cubs of a hungry tigress from whose jaws I preserved their lives by offering my own." (Mitra, Nepalese Buddhist Literature, 74)

And the following from the Suvarnaprabhasa, section XIX:

A Bodhisattva should sacrifice his own body for the good of others. The Lord in the course of his perambulation through the country of the Panchalas, entered a forest. He sat upon a grass plot, and struck the earth with the palms of his hands and the soles of his feet. Thereupon a great stupa made of gold, rubies, sapphires and precious stones rose like an apparition. The Lord ordered Ananda to open the doors of the stupa and found bones covered over with gems. The Bhikshus honored them with a salutation at the command of the Lord, and then the Lord, at the request of Ananda, gave the following history of the holy bones. (ibid, 201)

There follows an account, by the Buddha, of "The Hungry Tigress" jataka, which concludes, "I am, O Ananda, the prince Mahasattva. I obtained, by means of these bones, the great Bodhi knowledge which nothing can equal" (ibid, 248).

There is another interesting and especially bizarre (to modern sensibilities) version of this tale. As is the case with all oral traditions, many conflicting, but often mutually revealing, versions of tales exist. This is true of many of the jatakas. The version which follows reflects the remarkable lengths to which the jataka tradition will go in valuing compassionate, selfless action. It also reflects the cultural heritage of the time: Rupavati, the woman, must become Rupavata, the man, in order to proceed towards Buddhahood. Yet the Vimalakirti Sutra, as well as other traditional writings, make it clear that women and men are to be seen as equal in their ability to both attain Enlightenment and ultimately gain Buddhahood.

In a previous state of existence the Future Buddha was reborn as a woman of great beauty and virtue named Rupavati. Once she came upon a starving woman who under the uttermost pangs of hunger was about to eat her tiny infant son. Immediately Rupavati cut off her own breasts and gave them to the woman to eat as food. Her husband, making an Act of Truth, declared "If it is true such a sacrifice was never made willingly before may your breasts be restored." Immediately the breasts were restored.

Shakra, King of the Gods, fearing that by the merit of her sacrifice Rupavati might displace him from his high seat, went in disguise to Rupavati to test her. "Is it true," he asked, "that you sacrificed your breasts for the sake of a child?"

"It is true."

"Did you not, either in the act or afterwards, experience regret?"

"No."

"How could anyone believe you?"

"I will make an Act of Truth. If it is true that neither in the act nor after at any time did I experience the slightest regret; if, further, it is true that I acted without any desire whatsoever for gain—that I yearned not for worldly dominion, or that I might become either a great monarch or Shakra, King of the Gods, but rather, acted only out of spontaneous compassion and for the sake of the Supreme Enlightenment of all beings, then may I on this instant cease to be a woman and become a man."

Immediately she ceased to be a woman and became a man, named Rupavata, who became, in time, king of the city of Utpalavati. After a reign of sixty years Rupavata was reborn as the son of a merchant and was named Chandraprabha because of his beauty which outshone the moon. When he was eight years old the desire to offer himself for the welfare of others, without making distinctions of high or low, arose strongly in him. He went to the cremation grounds and cutting his flesh, bit by bit, gave it to the vultures to feed upon. He was next born as the son of a Brahmin named Brahmaprabha on account of the great radiance which shone from him. When he was sixteen he retired to the forest to undergo rigorous austerities. Near the hut one day he saw a starving tigress who in desperation was about to eat her newborn cubs. The youth immediately gave his own body to the tigress and saved the cubs.

The Buddha said, "The town of Utpalavati is the town of Pushkalavata now. She who was Rupavati before is now myself. The starving woman became the tigress. Those who were the parents of the youth Brahmaprabha became my parents Suddhodhana and Maya. The two cubs are now my attendant Ananda and my son, Rahula." (From the Divyadana Mala, a collection of Avadana [Noble Giving] tales purportedly related by the Buddha at Sravasti in the garden of Anathapindaka. Adapted from versions in Mitra, 315-16 and Burlingame, 313-4.)

"The Hungry Tigress," in all its versions, powerfully dramatizes the advice which the Buddha gave to his monks: "Even as a mother regards her child," he said, "her only child, so should one regard all beings."

A complete and lovely retelling of "The Hungry Tigress" can be found in Conze's Buddhist Scriptures. Conze's source is the Splendor of Gold, a Mahayana Sutra which he describes as having been "slowly composed over many centuries" (Buddhist Scriptures, 20).

In Aryasura's Jatakamala, the Bodhisattva is presented, not as a prince, but, more reasonably, as a mature religious teacher. Born into a devout and religiously skilled Brahmin family, he becomes a renunciate. His virtue draws disciples, and one day, as he walks with a young disciple, he comes upon the starving tigress and her cubs. The disciple is sent to find food for the starving beasts. The Bodhisattva then uses the opportunity to offer his own body—a joyous moment for the Great Being—so that the tigress's misery may be ended and her cubs spared. It is the moment of his most accomplished and complete teaching.

33. Great King Goodness (Mahasilava Jataka, No. 51)

This remarkably Gandhian tale of the transformative power of active nonviolence closely follows, with some adaptation, the Pali Jataka text. The scene of the king's meeting with the goblins and the corpse adds an entirely unexpected, yet fascinating (and very Indian), dimension to the story. The conclusion, addressing the rewards of persistence in goodness, are reminiscent of the conclusion of "The Brave Little Parrot," who persists in goodness not knowing how he can possibly succeed. Yet he does.

While this kind of story may seem preposterous, like some naive fairy tale, it has the power, nonetheless, to touch us deeply. Perhaps this is because it draws so clearly upon mythic-archetypal, wish-fulfilling territory of the psyche, territory common to us all. Stories are not true the way history is true. They are not true about what simply happened at one time or one place. They are true of the way of things in all places and times. They are as true as our most constant wishes and dreams. They speak for what we hope may be, and thus give us an accurate picture of the often unrealized dreams of the human heart. In stories, then, if not in life, we can fulfill the deepest wishes and make them real.

And then, too, there is the reality of Gandhi's nonviolent triumph in India.

At the conclusion of this story, the Buddha reveals that Devadatta was the evil minister, the one thousand heroes his (the Buddha's) present disciples, and King Goodness himself, the Buddha. Like the story "Give It All You've Got" the telling of this jataka was occasioned by a monk's temporary loss of faith.

34. The Naga King (Campeyya Jataka, No. 506)

This is an unusual and fascinating jataka. So many magical elements come together in it that its riches startle the mind. The nagas, wise and powerful serpent-spirits, are generally viewed as benign and are connected with all the earth's water systems. They are said to live in jewelled palaces beneath the waves of the ocean, rivers, lakes, and streams. Kala Naga Raja, a very ancient and wise Naga, even knew of the Buddha-to-be's impending great Enlightenment. (See "Enlightenment.")

There is a famous legend that says shortly after the Buddha's Enlightenment, a terrible storm arose. Then the serpent king, Mucalinda, rose up out of the earth and with his huge body encircled the Buddha, opening his great cobra hood to shelter the Enlightened One from the storm. Sculptures and paintings of this legendary event are especially popular throughout Southeast Asia.

The seemingly innocuous conclusion to this story—"and so the ground is gold even today"—is a traditional kind of story ending found worldwide. The point is not so much literal belief in this fantastic explanation (which seems to make the whole tale simply a kind of "pourquoi" or "just-so story") so much as the validating of the real emotions and values brought to life through the story. The conclusion returns us to literal reality, yet a reality transformed. When we look at the earth, we now see not just its form but something of its meaning.

The story's real meaning for traditional listeners, then, would be that, having heard the story, whenever we see the golden-colored earth, we too will naturally remember the preciousness of our own human birth—a treasure worth more than even the most vast amounts of gold—and strive, like the Naga King, for greater purity and wisdom. The seeming fiction of the story alters the reality of our lives. This is the story's (and the traditional storyteller's) job. This kind of ending is one of the tools of the profession.

To attain human birth—which Buddhist tradition insists is no easy task—and use it well—i.e., to further develop one's wisdom and compassion—is seen in Buddhism as the worthiest of all possible aims and accomplishments.

There is magic in this jataka. The many transformations—the rising of Sumana up into the air like a goddess, her rage and sorrow as she hovers shining in the air, the beautiful and astonishing touch of the great Naga King hiding himself in a flower and then reappearing as a handsome youth—give this tale unique distinction. Also noteworthy is the immediate willingness of both King Uggasena and the Brahmin snake charmer to release the Naga King. The brief verses in the Jatakastava describe the Naga King as a treasure himself: "pure and tranquillized the skin upon you was like gold, inlaid with precious stones" (Jatakastava, strophe 93).

Magical, treasure-filled underwater realms appear in the mythologies of many cultures, even those as widely separated as Ireland and

Japan. At the very least they suggest that in the depths are riches indeed. James Hillman points out in The Dream and the Underworld that Hades or Pluto can mean "riches" (20).

"Kogi, the Priest," an original tale of my own inspired by traditional sources, makes more contemporary reference to the nagas, great and wise dwellers in the seas.

SECTION III

35. Most Lovely Fugen

This story is based on a tale first put into English by Lafcadio Hearn. (Hearn identifies his English version as being from the old Japanese storybook, Jikkun-sho and titles his story "A Legend of Fugen Bosatsu.") Fugen is Japanese for the Sanskrit Samantabhadra, the Bodhisattva of Compassionate Action. Bosatsu is the Japanese equivalent of the Sanskrit bodhisattva.

In The Lotus Sutra the Buddha reveals that this ordinary, material universe is filled with countless bodhisattvas. No longer constrained by limited notions of Reality, they are free to appear in whatever forms necessary to alleviate suffering and help spiritually mature those still painfully bound by egoism, self-interest, and delusion. (See "The Black Hound" and "A Legend of Avalokitesvara"; also the commentary on "The Brave Merchant.")

36. The Dog's Tooth

A classic Tibetan tale about the transformative power of belief and faith. There is some sophisticated spiritual humor at work here, too. What we ourselves bring to our lives, our experiences, our teachings and practices may be more crucial than we think. That faith and the force of our creative imagination are essential aspects of reality and have their effects on the so-called "real world" is not surprising. What we think about and what we dream does clearly influence our behavior. This little story, however, quietly suggests that the mind's relation to the world is deeper than that. Mind and things—are they really separate? Buddhist tradition says not at all.

For two fascinating modern, scientific examinations of this, see The Tao of Physics by Fritjof Capra and The Dancing Wu Li Masters by Gary Zukav.

Spiritual humor is also embodied in the suggestive premise of the tale. Perhaps an old dog's tooth—and what, from our ordinary point of view, could be more lowly—is a holy relic, beyond all price. Indeed, what price could be put on such a thing? From an Absolute perspective one might say that everything is sacred, holy. And so the humor continues. For besides the fundamental ridiculousness of trying to separate Absolute and relative perspectives (or indeed, of establishing any labels, levels, and perspectives), if everything is holy then everything is simply what it is. A dog's tooth is . . . a dog's tooth. A rose is a rose is a rose. What is there left to do but laugh?

The remarkable, iconoclastic fifteenth-century Japanese Zen Master Ikkyu wrote a death verse that goes:

> Dimly for thirty years;
> Faintly for thirty years—
> Dimly and faintly for sixty years:
> At my death I pass my feces and offer them
> to Brahma.

> (quoted in Kapleau, Wheel of Death, 63)

Brahma is the Creator, one of the highest deities of Indian cosmology. Along with Vishnu, the Maintainer, and Shiva, the Destroyer, it is He who manifests all the worlds. The offering Ikkyu makes of his entire life is total and ordinary—in the profoundest sense. Everything, each thing, no matter how seemingly lowly, is an intrinsic aspect of the Great Mystery.

37. A Legend of Avalokitesvara

The path of the bodhisattva is given dramatic expression in "A Legend of Avalokitesvara." There is a Zen saying which likens this Path to the effort of trying to fill a well with snow. Compared to it, contemporary Roshi Philip Kapleau has said, Hercules' cleansing of the Augean stables seems almost child's play.

Throughout the traditional Mahayana countries (China, Japan, Vietnam, Korea, Tibet) magnificent paintings, as well as both cast and carved figures, of the Thousand-Armed Avalokitesvara bring this legend vividly to life. The eleven heads of the Bodhisattva are most often represented as a rising, tiered tower, like a wedding cake of heads, three and three and three topped by another head and finally, another. At each level the heads are smaller and smaller. The one thousand arms may be symbolized by as few as eight or even four arms. Yet in the palm of each hand is an opened eye. Lama Govinda explains the iconography in this way: ". . . in the palm of each hand an eye appeared; because the compassion of a Bodhisattva is not blind emotion but love combined with wisdom. It is the spontaneous urge to help others flowing from the knowledge of inner oneness" (Foundations of Tibetan Mysticism, 232).

Avalokitesvara, or Avalokita (Sanskrit for "Lord Who Looks Down from on High" or "Hearer of the Cries of the World") is known as Kannon in Japan, Kwan-Yin in China, Chenresig in Tibet. Many gentle, tender, and lovely iconographic forms of this bodhisattva exist. The most dramatic, however, is the thousand-armed one which vividly expresses the dynamic power of awakened compassion. It is visually gorgeous, intellectually daring, metaphysically heroic. These images show compassion exploding into every realm, looking simultaneously in every direction, responding with skillful, helping hands to every cry from every nook and cranny of the universe. In Zen, such images are understood to be presentations of one's own limitless and fundamental nature, the nature of the universe itself.

The unending task of Avalokitesvara, as of all buddhas and bodhisattvas, is to liberate sentient beings from their sufferings, including the root causes of suffering: attachment to greed, anger, and ignorance. One thousand arms are none too few for such a monumental task. Ultimately, as Avalokitesvara is none other than the compassionate activity of one's own Self-Nature, his or her exertions are none other than one's own. (See commentary for "Beginnings" and for "The Brave Little Parrot." Also see "Most Lovely Fugen," story and commentary, and "The Black Hound.")

The famous Surangama Sutra devotes an entire chapter to the saving power of the Bodhisattva Avalokitesvara.

The great Buddhist temple of Sanjusangendo in Kyoto, Japan has a vast central hall in which stand one thousand life-size, golden images of the Bodhisattva Kannon. In the very center of the hall, with five hundred Kannons on either side, sits a twelve-foot-high (seated!) thousand-armed figure whose face, crowned with ten small faces, radiates deep calm and limitless love. To stand in that hall is to feel the uncanny power of the Bodhisattva. Legend there springs to life.

The demons of the hell realms who appear in this retelling of the legend—"the horse-headed, tiger-faced, horned and fanged ones"—are the same apparitional beings who attack, or at least attempt to distract, the Buddha from his moment of Enlightenment. In that tale they serve in the armies of Mara, the Tempter. (See "Enlightenment.")

38. Stilson's Leap

The original stories of mine, "Stilson's Leap" and "Digit," are based on actual events. "Stilson's Leap" grew out of reading I did years ago on the Battle of Britain. I cannot place the exact source for this story. However, the story of an unnamed pilot's spontaneous self-sacrifice stayed with me. I began to see in it something of what a jataka occurring today might look like when viewed from outside the tradition. "Digit" is a kind of modern animal jataka, a contemporary version of "The Monkey King" in Aryasura's Jatakamala. (See commentary for "The Monkey and the Crocodile." Also see The Monkey Bridge in the bibliography.) Each is also a kind of modern analog to the classic jataka, "The Hungry Tigress"—also a tale of profound self-sacrifice.

In thinking about both these modern jatakas, a statement in Oscar

Wilde's De Profundis comes to mind: "The fatal errors of life are not due to man's being reasonable: an unreasonable moment may be one's finest moment. They are due to man's being logical" (88).

There is a profoundly universal element in certain jatakas, i.e. the classic tales of self-sacrifice, that remains mysterious and inexplicable. (In this collection see "The Lion, The Elephant and the Merchants' Cries," jataka and commentary; also "The Hungry Tigress," "The Banyan Deer," "The Golden Deer," "The Blue Bear" jatakas and their commentaries.) In these jatakas, a spontaneous, overwhelmingly altruistic desire to aid others, without taking thought for one's own welfare, comes to the fore and is given literary shape. This selfless desire is clearly not exclusive to any one tradition such as Buddhism, but permeates all peoples, all cultures, all nations. In times of crisis and danger it arises over and over—as has been well-documented. Animals and humans both seem to share this extraordinary impulse. Though scientists have tried to explain such behavior as an evolutionarily derived safety device, a clever stratagem of the "selfish gene" (through which the individual's sacrifice insures the continuity of the gene pool of the species), in the end this no more satisfactorily explains the matter than a spectral analysis explains the joy we feel upon seeing sunlight breaking through clouds. Nor does it satisfactorily explain interspecies compassion and self-sacrifice—dolphins coming to the aid of swimmers, dogs risking their own lives to save endangered humans, and so on. In the vision of the jatakas, animals and humans equally share the same fundamental heart-mind of compassion, the same fundamental Buddha-Mind of no-separation. Science and religion each have—and are—stories. At times they align perfectly, at other times they express two differing, yet intertwined, needs of the mind. One is the need to question and understand, the need to satisfy reason. The other rests with the interests of faith—not literalized belief in this or that dogma, which may often be the antithesis of real faith, but faith in the unknown itself, a curiosity and respect for what may be forever unknowable, a condition of wonder.

The following long quote is from Flight To Arras by author and aviator Antoine de Saint-Exupery. The book is the record of an almost suicidal reconnaissance mission he piloted during the Second World War. A later such mission claimed his life. He is writing here about flying towards the target through a barrage of deadly flak.

> Somehow those explosions . . . did not really count. They drummed upon the hull of the plane as upon a drum. They pierced my fuel tanks. They might have drummed upon our bellies. . . . But who cares what happens to his body? Extraordinary how little the body matters.
>
> There are things we might learn about our bodies in the course of everyday living if we were not blind to patent evidence. . . .

I used to wonder as I was dressing for a sortie what a man's last moments were like. And each time, life would give the lie to the ghosts I evoked. Here I was, now, naked and running the gauntlet, unable so much as to guard my head or shoulder from the crazy blows raining down upon me. I had always assumed that the ordeal, when it came, would be an ordeal that concerned my flesh. . . . It was unavoidable that in thinking about these things I should adopt the point of view of my body. Like all men I had given it a good deal of time. I had bathed it, fed it, quenched its thirst. . . . I had said of it, "This is me." And now of a sudden this illusion vanished. What was my body to me? . . .

Your son is in a burning house. Nobody can hold you back. You may burn up but do you think of that? You are ready to bequeath the rags of your body to any man who will take them. . . .

The flames of the house, of the diving plane, strip away the flesh; but they strip away the worship of the flesh too. Man ceases to be concerned with himself: he recognizes of a sudden what he forms part of. If he should die, he would not be cutting himself off from his kind, but making himself one with them. He would not be losing himself, but finding himself. This that I affirm is not the wishful thinking of a moralist. It is an everyday fact. But a fact . . . hidden under the veneer of our everyday illusion. Dressing and fretting over the fate that might befall my body, it was impossible for me to see that I was fretting over something absurd. But in the instant when you are giving up your body, you learn to your amazement—all men always learn it to their amazement—how little store you set by your body. . . . Here in this plane I say to my body . . . "I don't care a button what becomes of you. . . . There is no hope of surviving this, and yet I lack for nothing. . . ."

Man does not die. Man imagines it is death that he fears; but what he fears is the unforeseen, the explosion. What man fears is himself, not death. There is no death when you meet death. When the body sinks into death, the essence of man is revealed. Man is a knot, a web, a mesh into which relationships are tied. Only those relationships matter. The body is an old crock that nobody will miss. I have never known a man to think of himself when dying. Never. (104-107)

This version of the story "Stilson's Leap" leaves this modern jataka, like "The Hungry Tigress" and "Preacher of Patience," in a realistic mode, i.e., there is no "answer." No healing restoration occurs, no god magically descends from the skies to set everything right—as does happen in jatakas like "King Sivi" and "The Hare's Sacrifice." Both, of course, are equally traditional approaches. In the version "Stilson's Leap" which appeared in the original edition of The Hungry Tigress, there was a kind of restoration. It takes place years later, in the mind of one of the other pilots. Walking on a beach, watching the waves come in and roll out again, the bubbles rising and bursting and reappearing, he has this realization: "No effort is wasted; nothing dies. All things are transformed and all things live forever. Noble deeds, too, are never lost. Though they may seem fruitless they flower in the depths of time." It has been interesting to tell this modern jataka story from both sides of a traditional jataka pattern. The oral tradition, of course, allows for such constant experimentation and re-creation. The same teller may tell different versions of a story at different times, both as their own interests and understanding change, as well as to meet the varying needs of differing audiences.

39. Digit

"Digit" is another modern and original jataka tale of my own, loosely based on the now well-known incident of the death of Digit, the gorilla, so movingly related by the murdered naturalist, Dian Fossey, in her writings, and dramatically portrayed in the movie, Gorillas in the Mist. This modern jataka first came to mind after reading the original account of Digit's self-sacrifice and murder in an article in National Geographic. Later reflection made me realize that it is much like the jataka of "The Monkey King." (See commentary for "The Monkey and the Crocodile.") Modern research indicates that gorillas (and chimpanzees and orangutans) are, genetically speaking, 99 percent identical to humans. The differences between us, from the point of view of our genetic codings, are minuscule. There are even modern theories, based on this molecular evidence, that today's gorillas are actually the descendents of very early human groups which found their way into a lush and comfortable environment, and over the course of time evolved (i.e., adapted) to fit their near-perfect setting. Relieved from the constant stresses, pressures, and dangers that continuously shaped the rest of humanity, they never developed their intrinsic potential for complex communication and thought. Yet the potential is there—as evidenced by Koko, the female lowland gorilla, who has been taught to communicate in American Sign Language. Interestingly there is also a Mbuti (pygmy) legend that the "old man of the forest," the gorilla, was once a lazy man who liked to do nothing but lay around and eat. Gradually he grew a coat of fur and became a gorilla.

Gorillas do, of course, both actually risk and sacrifice themselves for their families. Hunters seeking to capture young gorillas for zoos—a practice which has hopefully ceased!—found they had to kill many of the group's adults to get the baby.

The jataka essence of this tale is the reality of an animal sacrificing itself for others.

The point of "Digit," of "Kogi, the Priest," and of "Stilson's Leap," as well as, for that matter, all as yet unwritten "jatakas," is simply that jataka tales need not simply be seen as tales of long ago. Mahayana teachings emphasize that there are countless buddhas throughout this endless universe, as well as countless beings aspiring, even now, at all different stages of the Bodhisattva Path. If we accept this vision then we can expect to see jatakas set in contemporary times. The jatakas offer a potential way of organizing some of the inexplicable realities of daily experience. Like all good stories, whether contemporary or traditional, their pretense throws open windows onto truth. This is part of the mystery of story itself. Fictions are tools for exploring both what is and what we dream might be. They deal with the mind's interaction with supposedly objective reality. (See commentaries for "The Golden Deer" and "Stilson's Leap".)

In "The Monkey King" (not in this collection but see the Pali Jataka as well as the Jatakamala; also The Monkey Bridge listed in the bibliography), as in the stories of "The Blue Bear," "The Golden Deer" and "The Banyan Deer," the human king learns a valuable lesson by seeing the actions or hearing the words of the wise animal. In stories like "Digit," the observer is no longer a king within the story but, rather, is ourselves, the readers and listeners. Whatever lesson or transformation occurs must now be within us. The king is dead; long live the king!

40. Kogi, the Priest

This original story of my own owes much to the traditional Japanese tale, "Kogi, the Priest." In that story a Buddhist priest-painter has a dream in which, for a time, he becomes a fish. Later it turns out that his dream was true. While in a coma in the human world, he really did, for a time, live as a fish. His subsequent paintings of fish were said to be so lifelike that they looked almost as if they might swim away. The story was transcribed from the Japanese by Lafcadio Hearn near the turn of the century. A recent retelling can be found in my book, Mysterious Tales of Japan (see bibliography).

This modern, whaling version of Kogi also owes a debt to Flaubert's masterful Legend of St. Julian Hospitator, as well as to a brief anecdote related by poet Gary Snyder in Earth House Hold about a Native American logger working in the Pacific Northwest who found that he could hear the trees screaming as he cut them down. The man gave up logging, grew his hair long, and returned to traditional ways.

The story is also a personal homage to the work of the Japanese Buddhist priest-sculptor, Enku, of nineteenth-century Japan, whose simple but dynamic carvings of buddhas and bodhisattvas have become treasures today, and to Herman Melville, whose masterwork, Moby Dick, still gives us unsurpassed insight into the hidden life of the sperm whale.

The naga realm, mentioned in this tale, appears more fully in the jataka of "The Naga King."

The name Eizo was actually the childhood name of the monk-poet Ryokan, one of the most beloved and tender figures in Japanese Zen. A noted poet and calligrapher, he was an accomplished Zen teacher in his own right but chose to live alone in a simple hut in the mountains. Playing ball with children, drinking sake with local farmers, teaching from the heart and by example, he began a legacy whose influence still grows today. One of his verses goes like this:

> O lonely pine
> I'd gladly give you
> My straw hat and
> Thatched coat
> To ward off the rain.

> (Stevens, tr., Dewdrops on A Lotus Leaf, 25)

There is a Buddhist legend to the effect that before his complete entrance into Nirvana, the Buddha entrusted certain precious Prajnaparamita (Highest Wisdom) teachings to the nagas. The nagas were to protect and hold these teachings until human beings were spiritually evolved enough to receive them. Contemporary readers, aware of the last thirty years' ongoing research, speculation, and experience with the intelligence (and essential gentleness) of whales and dolphins, can only wonder at the unique appropriateness of the naga legends of old.

The following quotes are also of interest.

> Sperm whale mothers invariably help their young escape (Beale, 1839), and "the mother may be seen assisting it to escape by partially supporting it on one of her pectorals" (Scammon, 1874). The rest of the pod either gets directly involved to distract the whalers or stands at close range, as if to encourage and coach those in mortal danger. Males and females alike have been known to risk their lives to rescue a distressed individual. (Cousteau, Whales, 213)

> In the far East stranded whales were looked upon as gods. The Montagnards of Vietnam believed that a child destined to redeem the world and deliver it from evil would be borne on a fabulous whale. This tradition had deep roots in Indonesia, the Philippines, China, Korea, and Japan, as

well as Indochina. (ibid, 247)

The first of the ten Buddhist precepts or "items of good character," upheld by Buddhists of all traditions and sects remains "not to kill but to cherish all life." One English translation of the precepts—which are not commandments so much as descriptions of our own fundamental aspiration and possibility—goes like this:

1) I resolve not to kill but to cherish all life.
2) I resolve not to take what is not given but to respect all things.
3) I resolve not to misuse sexuality but to be caring and responsible.
4) I resolve not to lie but to speak the truth.
5) I resolve not to take myself or to cause others to take substances that confuse the mind but to keep the mind clear.
6) I resolve not to speak of the misdeeds of others but to overcome my own shortcomings.
7) I resolve not to praise myself and downgrade others.
8) I resolve not to withhold spiritual or material aid but to give them freely where needed.
9) I resolve not to indulge in anger but to exercise control.
10) I resolve not to revile the Three Treasures (Buddha, Dharma, and Sangha), but to cherish and uphold them.

As mentioned at the end of "Kogi," Monjushri, or Monju in Japanese, is the Bodhisattva of Wisdom. The lion he sits upon is symbolic of the energy and vitality of one's True Nature, of Awakened Mind. In his hand Monjushri holds a sword capable of cutting through all delusion, all limitation. "Manjusri represents awakening, that is, the sudden realization of the Oneness of all existence and the power rising therefrom" (Kapleau, The Three Pillars of Zen, 377).

Samantabhadra, or Fugen, Bodhisattva of Action, appears in the story "Most Lovely Fugen." Fugen is usually seated on an elephant, an image of the power, sagacity, and dignity of one's own True Nature.

When the knowledge acquired through satori is employed for the benefit of mankind, Samantabhadra's compassion is manifesting itself. Accordingly, each of the Bodhisattvas [Manjusri and Samantabhadra] is an arm of the Buddha representing, respectively, Oneness (or Equality) and Manyness. (ibid, 377).

GREAT KING GOODNESS:
A MEDITATION ON THE MEANING OF A STORY

At first glance, the Buddhist jataka tale "King Goodness" seems to be nothing more than a propaganda piece for Buddhist values, specifically for the virtue of nonviolence.

Certainly traditional tales worldwide do dramatize values. In them specific causes are shown to lead to complex effects that lead to further causes, etc. But too easily tagged morals can also be the result of what happens when told tales get put into books. They get flattened out, abstracted from their oral performance base, and the "moral" replaces the live experience of hearing and seeing the tale. The story of "King Goodness" has been with us for twenty-five hundred years. I'd like to look at it here simply as a story, and see how it might serve its own meaning in ways that "King Goodness" as philosophy cannot.

To summarize the tale: King Goodness is a good king. He is noble, fair, generous, and virtuous. A vengeful minister asserts that the king's commitment to goodness has left his kingdom weak and helpless, that such commitment grows from a fundamental incompetence and naivete. This hypothesis is tested by another king via a series of raids into King Goodness's realm. The raiders are captured. But, when they explain that poverty alone motivated them, King Goodness gives them gifts and releases them. Not one is punished further for the crimes they have committed. Convinced that King Goodness's kingdom can be easily taken, the enemy king invades. As the army advances, King Goodness exhorts his mighty champions to refrain from violence. The army of the invading king wins easily. King Goodness and his one thousand champions are brought to the graveyard and are buried there, up to their necks, and abandoned to the jackals.

King Goodness remains alert and unfrightened. When the jackal king closes in for the kill he grabs on with his teeth to the jackal's ruff and lets the terrified beast pull him from his grave. Then he frees his men.

Two goblins are in dispute nearby, each claiming the greater portion of a corpse. Growing aware that a just man is in the graveyard, they go to King Goodness and ask him to divide the corpse for them. After bringing him his bath, clothes, and food from the palace, they present him with his sword. He splits the corpse perfectly into identical sections. In gratitude the goblins return King Goodness and his men to the palace.

The false king awakes, sees King Goodness standing by the bedside, and thinks it must be a ghost. In time the whole story of his liberation and return emerges. The false king repents. "Even goblins could recognize your worth," he admits, "while I, a man, could not. I am ashamed." He leaves, pledging to use his considerable power to protect King Goodness's realm. The evil minister is punished.

King Goodness has saved all people—those of his own realm as well as those of the enemy king—from the horrors of war. Joy arises in his heart, a joy greater than that which any victory in battle might bring. Sure now of the validity of his way, speaking from the ground of his own hard-won personal experience, he encourages all the people to persist, as he has done, in the ways of goodness.

Clearly the story, as the synopsis reveals, holds up an ideal, an exemplar of a tradition noted for compassion and nonviolence. But even King Goodness must learn from experience. And as the story unfolds, we, too, must determine for ourselves whether goodness has utility or not. I think we do see in the end that it works, but that the roots of its strength remain non-materialistic. Goodness requires faith. Through the narrative's action, we temporarily gain access to that faith. The process is experiential, not symbolic or didactic.

To review the story in greater detail: the tale begins with the birth of a royal child who is impossibly, perhaps monstrously, good. To balance this excess of goodness, an evil—selfish, callous, greedy, vengeful—minister is introduced. Cast out for his abuses, the evil minister seeks revenge and finds a ruler after his own heart, one interested in the normal perquisites of his role and office—power and possessions. Unlike King Goodness, this king's only compunctions about action are those of efficacy, not morals. If King Goodness is really weak then why not use force to take whatever he cannot hold? This second king is the king of this world and its timeworn, historic ways. He is the king of—with apologies to our reptile friends—"normal," lizard-brained, self-interested functioning.

King Goodness, on the other hand, embodies our potential for a more selfless life. Can such goodness really exist in this world? Does such goodness have a genuine place? Or is it a naive and childish weakness we must outgrow or hide away to succeed as adults? Which is real? We'll need to know if we are going to live well, even decently, on this earth.

The story becomes a tool for testing these two opposing visions, for revealing their interaction and for clarifying not just what is ideal, not only what may be possible, but what is necessary. King Goodness makes a vow to live by principle. "No violence," he says. And he demonstrates his integrity in his dealings with the raiding parties. He shows true Kingship—that deepest, royal aspect of the psyche—and protects even those who bring harm, showing them how to attain a better Path in life. He is, potentially, a great King, one who is not lost to the demands of ego but who wields power well. Yet for all that, he is incomplete. He remains a danger to his realm.

Can his way work? Do such vows empower? Or do they limit and cripple us? Without the willingness to rely on physical power he does appear emasculated as a leader. His kingdom is vulnerable and all his warriors, great champions though they are, are caught by his command and unable to resist. As a result all are cast into the graveyard. Here is the world's ordinary view dramatized. Goodness is equated, as the evil minister asserts, with weakness, and leads even those who might have had power to failure and destruction.

In the graveyard scene, failure gathers to a head and goodness seems to have no possible hope in this world. It is the time of night, darkness, and descent; the absolute bottom. King Goodness, the true king, and his men have been buried up to the neck; only their heads—the realm of thought that they have lived by—remain. And jackals are approaching—a vivid image for the failure that comes from attempting to live idealistically! Perhaps there is also the suggestion that living by vows—made just in the head—can bury us.

But King Goodness, if naive until now, does not remain so. He is not above tricking the jackal king and skillfully using the jackal's power to get free.

And there, at the darkest moment, at the bottom of the pit of the grave of the story with toothy old death creeping near, a hidden Path, a secret way opens. It is an ancient teaching, found in both folktales and religious literature worldwide. At the bottom of descent new life arises. Perhaps it is the remnant of an ancient, ritualized, initiatory moment informing literary form; its essence is: to live, one must die. One must enter the grave of all one's wonderful plans, ideas, stratagems. Like Dante, who at the bottom of the Inferno discovers that all has been simply upside down, King Goodness begins to ascend. It is a simple turn. He uses the jackal king's own power to get pulled free.

There is a Zen verse about feeling one's way in darkness along a wall. That is, there is a wisdom in "blindness," in having no plan or scheme or overarching system, a wisdom in being nakedly exposed to the intimate presence of each moment. Here is a bump in the plaster, here a shred of chipped paint, here a ridge line where the plasterer's arm wearied and the ripple in the wall remains to tell the tale. Each detail now comes fresh to us, distinct and unsequenced, and we must feel each one out, intimately absorbed. Without sight we have no overview. But such blindness may be true seeing, when no principles hide the Real in a fog of mental abstraction. Joshu (Chou-chou), the great T'ang-era Zen Master, was once asked, "Where is your mind focused?" He answered, "Where there is no design."

King Goodness descends in this manner—he has no plan, only a determination to follow his vows. And in this he finds his release, as do the heroes and heroines of folklore worldwide. He has entered a deep, synchronous place where, dead to the world, imposing nothing on what is, he lets go and all begins to work with him. It is the entrance into the super-natural.

The goblins, as it turns out, need a just and righteous man even as King Goodness needs magic to restore him to the palace. Without the goblins he has only one thousand mighty champions and the necessity of war—a just and righteous war it is true, but violent and bloody nonetheless. The only way to restore himself to the throne would be through the very violence he had originally sought to avoid. Without the corpse eaters he would have to recant his nonviolence or flee, abandoning his kingdom to the possessive claims of the worldly-wise king.

King Goodness meets the goblins graciously, and surprisingly, they come before him with respect. Instinctively, these creatures of darkness (the story actually treats them quite kindly; they seem no more evil than the bacteria which bring rot and decay, recycling dead stuff into humus and new life) begin working for him, providing him, out of gratitude, with all he needs to regain his throne. Even in this realm of bones, blood, and potential horror, he averts violence and brings peace. The goblins are grateful. Trust has been restored between them. Like squabbling siblings they simply wanted things to be fair.

The corpse and goblins appear at the moment King Goodness and his men free themselves. "Buried" in this scene is some sense that the goblins are devouring the corpse of King Goodness's old life, of his last illusions and attachments which this descent, in a kind of abbreviated story shorthand, signals us he has "died" to, been purged of. He has climbed up out of the grave, broken free of the earthly plane, leaving his illusions— including, perhaps, the inability to see how goodness implies action—behind. At that moment, the goblins appear dragging a corpse ready to be devoured and recycled. The descent is completed.

There are ancient graveyard rites in India and Tibet in which spiritual aspirants imaginatively offer the corpse of their wrong views, of their merely earthly life, of their material flesh, blood, and bones to the night walkers, the blood drinkers, the ever-hungry devouring ones—to all ghostly, suffering, hungry, incomplete beings. An ancient rite of compassion here serves the narrative's need.

In the end, the tale is the story of the initiation of the king. The false king who rules by physical might discovers the power of true Kingship conceived on spiritual ground—and bows in humility to the greater presence. The world is restored, the true king's power tested and confirmed. The world is restored, too, to harmony; the lesser power, which had sought to usurp control, in the end must revolve rightly around the greater.

But King Goodness grows, too, and if he was naive to start, by the end is so no longer. He has learned to use his wits and to make use of circumstance. And we—like the usurping king—have learned that vows do have power, that faith may be insight into the way things happen. There has been a ritual descent into death and the graveyard and darkness. We meet the blood drinkers who dwell there—and we meet, too, those who, while seeming human, have lost their human vision and hearts. The goodness of the king (we should call it more truly, "Goodness," for it is not "goodness" as opposed to "badness," as opposed to anything) has not guaranteed him an easy Path. He does however find, along with hardships, unexpected connection, confirmation, and joy. The story dramatizes, and so for the imagination makes once again Real, an ancient Way or Path.

"King Goodness" is not simply a tale with a moral. The nonviolent moral is not the full meaning of the story. The meaning lies in our experience of the story as it comes alive, forming its complex images within us. Traditional stories help us regain this territory. They are the encodings of wisdom.

Woven within and throughout the incidents and details of this twenty-five-hundred-year-old Buddhist jataka tale is a more complex story. "Great King Goodness" is more than the ancient advertisement for nonviolence it might at first seem to be.

Liking Jatakas

A storyteller, unlike a historian, must follow
compassion wherever it leads.
—Norman Maclean, Young Men and Fire

While tradition asserts that the original narrator of the jataka
tales (stories of the Buddha's earlier births) was the Buddha himself, history remains equivocal. Textual analysis reveals
strata within collections of jatakas that indicate a range of possible originators. Nonetheless, whoever that first narrator, or
narrators, may have been, he, she, or they clearly felt the primal
impulse of storytelling towards compassion. Because of this, the
jatakas today are not just the old tales of a particular religious
or cultural tradition. Rather, they remain expressions of a core
place in the imagination. In the jatakas—taken at their best—
compassion is not only given the freest rein but is liberated to
reshape the world as it desires. In the jatakas, we see the world
as a realm of bodhisattvic impulse, bodhisattvic vision.

It can be unnerving. Ordinary perspectives can be overturned
and strange things happen: a prince offers his own body to a
starving tigress so that she and her cubs may live; a king slices
healthy flesh from his bones to save a dove and feed the hawk
that sought her life; a lion and an elephant spontaneously risk—
and lose—their own lives in order to protect shipwrecked men;
a deer leaps into a swollen river to carry a drowning swimmer
to safety. The tales can be uncompromising and bizarre. But
they express, too, a tenderness between the realms—human and
animal; god, demon, or nature spirit—such as we might hope to
find in an as-yet-uncreated literature of deep ecology. In these

tales humans are not "higher" than animals. Indeed, animals are often wiser than humans. And compassion, springing from insight into the fundamental equality of all living things, precedes preoccupation with self.

Each jataka is traditionally viewed as the recounting of a past life of the Buddha. Amazingly, many of the 550 Pali jataka tales that comprise The Jataka, as well as those of the more varied Mahayana jataka tradition, are stories of animal births. The Great Teacher, it seems, spent many of his past lives not in lofty human or divine states but among the animals. (Of course, this may also spring from the interest of early Buddhist storytellers in recycling animal fables already known to them from the classical Indian story tradition.) But what is low, after all, and what high? As Henry Beston's well-known words from his classic Outermost House put it:

> We need another wiser and perhaps more mystical concept of animals. . . . We patronize them for their incompleteness, for their tragic fate of having taken form so far below ourselves. And therein we err. For the animal shall not be measured by the man. In a world older and more complete than ours they move finished and complete, gifted with extensions of the senses we have lost or never attained, living by voices we shall never hear. They are not brethren. They are not underlings; they are other nations caught with ourselves in the net of life and time, fellow prisoners in the splendor and travail of the earth. (25-6)

Zen students may think of the second koan in The Mumonkan, a training text of forty-eight koans, or spiritual challenges, designed to open the Mind's Eye, and then further refine understanding. Zen Master Mumon's commentary to the koan, known as "Hyakujo's Fox," concludes: "If you have an eye to see through this you will know that the former head of the monastery [who was, the koan states, reborn as a fox] did enjoy his five hundred happy blessed lives as a fox." And there is that most central koan—Joshu's "Mu"—in which a monk asks: "Does [even] a dog have the Buddha-Nature?" So then, where is high and where low?

As naive, simple, and "folklorish" as the individual tales may be, the vision of the jatakas as a whole is not quite so quaint. In these stories equal attention is given to the needs and interests of the nonhuman—a very contemporary perspective after all. I am reminded of Pulitzer Prize–winning poet Gary Snyder's fine, brief definition of deep ecology which he presented in a workshop a few years back: "Deep ecology," he said, "is one which gives equal weight to the needs of the nonhuman." Through the jataka tales an ethos connecting all living things is given life.

However, until recently, the jatakas were viewed by Westerners as mere children's fables. They seemed to throw Buddhism—initially characterized by Western scholars as rationalistic (and pessimistic!)—back into the morass of emotion and myth, back among the talking animals of the nursery. But perhaps these are not such juvenile places after all. Myth, we now understand, is one of humanity's most profound and subtle forms of thinking. And is there anything intrinsically childish about talking animals—except, that is, for what we ourselves imagine them to be saying? Dolphins, gorillas, whales, crows, wasps, bees—in reality none are silent. Are stones silent? Are stars or trees?

Such tales may seem childish, but the archetype they open to us, of a world buzzing with life and communication, is intrinsically mature, even powerful. The universe they thrust before us is like an endless, ongoing, multitiered conversation, with everyone and everything having its voice. Many jatakas, like the best folktales around the world, are in actuality not so much childish as childlike—and hooray, I say, for that. They restore to us a realm of Mind that we abandon to our peril, a realm of wonder in which everything is alive.

And how mature are we, anyway? The chaos and violence of our human-centered world and of our often insane policies and politics rarely offers proof of true adulthood. Reimagining the old, intimate ways of fur and teeth, hooves and claws, whinnies, grunts, barks, chirps, moans and roars may be just the tonic we need. "Not-knowing is most intimate," as one old Zen Master put it. Maybe we think—and think we know—too much. And we are suffering from it.

Perhaps, then, it is among the animals, in the world of unknowing, of "dumb" instinct, that we may find a deep, abiding vision. "Shujo honrai hotoke nari—from the beginning all beings are Buddha," said Hakuin Zenji, one of the great elders of Japanese Zen and of American Zen today. All beings are Buddha—wasp, donkey, lynx, otter, raven, sperm whale. Each its own being, each its own realm, each whole and complete, each the Universe itself, each interwoven seamlessly with all other beings, all other universes. To drop one's tedious burdens of mind and enter this realm in that timeless company is to rediscover delight. From the beginning it has been just so.

The jatakas, a traditional part of the Buddhist canon, are not simply children's tales but a dramatic and popular teaching presenting this heart of Buddhist vision. In them the highest ethical and spiritual principles may be dramatized from within the furred, feathered, clawed, "dumb" animal realm. The Mahayana, or Great Vehicle, which supports all beings, is demonstrated, little doorways to it kept open, by such jatakas. The carvings at the Indian Buddhist shrine of Sanchi, the paintings of the Ajanta caves, the vast monument of Borobudur all show that the tales spring from the oldest layers of the 2,500-year-old Buddhist tradition. And at the heart of the jataka tradition at its best (there are, alas, admittedly tales that fall far short of the tradition's own highest ideals) are animals.

Indeed, at the heart of the imagination itself, as evidenced by cultural traditions worldwide, are oracular and numinous animal presences. Children in every neighborhood can claim this same visionary mind. I knew, as did you, that the neighborhood cat stalking among the bushes or prowling along the brick wall was endowed with all the burning mystery of Blake's "tyger" or of Christopher Smart's cat, Geoffrey, or of Mowgli's awesome companion, Bagheera, the black panther. I knew, as did you, that clay, wooden, or plastic animals, carried amiably through the day in the pockets of one's bluejeans, could come alive.

As an adult I found that the jatakas spoke directly to this missing area of the imagination, a realm I had known intimately as a child. In their excesses I found a literature which spoke a simple truth: all living things have consciousness and meaningful destinies. The tales showed, too, what pure compassion looks and feels like—compassion which no longer cares what the world or ego thinks, compassion which doesn't look down on other species but lives harmoniously with and among them.

In the jatakas, compassion, like some great, wildly talented genius of a shape shifter, takes every possible form, extending one thousand helping arms and eleven clear-seeing heads into every realm of being. In them we discover that animals and humans are members of a living, mysterious universe. We find, too, that animals may be our teachers and benefactors. Having been on this earth longer than us, they are the elders. Which is not to say that they might not be as completely foolish as humans in these tales. They can be. But they can also point the Way to maintaining what we have all too often lost—the wisdom of the heart. And sometimes, under the right conditions, even we humans, as lost in our heads as we so often are, can regain a dignity and wisdom equal to theirs. Certainly it is an idealized view. But the imagination—and the world—would be the poorer without it.

So, still guiding us from the heart of Buddhist life and practice after twenty-five hundred years are the jatakas. Recite the first of the Four Great Buddhist Vows, "All beings without number I vow to liberate," and you will find yourself coming again into their domain. It is archaic territory, but strangely, in this time of the wholesale dying of species, very close to us today.

In light of these tales' contemporary relevance, I asked some noted Buddhist teachers and writers what their favorite jataka tale might be and why. Here are their responses.

Andrew Schelling, Assistant Director of the Naropa Writing Project wrote: "My favorite is 'The Monkey King.' A human despot, angered that a band of monkeys that lives in a magic mango tree is feeding on its fruit, orders his bowmen to slaughter them. The king of these monkeys makes an escape bridge out of his own body, sacrificing himself so that his tribe can flee to safety. Then occurs one of those insistent dreams, so historically rare as to seem nearly hopeless: the human tyrant, stunned at this brave selfless act, loses his taste for slaughter and begs to hear what teachings the battered, dying Monkey King holds.

"How rare are such 'turns of heart' in the annals of any nation! Not since the Buddhist King Ashoka has a powerful warrior so swiftly realized the power of laying aside the bow!

"Until this failed human experiment we call 'the State' withers away, dropping its arrows and leaving government in the hands of local decentralized communities—until that time the great Buddhist dream for this world is that kings and prime ministers, presidents and generals, anyone who controls the fate of another, may be touched and transformed by tender acts. May all beings attain unsurpassable enlightenment!"

"'Prince Five-Weapons,'" answered author, eco-philosopher, and peace worker, Joanna Macy, "a story in which the Buddha, as a young prince, risks his life to subdue a huge, sticky-haired monster, converting him at last to harmlessness and good. It celebrates," she adds "the indomitability of raw courage. Even when all his weapons were of no avail, even when horrifyingly stuck to the huge, sticky monster—by limbs and head—the prince still trusted in 'the sword of truth within.' And that freed him. And as it turned out it freed the monster too."

"I won't try to pick my very favorite," wrote Robert Aitken Roshi, "just one among many. The one I have chosen illustrates the Dana Paramita. It is the story of 'The Hare's Sacrifice,' a story of offering oneself to be eaten. In it the Buddha is a little hare who offers his own body as food to a starving beggar. The beggar is really the king of the gods who has taken this form to test the hare. 'The Hungry Tigress' story in which the Buddha offers his body to a starving tigress and her emaciated cubs is similar. However, the renewal of the hare through self-giving, the imprinting of the hare on the moon as the embodiment of the gift and (in some versions), the return of the hare to his friends to continue their karma, complete the gift cycle in a way that 'The Hungry Tigress' does not.

"The gift worthy of the name is always a gift of the self as food. 'This is my body, broken for thee.' Without a single thought of survival or reward, I gladly give myself to eat. Unexpectedly I am not only unharmed, but my life is enhanced. The many beings are nourished and the gift itself unexpectedly becomes a model for others to emulate. I live out my life with my friends and we enrich our mutual interdependence and the mutual interdependence of all beings."

"An unpopular idea with many people: animals and humans are part of a continuum and share in a spiritual nature," answered animal rights activist Elsie Mitchell of the Ahimsa Foundation. "The jatakas do not make the modern assumption that only humans who exhibit violent or cruel behavior are 'animals.' In the jatakas, all sorts of behaviors are to be found among both humans and nonhumans. Buddhist behavior is also known and practiced by nonhumans according to their circumstances. One of my favorite jatakas is 'The Three Wise Birds.' In this tale man learns, and greatly benefits, from his association with nonhuman creatures."

"The story of the Buddha's last birth before his birth as Siddhartha Gautama—'The Vessantara Jataka,'" said Lama Kongtrul Rinpoche. "It is a most difficult story with many interesting turns about a king who offers all his possessions, even his wife, children, and his body. It's a long one and a nice piece. At the end everything is given back. It might be frightening to take the idea that a Bodhisattva would offer his own body but I think it is OK."

Storyteller and author Laura Simms, who passed on this information to me, commented to the Rinpoche: "I think this is a tale of unrelenting compassion."

"Exactly," he replied.

Laura added that her favorite jataka to tell to children is "The Rabbit in the Moon," also known as "The Hare's Sacrifice." "I love telling it to children because they have a natural sense of compassion and they not only feel sympathy for the rabbit who offers his body to the flames, but can also delight in experiencing—in the safety of the story—their own greed and ignorance through the refusal of the other animals to share their food—without having to act it out in life. But for adults my favorite is 'The Banyan Deer,' a tale in which the Buddha, as a Deer King, saves his own herd through his self-sacrifice and courage and then goes on to liberate yet another herd, then all four-footed, all flying, and all swimming creatures as well from the hunters' bows and spears. I tell it because of its clear emphasis on the nature of compassion and on ruling for the benefit of all—and because hunting for pleasure breaks my heart."

Zen Teacher Sunyana Graef of Vermont responded that she had two favorites. First for her also was "The Banyan Deer," which she loved, she says, "as soon as I heard it—even before I became a Buddhist. I was a vegetarian before becoming a Buddhist and this story of a deer who leads a human king to respect all life—and so essentially to become a vegetarian—moved my heart deeply.

"My other favorite is 'The Spade Sage,' in which the Buddha, as a gardener long ago, tries six times to give up his attachment to his own skill before he at last succeeds with the seventh effort. If even the Buddha had to work so hard at it—had to try and fail over and over before success—then there's surely hope for all of us."

Buddhist scholar and author Ken Kraft raised some other issues: "A few years ago, at an exhibition in Japan, I saw a beautiful depiction of the well-known jataka story about the hungry tigress. It was on a lacquered panel on a seventh century shrine. The key points were unmistakable: a prince (the future Buddha) jumps off a cliff to feed a hungry tigress who is about to eat her own cubs.

"Because all three figures of the prince (hanging his shirt on a tree, diving off the cliff, laying on the ground about to be eaten) are in the same pictorial space one's eye naturally traces the elegantly depicted jump over and over again. Visually, at least, the prince/Buddha is recycled, reborn. Eventually the poses acquire a simultaneity, then an equality, and the effect dispels conventional judgements about the three states depicted. The prince becomes the tiger, the tiger becomes the prince; it's fine to eat, it's fine to be eaten.

"If, like the unknown shrine artist, we can savor the spirit of the story it becomes a powerful metaphor for the many forms of selflessness—a selfless thought, a selfless act, a selfless moment, a selfless state. In our everyday behavior, even when we know we need to give ourselves away we usually resist. Yet in the actual doing we discover the liberating nature of compassionate self-sacrifice.

"Of course the story also works as a metaphor for the tremendous selflessness that some spiritual traditions require at a critical stage of practice. As so many masters have said, unless the small self can take the plunge into the abyss of its own extinction, one will never know the unsurpassed joy and freedom that follow.

"In a simple yet subtle way, the Japanese shrine panel conveys the naturalness and grandeur of that timeless leap."

Roshi Philip Kapleau answered by saying, "There are many jataka tales that move me deeply. However, for personal reasons—my own life experience and Zen training—the jataka which I've seen titled 'Give It All You've Got' strikes the deepest chord. In that tale a caravan leader strengthens the courage of a young man who is down at the bottom of a dry well, digging for water. If he fails they will all die. The rock at the bottom of the well must be broken, but so far it has resisted all efforts. It's a claustrophobic moment, the sand is trickling down, the well shaft threatening to collapse. The youth feels he cannot go on. The caravan leader reassures him that the water is there. 'Be calm and steady,' he says. 'Give it one more shot and give it all you've got.' The youth rouses his energy, tries again, and this time breaks through to the lifesaving water.

"Though simple in plot, direct, and unadorned, the story has powerful implications: that determination and persistence are the two indispensable ingredients for success in any endeavor. For me that relates especially to Zen training. My Zen teacher Harada Roshi added another element: conviction. 'When a Zen aspirant is convinced he can awaken to his True Self,' he would say, 'that conviction will generate strong determination and strong determination results in a persistent all-out effort. Given this mind-state the aspirant can no more miss becoming enlightened than he or she can miss the ground with a stamp of the foot.' The story reinforces this as well as pointing to the indispensable aid that spiritual friends—one's teacher and Sangha—can offer.

"In my own training in Japan I often felt very much like that youth in the jataka tale. When at last my breakthrough was confirmed I remembered the words on a postcard which my friend Tangen-Roshi had once sent me: 'Sometimes even in the driest hole one can find water.' It was the spur I needed and my gratitude to him is boundless.

"In this jataka I found that such experiences have been part of the Buddhist tradition from the beginningless beginning. And my gratitude arises once more."

As for myself, my personal favorite jataka is "The Brave Little Parrot," a tale in which a parrot tries to put out a raging forest fire. ("Oh monks," said the Buddha in the Fire Sermon, "this world is on fire.") Dipping himself in a river, the parrot flies back and forth through the flames, sprinkling the few drops of water which cling to his feathers. Though the task seems hopeless, he continues. Seeing him continuing on and on beyond thought's despair, despite dangers and fears, the gods themselves are moved. They intervene, rain pours down, and the fire is quenched.

Why do I like it? First, because it shows the transformative power inherent in wholehearted action, wholehearted response. I think of Oscar Wilde's De Profundis. In that painful collection of letters from prison he writes: "The fatal errors of life are not due to man's being unreasonable: an unreasonable moment may be one's finest moment. They are due to man's being logical" (88). Logically, a few sprinkles of water can't possibly save a burning world. But the brave little parrot acts out of deepest intuition, does fully that one little thing that he—or she—can, and all is changed.

Each of us, this story reminds me, lives in a burning, transient world. Yet, like the little parrot we each have a tiny sprinkle of water we can offer. Logically, there is no hope. But . . .

BIBLIOGRAPHY

LIFE OF BUDDHA AND THE JATAKAS

Beyer, Stephen. The Buddhist Experience: Sources and Interpretations. Encino, Calif.: Dickenson Publishing Co., 1974.

Burlingame, Eugene, tr. Buddhist Parables. New Haven: Yale University Press, 1922.

Carus, Paul. The Gospel of Buddha. Chicago: Open Court Publishing, 1915.

Conze, Edward. Buddhist Scriptures. New York: Penguin Books, 1973.

Coomaraswamy, Ananda K. Buddha and the Gospel of Buddhism. New York: Harper & Row, 1964.

Cowell, E.B., ed. The Jataka, or Stories of the Buddha's Former Births. Translated from the Pali. 3 volumes. 1895. Reprint, London: Pali Text Society, 1973. Distributed by Motilal Banarsidass, Delhi.

Dayal, Har. The Bodhisattva Doctrine in Buddhist Sanskrit Literature. Delhi: Motilal Banarsidass, 1978.

De Silva-Vigier, Anil. The Life of the Buddha Retold from Ancient Sources with 150 Masterpieces of Asian Art. London: Phaidon Press, 1955.

Dorjee, Tenzin, tr. Generous Wisdom: Commentaries of His Holiness the Dalai Lama XIV on the Jatakamala Garland of Birth Stories. Dharamsala: Library of Tibetan Works and Archives, 1992.

Dresden, Mark J., tr. The Jatakastava, or Praise of the Buddha's Former Births, vol. 45, part 5 of New Series. Philadelphia: Transactions of the American Philosophical Society, 1955.

Francis, H.T. and E.J. Thomas, tr. Jataka Tales. Bombay: Jaico Publishing House, 1956.

Grousset, Renee. In the Footsteps of the Buddha. New York: Grossman Publishers, 1971.

Herold, A. Ferdinand. The Life of Buddha. Tokyo: Charles Tuttle Co.,

1954.

Johnston, E.H., tr. Asvaghosha's Buddhacarita, or Acts of the Buddha. Delhi: Motilal Banarsidass, 1978.

Khoroche, Peter, tr. Once the Buddha Was a Monkey (Aryasura's Jatakamala). Foreword by Wendy Doniger. Chicago: The University of Chicago Press, 1989.

Kohn, Sherab Chodzin. The Awakened One: A Life of the Buddha. Boston: Shambhala, 1994.

Mitchell, Robert Allen. The Buddha: His Life Retold. New York: Paragon House, 1989.

Mitra, Rajendralala. Nepalese Buddhist Literature (Sanskrit Buddhist Literature of Nepal). Calcutta: Asiatic Society of Bengal, 1882.

Nhat Hanh, Thich. Old Path, White Clouds: Walking in the Footsteps of the Buddha. Berkeley: Parallax Press, 1990.

Pal, Anjali. Jataka Tales from the Ajanta Murals. Bombay: IBH Publishing Co., 1968.

Percheron, Maurice. The Marvelous Life of the Buddha. New York: St. Martin's Press, 1960.

Poppe, Nicholas, tr. The Twelve Deeds of the Buddha: A Mongolian Version of the Lalitavistara, no. 16 in Studies of Asia. Seattle: University of Washington Press, 1967.

Pratt, J.B. The Pilgrimage of Buddhism. New York: The Macmillan Company, 1928.

Rhys Davids, Caroline A.F., tr. and ed. Stories of the Buddha: Being Selections from the Jataka. New York: Dover, 1989.

Rhys Davids, T.W., tr. Buddhist Birth Stories (Jataka Tales): The Story of the Lineage. London: George Routledge and Sons Ltd; New York: E.P. Dutton and Co., n.d.

Saddhatissa, H. The Life of the Buddha. New York: Harper & Row, 1976.

Sangharakshita, Bhikshu. The Three Jewels: An Introduction to Modern Buddhism. Garden City: Doubleday and Co., 1970.

Wray, Elizabeth, Carla Rosenfield, Dorothy Bailey, Joe Wray. Ten Lives of the Buddha: Siamese Temple Paintings and Jataka Tales. New York: Weatherhill, 1972.

BUDDHIST TEACHING AND PRACTICE

Aitken, Robert. Taking the Path of Zen. San Francisco: North Point Press, 1982.

_____. The Mind of Clover. San Francisco: North Point Press, 1984.

_____. Encouraging Words. New York: Pantheon, 1993.

_____. The Dragon Who Never Sleeps. Berkeley: Parallax

_____. The Gateless Barrier. San Francisco: North Point Press, 1991.

_____. Original Dwelling Place. Washington, D.C.: Counterpoint,

1996.

_____. The Practice of Perfection. Washington, D.C.: Counterpoint, 1994.

Cleary, Thomas. The Flower Ornament Scripture: The Avatamsaka Sutra, volume 3. Boston: Shambhala, 1987.

de Bary, William Theodore. The Buddhist Tradition in India, China, and Japan. New York: The Modern Library, 1969.

Eppsteiner, Fred. The Path of Compassion: Writings on Socially Engaged Buddhism. Berkeley: Parallax Press/Buddhist Peace Fellowship, 1988.

Govinda, Lama Anagarika. Foundations of Tibetan Mysticism. New York: Samuel Weiser, 1973.

_____. A Living Buddhism for the West. Boston: Shambhala, 1990.

Hakeda, Yoshito S. The Awakening of Faith. New York: Columbia University Press, 1974.

Hurvitz, Leon. Scripture of the Lotus Blossom of the Fine Dharma (The Lotus Sutra). New York: Columbia University Press, 1976.

Jivaka, Lobzang. The Life of Milarepa: Tibet's Great Yogi. Translated by W.Y. Evans-Wentz. London: John Murray, 1962.

Kapleau, Philip. Awakening to Zen. New York: Scribners, 1997.

_____. The Three Pillars of Zen. Revised and expanded edition. Garden City: Doubleday, 1988.

_____. Wheel of Death: Writings from Zen Buddhism and Other Sources. London: George Unwin & Allen, Ltd., 1972.

_____. The Zen of Living and Dying. Boulder: Shambhala, 1998

_____. Zen: Merging of East and West. Revised edition. Garden City: Doubleday, 1989.

Kraft, Kenneth, ed. Zen: Tradition and Transition. New York: Grove Press, 1988.

Ross, Nancy Wilson. Buddhism: A Way of Life and Thought. New York: Vintage Books, 1981.

Shantideva. A Guide to the Bodhisattva's Way of Life (Bodhicaryavatara). Translated by Stephen Batchelor. Dharamsala: The Library of Tibetan Works and Archives, 1979.

Shibayama, Zenkei. Zen Comments on the Mumonkan. New York: Harper & Row, 1974.

Soothill, W.E., Wilhelm Schiffer and Pier P. Del Campana. The Threefold Lotus Sutra. Translated by Bunno Kato, Kojiro Miyaska and Yoshiro Tamura. New York: Weatherhill/Kosei, 1975.

Suzuki, Shurnyu. Zen Mind, Beginner's Mind. New York: Weatherhill, 1973.

Thurman, Robert. The Holy Teaching of Vimalakirti: A Mahayana Scripture. University Park, Pa.: The Pennsylvania State University Press, 1976.

Trevor, M.H. The Ox and His Herdsman: A Chinese Zen Text. Tokyo: Hokuseido Press, 1969.

Woodward, F.L. Some Sayings of the Buddha. New York: Oxford University Press, 1973.

Yokoi, Yuho, with Victoria Daizen. Zen Master Dogen: An Introduction with Selected Writings. New York: Weatherhill, 1976.

BUDDHIST LITERATURE, ART, AND TRAVEL

Blofeld, John. The Wheel of Life: The Autobiography of a Western Buddhist. Boston: Shambhala, 1978.

Blyth, R.H. Haiku. 4 volumes. Tokyo: Hokuseido Press, 1952.

David-Neel, Alexandra. Magic and Mystery in Tibet. New York: Penguin Books, 1973.

Dotzenko, Grisha F. Enku, Master Carver. Tokyo: Kodansha International, 1976.

Govinda, Lama Anagarika. The Way of the White Clouds: A Buddhist Pilgrim in Tibet. Boston: Shambhala, 1966.

Harrer, Heinrich. Seven Years in Tibet. New York: E.P. Dutton, 1954.

Harvey, Andrew. A Journey in Ladakh. Boston: Houghton Mifflin Company, 1983.

Hearn, Lafcadio. Kwaidan: Stories and Studies of Strange Things. Rutland, Vt. and Tokyo: Charles Tuttle Company, 1971.

_____. The Buddhist Writings of Lafcadio Hearn. Introduction by Kenneth Rexroth. Santa Barbara: Ross-Erikson, Inc., 1977.

Ishigami, Zenno, ed. Disciples of the Buddha. Translated by Richard Gage and Paul McCarthy. Tokyo: Kosei Publishing Co., 1989.

LaFleur, William, tr. Mirror for the Moon: A Selection of Poems by Saigyo (1118-1190). New York: New Directions, 1978.

Mathiessen, Peter. The Snow Leopard. New York: Bantam, 1980.

Reischauer, Edwin O. Ennin's Travels in T'ang China. New York: The Ronald Press, 1955.

_____, tr. Ennin's Diary: The Record of a Pilgrimage to China in Search of the Law. New York: The Ronald Press, 1955.

Reynolds, Christopher, ed. An Anthology of Sinhalese Buddhist Literature up to 1815. London: George Allen & Unwin, 1970.

Sangharakshita. The Drama of Cosmic Enlightenment: Parables, Myths, and Symbols of the White Lotus Sutra. Glasgow: Windhorse Publications, 1993.

Snyder, Gary. Earth House Hold: Technical Notes and Queries to Fellow Dharma Revolutionaries. New York: New Directions, 1969.

_____. A Place in Space. Washington, D.C.: Counterpoint, 1996.

Stevens, John. One Robe, One Bowl: The Zen Poetry of Ryokan. New York: Weatherhill, 1977.

_____. Dewdrops On A Lotus Leaf: Zen Poems of Ryokan. Boston:

Shambhala, 1993.

Tanahashi, Kazuaki. Penetrating Laughter: Hakuin's Zen and Art. Woodstock: The Overlook Press, 1984.

Tucci, Giuseppi. To Lhasa and Beyond. Rome: Instituto Poligrafico Dello Stato, 1956.

Watson, Burton, tr. Ryokan: Zen Monk-Poet of Japan. New York: Columbia University Press, 1977.

Zimmer, Heinrich. Myth and Symbol in Ancient Indian Art and Civilization. Edited by Joseph Campbell. New York: Harper & Row, 1962.

EARTH, ANIMALS, AND THE ENVIRONMENT

Aisenberg, Nadya, gen. ed. We Animals. San Francisco: Sierra Club Books, 1989.

Badiner, Allen Hunt, ed. Dharma Gaia: A Harvest of Essays in Buddhism and Ecology. Berkeley: Parallax Press, 1990.

Beston, Henry. The Outermost House: A Year of Life on the Great Beach of Cape Cod. 1st Owl Book edition. New York: Henry Holt & Co., 1992

Cousteau, Jacques-Yves and Yves Paccalet. Whales. New York: Harry N. Abrams, Inc., 1988.

Fossey, Dian. Gorillas in the Mist. Boston: Houghton Mifflin, 1983.

Hillman, James. Dream Animals. San Francisco: Chronicle Books, 1997.

Kapleau, Philip. To Cherish All Life: A Buddhist Case for Becoming Vegetarian. New York: Harper & Row, 1982.

Lopez, Barry. Arctic Dreams: Imagination and Desire in a Northern Landscape. New York: Bantam, 1987.

_____. Crossing Open Ground. New York: Vintage Books, 1989.

Lovelock, James E. Gaia: A New Look at Life on Earth. New York: Oxford University Press, 1987.

Mowat, Farley. Woman in the Mists. New York: Warner Books, 1987.

Thomas, Elizabeth Marshall. The Tribe of Tiger. New York: Simon & Schuster, 1994.

Thomas, Lewis. The Lives of a Cell: Notes of a Biology Watcher. New York: Bantam, 1984.

Wylder, Joseph. Psychic Pets: The Secret World of Animals. New York: Harper & Row, 1978.

MYTH AND STORY

Ausubal, Nathan, ed. A Treasury of Jewish Folklore. New York: Bantam, 1980.

Campbell, Joseph. The Hero with a Thousand Faces. Princeton: Princeton University Press, 1973.

_____. The Way of the Animal Powers. New York: Harper & Row, 1988.

Campbell, Joseph with Bill Moyers. The Power of Myth. New York: Doubleday, 1988.

Colum, Padraic. Storytelling: New and Old. New York: Macmillan, 1968.

Erdoes, Richard and Alfonso Ortiz, eds. American Indian Myths and Legends. New York: Pantheon Books, 1984.

Grimm, Jakob and Wilhelm Grimm. The Complete Grimm's Fairy Tales. Introduction by Padraic Colum. Commentary by Joseph Campbell. New York: Pantheon Books, 1972.

Kane, Sean. The Wisdom of the Mythtellers. Peterborough: Broadview Press, 1994.

Piggott, Juliet. Japanese Mythology. London, Paul Hamelyn, 1969.

Ramsey, Jarold, ed. Coyote Was Going There: Indian Literature of the Oregon Country. Seattle: University of Washington, 1980.

Van Der Post, Laurens. The Heart of the Hunter: Customs and Myths of the African Bushmen. San Diego: Harcourt, Brace, Jovanovich, 1961.

Waters, Frank. Masked Gods: Navaho and Pueblo Ceremonialism. New York: Ballantine Books, 1970.

ESPECIALLY FOR CHILDREN

Coatsworth, Elizabeth. The Cat Who Went to Heaven. Illustrated by Lynd Ward. New York: Macmillan, 1928.

Khan, Noor Inayat. Twenty Jataka Tales. The Hague: East-West Publications Fonds b.v., 1975.

Laidlaw, Jonathan and Janet Brooke. Prince Siddhartha: The Story of Buddha. Wisdom Publications, 1984.

Martin, Rafe. Brave Little Parrot. Illustrated by Susan Gaber. New York: G.P. Putnam's Sons, 1998.

_____. Foolish Rabbit's Big Mistake. Illustrated by Ed Young. New York: G.P. Putnam's Sons, 1985.

_____. The Monkey Bridge. Illustrated by Fahimeh Amiri. New York: Alfred A. Knopf, 1997.

_____. Mysterious Tales of Japan. Illustrated by Tatsuro Kiuchi. New York: G.P. Putnam's Sons, 1996.

Martin, Rafe and Manuela Soares. One Hand Clapping: Zen Stories for All Ages. Illustrated by Junko Morimoto. New York: Rizzoli, 1996.

Dharma Press, of Berkeley, California, has published a series of children's picture book versions of the jatakas. These are translated directly from the original texts, edited where necessary to make them more accessible to young readers/listeners. There are about twenty books in the series so far. Among them are:

The Parrot and the Fig Tree, illustrated by Michael Harmon, 1990.

The Rabbit and the Moon, illustrated by Rosalyn White, 1989.

A Precious Life, illustrated by Rosalyn White, 1988.

GENERAL

Alighieri, Dante. The Inferno. Translated by John Ciardi. New York: Mentor, 1954.

Capra, Fritjof. The Tao of Physics. Boston: Shambhala, 1975.

De Saint Exupery, Antoine. Flight to Arras. New York: Harcourt, Brace and World, 1942.

Eliade, Mircea. Shamanism: Archaic Techniques of Ecstasy. Princeton: Princeton University Press, 1974.

Flaubert, Gustave. Legend of St. Julian Hospitator. In Three Tales. Translated and with introduction by Robert Baldick. Baltimore: Penguin, 1961.

Hillman, James. The Dream and the Underworld. New York: Harper and Row, 1979.

Jablonski, Edward. Air War. 2 vols. Garden City: Doubleday, 1971.

Jung, C.G. Memories, Dreams, Reflections. New York: Vintage Books, 1965.

_____. Modern Man in Search of a Soul. San Diego: Harcourt, Brace, Jovanovich, 1933.

Melville, Herman. Moby Dick, or The Whale. New York: Modern Library, 1992.

Seed, John, Joanna Macy, Pat Fleming and Arne Naess. Thinking Like a Mountain: Towards a Council of All Beings. Philadelphia: New Society Publishers, 1988.

Singer, Isaac Bashevis and Richard Burgin. Conversations with Isaac Bashevis Singer. New York: Farrar, Strauss, and Giroux, 1986.

Wilde, Oscar. De Profundis. New York: Avon Books, 1964.

Zukav, Gary. The Dancing Wu Li Masters. New York: Bantam, 1980.

Want cash for this book?

It's Easy!

1

Go to
textbooksNow.com
and click "sell."

2

Get an instant quote
on your book.

3

Send it back -
we'll pay the postage!

4

We'll send you
a check.

Ship To:

William Thomas Moore
601 17th St
Bellingham, WA 98225

Ship From:

MILLIE'S BOOKS-AMAZON
8950 W PALMER ST
RIVER GROVE, IL 60171

Date: 03/25/2009

SKU	Qty	Condition	Title	Price	Total
4941274U	1	Used	3 9780938756521 Hungry Tigress	$ 5.89	$ 5.89

Sub Total	$ 5.89
Shipping & Handling	$ 3.99
Tax	$ 0.00
Total	**$ 9.88**

Order #: 058-7992894-4277311

Refunds: All items must be returned within 30 days of receipt. · Pack your book securely, so it will arrive back to us in its original condition. To avoid delays, please use the return section and label provided with your original packing slip to identify your return. Be sure to include a return reason. · For your protection, we suggest using a traceable, insured shipping service (UPS or Insured Parcel Post). We are not responsible for lost or damaged returns. · Item(s) returned must be received in the original condition as sold and including all additional materials such as CDs, workbooks, etc. · We will initiate a refund of your purchase price including applicable taxes within 5 business days of receipt. Shipping charges will not be refunded unless we have committed an error with your order. · If there is an error with your order or the item is not received in the condition as purchased, please contact us immediately for return assistance.

Reason for Refund/Return:
Condition   Incorrect Item Received   Incorrect Item Ordered   Dropped Class   Purchased Elsewhere   Other

Contact Us: For customer service, email us at customerservice@textbooksNow.com.